MANAGING BY REMOTE CONTROL

How to More Effectively Manage People and Resources When You Can't Always be There

PETER R. GARBER

St. Lucie Press
Boca Raton   London   New York   Washington, D.C.

"Different Perceptions of the Job" figure concept from Games Trainers Play, by J. Nystrom and E. Scannel, 1980. With permission of the McGraw-Hill Companies.
Concept and use of the term "Sanctioning Team" courtesy of Don Jewell.
"Your Life as a TV Host" concept from "Adventures at Work: Experiencing Work as A Movie," 1995 Annual, Vol 1, "Training." Courtesy of Jossey-Bass Pfeiffer.
"Today's Supervisor" concept from "Today and Tomorrow," 1998 Annual, Vol 1, "Training." Courtesy of Jossey-Bass Pfeiffer.

Library of Congress Cataloging-in-Publication Data

Catalog record is available from the Library of Congress

Contents

About the Author

Peter R. Garber is Manager of Teamwork Development for PPG Industries, Inc., Pittsburgh, Pennsylvania. Mr. Garber has been with PPG since 1980 where he has held a variety of Human Resource positions at a number of the company's manufacturing facilities prior to his current assignment at their Corporate Offices in Pittsburgh.

He is the author of a number of other business-related books including: *Coaching Self-Directed Workteams, 30 Easy-to-Use Reengineering Activities, 25 SkillBuilding Activities for Supervisors and Managers, Diversity Explorations, 101 Stupid Things Supervisors Do To Sabotage Success, Team Skillbuilders, 25 Customer Service Icebreakers and Activities, 101 Ways to Build a Better Relationship with the Customer,* and 25 sales strategies and teaching activities. He has also published a number of shorter articles and teaching tools on a variety of Human Resources subjects.

Today, Mr. Garber specializes in helping drive organizational change and creating greater levels of involvement and empowerment. In his work he has found that managers are being asked to accept ever more responsibilities often with limited additional resources being made available to them. The concepts presented in this book are a result of his experiences helping managers deal with these expanding accountabilities and in finding ways to add value to everyone's role in today's organization by *Managing by Remote Control.*

Mr. Garber received his B.A. in English from the University of Pittsburgh and his Masters Degree in Guidance and Personnel from St. Bonaventure University. Mr. Garber currently serves on the Human Resources Advisory Committee for Duquesne University in Pittsburgh. He is married and has two daughters.

Introduction

We truly do live in a television society. Few, if any, other inventions in recent history have had such a dramatic influence on our lifestyle and habits as that of television. However, as television has become such an integrated part of our culture today, we may not always be aware of its tremendous influence in our lives. The television set has become the main source of information and entertainment in virtually every American home during the past half century. What first started as a tiny fuzzy black and white viewing screen that the family of the 1950s huddled around to see Milton Berle wearing a dress, now is so advanced that it is sometimes hard to comprehend the sophistication and capabilities of television today. Not the least of these technological advances is that of the remote control device. The remote control has changed our television viewing habits by allowing us to effortlessly change from one to the next channel without ever leaving the couch. We are now completely in control of what we choose to watch. The remote control device has created an entirely new favorite pastime — channel surfing!

Much of the information we receive about what is occurring in the world today is received via the television. Images of natural disasters, politics, world events, sports, weather, and even wars are transmitted instantaneously into our living rooms through our television sets. Television's influence is so great that it even carries over into our work lives, though we may not always be aware of it. Last evening's television programs are a frequent source of conversation during the morning coffee break or around the water cooler. Television's influence even impacts the way we manage our organizations.

Many of the changes we see in our organizations today are directly influenced by what may be occurring in our culture. To illustrate, think about how television programming has changed in the past several decades and those changes that we have seen in the workplace. These parallels are more than just coincidence. They reflect real life in many of its most important aspects. Television shows provide a mirror of ourselves and the times in which we live. To dismiss them as trivial would be to ignore an important part our culture. We manage our organizations within the culture in which we live. Organizational culture is determined as much by what is occurring outside its walls as from within.

In keeping with the concept of Remote Control Management, which derives its name from this now essential piece of television hardware, analogies between television programs and management styles will be made throughout this book. They are intended not only to be fun to read, but to uniquely illustrate how we are evolving both as a society and also as managers as we experience the evolution of the age of television and organizational change and their influence on one another.

> Information concerning seminars on
> Remote Control Management
> are available by calling (724) 934-9649.

Managing by Remote Control

T he world used to be more "hands-on" than it is today. There were so many things that we used to do on our own. For instance, you may be old enough to remember actually getting off the couch and manually changing the channel dial on your television set. It is amazing what a burden this would be to most of us today when a misplaced TV remote control device might qualify as a family emergency! As the electronic and communication age continues to evolve, we are provided with more and more ways to automate our lives. We have self-propelled lawn mowers, electronic locking systems, automatic tellers, and countless other labor-saving devices intended to make our lives easier and better. We are constantly being bombarded with television commercials trying to convince us how the quality of our lives would improve by simply purchasing their product. Our homes are becoming more like scenes in Future World at Epcot depicting how the family of the future might live in the next century. Home personal computers are changing our lives, providing us instant access to unlimited data via the Internet and linking us electronically with the world through E-mail. No longer do we need to fantasize about what the future might be like — the future has arrived!

Sometimes it seems we may be more accepting of the life-style changes in our personal lives than of what is occurring in our professional lives. We anxiously wait for the next software upgrade our home personal computers enabling us to experience the virtual reality of commanding spaceships to other galaxies. Even our microwave ovens and videocassette recorders contain more powerful computers than those that guided the Apollo spaceships to the Moon. But what about changes that these advances in technology are creating in the workplace? Are managers always as receptive to these changes at work as they are to those introduced on their new 50-inch big screen TV with every available feature including surround sound, picture-in-picture, and sleep timers, purchased just in time for this year's Superbowl? Probably not. Why is it that we often perceive these new advances that affect us personally as life-style improvements, and similar shifts in the workplace as threats?

How these changes in our world are affecting our work lives may be perceived in many different ways. Technology can be both a blessing and a curse. It provides better ways in which to get work done, but also complicates another aspects of life. Just keeping up with the latest technology on the market can be a humbling and frustrating experience. The life cycle of the latest computer technology is just slightly longer than that of a fruit fly! Technology can enable a Manager to stay in close touch with parts of the organization in faraway locations. On-line computers allow the Manager to keep abreast of real-time operational details previously not even accessible to him. With these improved communications, Managers are able to enlarge their span of control in the organization. They can be responsible and accountable for more aspects of the operation. Managers are able to manage greater numbers of people as a result of their ability to be linked on-line to this important business information. In other words, they can have immediate access to business information as it happens. It is no longer necessary to employ people whose job is to report information upward in order for sound decisions to be made. They are no longer dependent on others to be "good and faithful" translators of vital data necessary for important decisions to be made. However, this power can be intimidating, even frightening. The Remote Control Manager may find him- or herself responsible for a vast array of functions. Some of these responsibilities may not be very familiar to the Manager. These responsibilities may be outside the Manager's area of expertise. The Manger must often rely on the experience and talents of others who report to him or her. This requires a different set of skills than more traditional "hands on" management situations dictate.

The Remote Control Manager's name can be deceiving. Don't be fooled; the Remote Control Manager cannot be aloof or detached from what he/she is responsible for. Nor is this manager a "control freak." *Control* in this sense is similar to its usage in the definitions of *quality control* or *process control*. This is control in its most positive application. Being in control means that the organization or process is operating as it was designed and intend to do. Like any good manager, the Remote Control Manager is still responsible for those aspects of the organization that he or she is held accountable. The Remote Control Manager must ensure that everything operates as it should according to design. The Remote Control Manager must be an integral part of the organization. Not being there can no longer be a legitimate excuse for poor performance in others. The Remote Control Manager is just as accountable for results as a Traditional Manager. The good news is that it is possible for Managers to make even more significant contributions to their organizations with this expanded scope of responsibilities. By better understanding the concept and philosophy of remote control management, Managers can become more effective leaders and maximize the potential of those who report to them.

Our world is getting both smaller and larger at the same time. It is getting smaller in the sense that we are able to easily communicate with virtually anyone, anywhere in the world. It is getting larger in the sense that a Manager could find him- or herself responsible for the business of an organization covering a vast geographic area of the globe. This far-reaching scope of responsibility would have been considered unmanageable just a decade or even a few years ago. The Remote Control Manager must use all of the tools and resources he has available to him. Included in these resources are not only latest communications technology but the eyes, ears, creativity, experience, and efforts of those who report to him in these remote locations. These become the Manager's *Remote Control.*

Remote Control management fits well into the philosophies of empowerment and teamwork so popular in many organizations today. These approaches to people management rely extensively on the same basic systems as that of Remote Control Management. The commonality is trust. Both empowerment and remote control management involve a "letting go" of what traditionally would have been considered exclusively the manager's responsibility. In the past, to delegate these types of assignments would have been considered a challenge or threat to the manager's authority, even job security. These were the duties of what Managers believed he or she got paid to perform.

Remote control as with empowerment, does not diminish a manager's accountability or authority in any way. What remote control does is change the way the manager fulfills these accountabilities and exercises their authority. Like changing channels on a remote control, the manager gets these tasks completed, but without actually being there physically to ensure that the work gets done.

The Changing Role of the Manager

There is no doubt that the role of the Manager is changing as a result of the new structure of organizations today. Diversity and globalization are setting the direction for today's organization and management philosophies. Diversity addresses not just the make up of an organization's employees in regards to race, gender, age, or national origin but in its business as well. Organizations are becoming more diverse in the products and/or services they provide, as well as the type of business and markets they enter and in the geographic areas in which they locate. Diversification is becoming a required survival skill of successful organizations. These changes create rippling effects throughout the organization. Not the least of those impacted are managers and what is expected of their roles. Paradoxically, perhaps, managers are being asked to achieve even more with less resources along with their expanded accountabilities. The logic of his would be that, if a manager has a greater scope of responsibility, then his/her output should also increase. The only way that this greater challenge can be met is through empowering other people to accept greater levels of responsibilities. Remote Control Management goes a step beyond empowerment. Empowerment involves moving decision making and responsibility to lower levels in the organization. Remote Control Management encompasses these principles, but does it from a distance. The Remote Control Manager empowers without being there. The difference is that in many ways, it may be one thing to empower others while you are still physically present just in case something unusual happens in which you need to intervene, but what about the cases when you are almost never able to physically be there? Remote Control Management takes empowerment to highest level.

The realities of today's business world are making Remote Control Management more of a necessity than simply something that might be "nice" to do. Managers need to take a step back and to get a broader perspective, a bigger picture view of the part of the organization for which they are now responsible. They can't possibly deal with every detail of the expanded scope of their responsibility. Even if they tried, this would make them too focused on the details of that for which they are responsible and cause them to lose sight of the overall direction of the business. This is the classic "can't see the forest for the trees" syndrome. However, it can be an insecure feeling when you don't know something, particularly if you are a manager. Especially when your boss asks you if you know! Those three little words, "I don't know," can sound like a self-imposed career death sentence when uttered to your boss.

Part of Remote Control Management, or any system that involves these changing roles of management, is a clear understanding on the part of everyone in the organization concerning what to expect and not to expect of people in these new roles. If the reaction to "I don't know" from a subordinate is, "Well, you had better damned well find out!," the likelihood of any change in the management style of the organization is highly unlikely.

This is why it is critically important how changes such as how Remote Control Management are introduced are viewed by others in the organization. It must have the support of everyone in the organization, particularly at the top executive levels. Without this support and "buy-in," the organization could actually extinguish those behaviors that are intended to be steps moving in the direction of changing the management style of the organization. What would happen if, during this transition, a manager is chastised for not knowing a particular process-related detail of something within his accountabilities that he typically could recite on command in the past? Most likely, the Manager would find out this level of detail and ensure that he was always prepared with it in the future. What then does this do to the Manager's efforts to focus on the "bigger picture"? So often, it is not those who are being asked to change who have the greatest difficulty making the transition, but those who requested that the change be made.

This is where most difficulties concerning changing Managers' roles manifest themselves. There is often great confusion between the distinction of changing someone's role in an organization and their accountabilities. Remote Control Management does not necessarily change the manager's accountabilities. As mentioned, these accountabilities may actually increase in this system. What does change is the way in which these accountabilities are exercised. A Manager can accomplish more if he uses the resources that are available in a more effective and efficient manner. A Remote Control Manager learns to realize that often these resources work more effectively when managed less directly. This involves placing greater trust and responsibility in those who report to the manager. For this system to work, both the Manager and his or her direct reports must understand each other's roles and responsibilities. They must understand why things are being done in certain ways and support the new initiatives, rather than sabotage their progress. Information and communications become critical in this process.

A Remote Control Manager must believe in those who report to him or her and trust not only them but their intuitions as well. The Manager needs to understand the perspective in which others give advice and direction concerning operation of the part of the organization for which they have been given responsibility. If the Manager is not going to be there, some level of the responsibility for that part of the operation must be assigned to those who are there all the time. If the Manager is still going to make all critical decisions and at the same time remain remote from that location, he or she will be making decisions based on incomplete data. Sometimes, Managers need to have so many numbers before they can make a decision that by the time they have all the data, it is too late. This "analysis until paralysis" can allow competitors to get a jump on you in entering new markets or cause old methods to be retained long beyond their usefulness. The Remote Control Manager must believe that others who report to him would make the same decisions that he would, provided they had the same information on which to base these decisions.

This can be both an enlightening and humbling discovery for a Manager. It may be viewed in either two ways: "What is my value to the organization anymore if those who report to me are now making the same decisions I made in the past?"; or "If I can now trust those who report to me to assume responsibility for these aspects of the operation, I can focus on other bigger picture things." To a large extent, it is up to each Manager to choose which of these ways he or she chooses to view the new role. The outcome of this decision will have the most profound effect on the success or lack thereof of any major cultural change that is even contemplated by the organization. This can become a career crossroads for a future Remote Control Manager. It may appear to more like Robert Frost's "Road Less Traveled."

This is not the way that most Managers are used to traveling. Remote Control Management creates a whole new paradigm of leadership, not one that necessarily comes easily or naturally. It can be a very confusing transition. There are many decisions to make and new ways of looking at working relationships. At times, it may seem that the Remote Control Manager is venturing into uncharted territory. It may seem that the only directions you get sound like the immortal words of the former great baseball player, Yogi Berra, "When you come to a fork in the road, take it!" You desperately try to use the clicker on your remote control but the picture remains the same. There are no signposts ahead — you have now entered the Twilight Zone of Management!

Creating the Culture of Remote Control

"What is the culture of an organization and how does it affect its management systems?" is a question that must be addressed before any change initiative is embarked upon. This book will explore the question of culture and how it impacts the role of the Remote Control Manager. The Remote Control Manager influences the culture of the organization as well as being impacted by it.

For the purposes of this discussion, let's define culture as it relates to the workplace as:

> **The rules, both formal and informal, which determine how people behave in an organization.**

One might quickly surmise that if all an organization needs to do to create a culture of Remote Control Management, they simply change the rules and it's done! Unfortunately it is not that easy. To illustrate, think about the rules in your organization. Are they all being followed to the "letter of the law"? Most likely, they are not. Why? Probably because it is relatively easy to write down and distribute what you want the rules of an organization to be. It is an entirely different challenge to ensure that everyone complies. There are even rules that are written that may never really be expected to be adhered to by anyone in the organization. For instance, many organizations have rules concerning solicitation in the workplace by co-workers. These rules are intended to prevent employees from being bothered, even harassed by others to purchase something during their workday. This can be not only irritating but nonproductive. There are typically signs in visible locations at entrances of most places of employment that say NO SOLICITATION. However, how strictly are these rules typically followed? If a group of Girl Scouts selling cookies show up at the receptionist's desk, are they informed about the company's no solicitation rule and shown to the door? More likely, an order form for this year's cookie drive is circulated throughout the office — and besides, wouldn't you hate to miss out on those great cookies each year?

This is an important point concerning Remote Control Management. You can not simply dictate organizational and cultural change. It is like the old saying, "Those convinced against their will are of the same opinion still." These things need to be managed, and in more and more circumstances today, they have to managed remotely. As much as we would love to be able to simply send out a letter or E-mail message and change the culture of the organization, this would probably have little or no effect. Of course, this does not mean that this approach has not been tried many times!

What is needed is a systematic and designed approach to organizational change. Enabling people to manage remotely is not something that can be dictated, but rather something that has to be developed. It probably took years for the existing culture of the organization to be established. It will take at least a number of years to change it. Unfortunately, often organizations have little patience for designing organizational change. We live in an "I want it now" society. The suggestion that achieving desired cultural change would be a long-term process might be met with the same mindset as your New Year's resolution to lose weight next year. It might begin with the best intentions, but quickly degenerate to trying to find the easiest way to meet your goals with the least amount of sacrifice. This is why there is such a huge market for all those gadgets and gimmicks promising you "buns of steel" in just 30 seconds a day that are constantly being advertised on television. Unfortunately, there is no "30-second" approach to organizational change, no magic dust, no Organizational Change Fairy Godmother!

The rate at which some organizations are able to change is clearly demonstrated in the following brief look of a work environment with a very domineering manager in charge:

The Discovery

The situation had not changed very much at the facility for many years. The manager of the facility ran it with an "iron fist." He pretty much dictated what everyone was to do and as a result there was very little input from anyone concerning their ideas or opinions concerning changes in the workplace. Employees' attempts to share their ideas to improve the process were typically meet with displeasure and a stern warning to "worry about your own responsibilities and I'll worry about running this place," from the manager.

Despite the frustration this work environment created in the organization, things still seemed to run pretty well. The facility had exceeded the goals set for them by the company for the past 5 years. From the manager's viewpoint there really wasn't any reason to change anything. "If it ain't broke — don't fix it" was heard a lot around the company.

However, one day a technician in the facility noticed something. With just a few computer programming changes, the entire process could be made more efficient. This could save significant equipment downtime and reduce maintenance costs. Apparently this programming logic had been inadvertently left out during its installation several years before. The technician discovered the omission while researching another computer problem in some documentation he had found. He immediately told his supervisor about his discovery.

The necessary changes will require the approval of the facility manager to be implemented and will result in significant downtime that could prevent the facility from meeting their goal for the month. This is something that had not happened for the past 5 years.

What do you think will happen in this organization concerning this discovery? Do you think that this discovery will get the attention it needs to be implemented? How could this situation be changed? What do you think the potential benefits versus losses were to the company as a result of this management style?

Creating a culture which supports Remote Control Management must begin with the support and direction of the leadership of the organization. Many attempts to change organizational culture are initiated at the grass roots level. That is, it is believed that to change the roles of the people in the organization you need to go immediately to those who are directly affected by these changes. After all, they are the ones you are asking to change. This approach, it is reasoned, will save you many unnecessary steps in the process. Typically these grass roots approaches to organizational change begin with promising results. Those who are being asked to change are told about the changes and encouraged and reinforced for displaying different behaviors. Everyone is excited by the initial changes they see and they have no reason to believe that they won't become the new cultural norm in the organization. However, change doesn't happen in a vacuum. The new ways of managing begin to affect virtually every aspect of the organization. The changes begin to migrate to the higher levels. Eventually, those at the highest levels are affected. Unless they understand and support the change, they may feel threatened by its existence and want it to go away. They will quickly begin to dismantle the changes and try to return things to the way they were.

Profile 1.2

At a medium-sized manufacturing facility located in the Midwest, a young engineer became excited about the possibilities that the concepts of empowerment could create in his department. He developed a plan to implement empowerment concepts on his production line and went to the plant manager for approval. Without giving it much thought, the plant manager gave his blessing, but had little understanding of what would be involved in this change process. The engineer proceeded to talk to a group of production workers about giving them more decision-making and problem-solving responsibility on the job. This was met with great acceptance from these employees who felt that it was about time that someone asked what they thought after all these years of performing their jobs. A number of changes concerning running the production process were made that gave the production employees greater responsibilities. For a short time, with the knowledge of these experienced production employees now being more fully utilized, the production process was running more efficiently than ever. The plant manager was delighted with the engineer's suggestion.

However, unintentionally, the engineer had left their supervisors out of this empowerment process. Concerned about what their future role was to be in this new scheme of things, they had little reason to support this new way of operating the production line. In their own way, they began to do what they could to make it go away. This quickly became counterproductive, and the production process began to be negatively affected, as was the goal of the supervisors. It wasn't long before the plant manager called the young engineer into his office and told him that he didn't know why things were suddenly going so wrong but to go back to their original system of managing. The engineer thought about what he had done wrong and asked for one more chance to correct this problem. The plant manager reluctantly agreed.

The engineer met with the supervisors and asked them what they thought was the problem with this new system that had started out in such a promising manner? The supervisors told him that what they thought he said to them was something like this, "We are going to give the people that work for you most of the responsibilities and decisions that have been a major part of your jobs all these years. Now just get out of the way while we begin this important experiment to see if we can run this factory without you!"

The engineer assured these supervisors that wasn't what he meant, and he realized at least some of the mistakes that he had made. He had not done a good job of communicating to all levels of the organization what the changes were designed to accomplish and what roles everyone needed to play. In fact, the supervisors needed to support this process and be intimately involved in helping move the decision making process to lower levels in the organization. Without their support, the true potential of this process would never be realized. He went back and spent the necessary time to educate the supervisors as well as the other levels of management in the organization about the empowerment process and how they might be affected. He developed a committee to direct the process comprised of the managers and supervisors from various departments in the organization. He made sure that everyone was comfortable and ready to move on the next step in the process. The result was that empowerment produced better results than anyone ever expected and at the same time made everyone feel that they were more an important part of the overall team than ever before.

Thus, if neither dictating organizational change nor a grass-roots approach is the answer to creating cultural change, how then is it achieved? The following key principles are significant in achieving the desired organizational change and culture supportive of Remote Control Management.

Remote Control Management Key Principles

1. There needs to be a clear vision of what Remote Control Management means to the organization.
2. There needs to be an understanding that remote control may or may not be the most effective way of achieving the objectives of an organization.
3. Continuous learning and improvement are essential to Remote Control Management.
4. Responsibility and accountability are required of everyone in the process, including those who had little or none in the past.
5. The roles that most people presently play may be changed as a result of Remote Control Management.
6. The structure of the organization will be reviewed and possibly changed as the concept of Remote Control Management is introduced.
7. Remote Control is not abdication of management responsibilities. However, the way that management manages may change.
8. The top management of the organization must (a) understand this process and (b) support its implementation accepting that there will be problems along the way.
9. Most people in the organization are capable of accepting greater levels of responsibility than they have now.
10. The goal is to establish an environment supportive of Remote Control Management. This may include creating organizational structures to enable Remote Control Management to exist and to provide the skills training that everyone needs to work in this new environment.

How Will We Know When We Get There?

The concept of continuous improvement is also important to Remote Control Management. Remote Control Management must continuously find new and better ways to maximize peoples' abilities and potential.

The goal for Remote Control Management should be to support the people management systems of the organization. Remote Control Management can be the "vehicle" to more closely link operational capability to individual competency. Without Remote Control Management, it is likely that our organizational capability will always exceed our individual competency as illustrated in the diagram below:

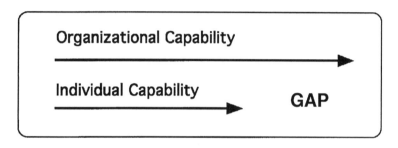

Our goal should be to narrow this gap as much as possible in the future.

What Is Remote Control Management?

Remote Control Management can be difficult to define and will be different with each application and location. Basically, Remote Control Management describes an overall management philosophy and subsequently an organizational structure that has the potential to change the responsibilities and accountabilities of everyone involved in the process.

Through Remote Control Management, responsibilities are moved to the lowest level in the organization in which they would be most appropriate and effective. Managers no longer have to be physically present to be responsible for their areas of responsibility.

The key to Remote Control Management is the roles that people play in an organization. For example, the role that a Manager plays in a traditional organization would be quite different than that in a remote control organization. Traditionally, a Manager's role was to tell people what to do and to be there to ensure that it got done. In a Remote Control-Managed organization, the Manager's role is to enable those who work for her or him to make decisions and accept responsibilities for themselves. This requires new skills, expectations, goals, and measures for everyone in the organization.

Measuring Success

Success, as it relates to Remote Control Management, can be difficult to measure. Remote Control Management is more a continuous series of small steps (and hopefully successes) leading toward the ultimate objective of more fully utilizing our people's potential. Success might be better termed "milestones."

Remote Control Milestones

- Create a better understanding throughout the organization concerning what the concept of remote control is all about.
- Support (champion) from top management concerning Remote Control Management and its strategic importance to the business.
- Remote Control Management must be viewed as a process, not a program — that is, something that will continue on and on, as opposed to a program with a defined beginning and endpoint.
- An acceptance throughout the organization of the commitment (including time) required to implement Remote Control Management.
- Thinking of Remote Control Management as a "cultural change" rather than a fad or training initiative.
- Documented improvements in performance indexes supporting the gains achieved through Remote Control Management.
- Sharing of resources, knowledge, principles, tools, training, practices, etc. throughout the organization concerning what we have collectively learned about Remote Control Management.
- Remote Control Management must become part of the overall business strategy (similar to safety, quality, diversity).

Competitive Advantage

There should only be one reason for an organization to be interested in implementing Remote Control Management — to create or sustain a competitive advantage. In order to remain competitive, we need to continuously improve our management systems. Because Remote Control Management can have such dramatic bottom-line results on performance, we can only help ourselves to remain competitive leaders through the implementation of these principles.

The inherent problem with Remote Control Management, as with any other change process that involves a cultural change, is the complexity and time required to ultimately achieve the organization's goals utilizing this concept. It might be easier to continue to manage the way we always have in the past. If this process is not initiated before you find yourself at a competitive disadvantage with other organizations utilizing these concepts, it may be difficult if not impossible to "catch up." Remote Control Management requires time to be effectively introduced and implemented. To attempt to hurry this process in a crisis mode would not work. The time to begin Remote Control Management initiatives is before there is a crisis situation and there is still the opportunity to *do it right.*

Remote Control Tools

The most powerful tool is knowledge. This knowledge relates to what Remote Control really involves and the process needed for implementation. A Remote Control tool kit would include the following tangible and intangible resources:

- **Remote Control Management Coordinator** — to provide support throughout the organization in the implementation of these concepts
- **Remote Control Management Advocates** — at all levels of the organization, but particularly at the top positions
- **Educational Resources** — state-of-the-art books, videos, learning instruments, and assessments that support the concepts of Remote Control Management
- **Outside Resources** — to share what other companies are accomplishing in this area and how. This might include benchmarking visits, outside consultants, seminars, conferences, meetings, organization, and affiliations

- **Vision** — a plan is needed describing what the organization expects to achieve through Remote Control Management
- **Structure** — a management system and structure must exist which enables Remote Control initiatives to move forward toward the organization's goals

Remote Control Organizational Change Model

The following Remote Control Organizational Model can help establish a culture of Remote Control Management. This structure is designed to allow the support, approval, direction, design, and implementation of a Remote Control to take place:

	Sanctioning Team ➤	Steering Team ➤	Design Team
Who are they?	Business Managers	Facility's Leadership	Key people from various areas of the organization
What do they provide?	Commitment and Support	Vision and Direction	Develop and implement plan

The Sanctioning Team

The term "sanctioning" means to give approval or consent. In the business world, sanctioning takes on even greater meaning: it involves providing the necessary resources to allow organizational change to happen. The Sanctioning Team should be comprised of upper management who have the authority to grant approval, not only for the financial resources needed but also for the emotional resources. Those in upper management can do as much to drive organizational change by providing this emotional encouragement and recognition as they can by approving budgets to finance these initiatives. The Sanctioning Team will play the least active role in the change process, but also the most important. Organizational change must start at the top.

No company worth its salt would go forward without a business plan to be successful in the marketplace in which it must compete. Sales, marketing, budgeting, productivity, quality, safety, and many other indexes are identified and goals established in each of these areas. The organization will measure its progress towards these goals and make necessary adjustments on a frequent basis. However, where an organization needs to be headed in terms of its management style and culture is not typically thought of as something that needs to be planned. It is often something that everyone hopes will just happen somehow or that the organization will eventually evolve to. But few things of value happen without insight, planning, and resources. The purpose and existence of this Steering Team is to establish this direction for organizational and cultural change. If not for this direction by the Sanctioning Team, these changes might never come to fruition.

As mentioned, change will hit a "wall" as it moves upward in the organization if the way has not been "paved" in advance. Part of this prework is ensuring that upper management is aware and supportive of these initiatives. They need to understand and feel comfortable with the changes that will begin to take place. Systems and procedures that they have grown accustomed to will begin to change. This can take everyone out of their comfort zones, including top management. If someone doesn't feel part of something new, he or she may instinctively resist it. On the other hand, if people feel that they have been included in the process and play a key role, they will work hard to help achieve the success of the change. The latter is definitely what upper management of your organization needs to feel about the concepts of Remote Control Management. If they have little or no patience for a manager saying "I don't know; I have given someone else who works for me that direct responsibility," then a traditional style of management will quickly return.

The bottom line is this: it is not enough to merely *want* to establish an organizational culture of remote control — you have to provide the resources necessary to achieve this goal. Ultimately, the bill goes to the Sanctioning Team for approval.

The Steering Team

Think of organizational change as a ship that needs to be guided into uncharted waters on the high seas. Someone needs to chart the course that it must take to reach the ultimate destination. The Steering Team plays this role. Once the support and approval is given by the Sanctioning Team, there needs to be another group that begins to identify the specific direction and goals that the changes are intended to achieve. The Steering Team plays a more active role in the change process. They develop the vision for the process. They create the view into the future of what the changes will look like at some future time. The Steering Team needs to keep in touch with the Sanctioning Team to the extent that they are interested in this level of detail. Remember, the Sanctioning Team is busy running the business. They are flying at 30,000 feet. The Steering Team is more comparable to being in the control tower, directing air traffic, and ensuring that everyone is performing their jobs in the correct sequence and according to plan. The Steering Team should consist of those who have direct responsibilities for that part of the organization that will be directly affected by these changes. They are the ones who ultimately will be held accountable for the results that are achieved by the changes. The Steering Team are those with a vested interest in the success of the organizational changes that are being proposed.

The Design Team

The Design Team is charged with the responsibility of developing the plan to actually implement the changes being proposed. The Design Team must find a way to achieve the vision and direction given to them by the Steering Team. There needs to be a strong linkage between the Steering Team and Design Team. This is often best achieved by having a member of the Steering Team also serve on the Design Team. This ensures that there is frequent communications between these two teams as the change process continues to move forward. The Design Team's responsibility is to develop and implement a plan to achieve the objectives of the changes that have been identified as important and necessary. The Design Team should consist of individuals who will be directly affected by the changes and can represent the interests of others who are in a similar circumstance. They should be close enough to the "action" to understand what is possible and what is not. They are the "reality checkers." The Design Team must ensure that a plan is not proposed that is impossible to implement. If they find themselves being asked to do this, then they need to go back to the Steering Team and communicate this fact.

The Design Team needs to look at the specific details of the change that is being proposed. They need to identify specifically what needs to be done to achieve the goal that has been developed. For example, a Design Team might identify the following areas that need to be developed in the organization to create a culture supportive of Remote Control Management: Rewards and Recognition, Communications, Training (for both managers and those that report to them), Organizational Structure, Roles and Responsibilities, Financial Reporting, Technical Capabilities, and Process Improvements.

Journeys and Expeditions

Many organizations, during the past decade or so, have initiated organizational change initiatives such as a Quality Improvement Process to improve the service and/or products delivered to their customers. They were taught to describe these changes as a "journey," one that must begin with the first step with others to follow in a specified sequence. The problem with many of these attempts to change the culture of the organization was the use of the term "journey." A journey implies going someplace relatively easily reached and without taking any significant risks. A journey is something more like what a tourist may go on, a safe destination of sorts. On the other hand, an *expedition* is something quite different. An expedition is for adventurers. In many ways, a Remote Control Manager must be an adventurer. He will probably find himself venturing into uncharted territory as this concept begins being introduced and utilized. The sounds of the wild that you might hear on this expedition might be uttered from your boss and sound like, "What do you mean you don't know. That's what I pay you to know. Now go find out!" Becoming a Remote Control Manager can certainly be a dangerous expedition.

An expedition involves exploring places that you have never been before and that once reached will change you in ways that you never imagined. Going on this type of an adventure requires resources, planning, preparation, and a commitment to reach your ultimate destination. An expedition also can involve taking risks. Sometimes organizations get discouraged and frustrated when trying to change their corporate culture. They set off on their "journeys" with unrealistic expectations about achieving their goals and what it will take to reach their destinations. They are like the early explorers centuries ago, who expected to sail to the new world to find piles of gold waiting for them on every shore they reached. Even Columbus did not begin to realize the significance of his discoveries during his lifetime. He had no way to comprehend the vast potential and resources discovered during his voyages to the new world. In many ways Remote Control Management is just beginning to realize how many benefits have yet to be discovered as a result of this process.

A Remote Control Manager needs to view these changes as embarking on a long and great adventure as if you were setting out to discover new worlds. The most essential resource you must have is a clear understanding of your goals and objectives. Most important is that you have the wisdom to realize that achieving these goals will not happen overnight and to be able to see and appreciate the successes you achieve along the way.

Q.U.E.S.T.

The adventurers of yore had a quest. A quest is something of value that you pursue, search, or seek. The Remote Control Manager, too, must also have a quest. However, in this case the letters "QUEST" also represent a set of standards to follow on this expedition. They represent:

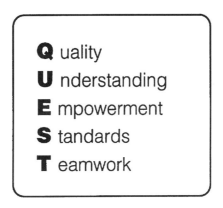

Q uality
U nderstanding
E mpowerment
S tandards
T eamwork

Quality

Any quest must begin with the search for quality. In the past few years, great effort has been expended trying to find a universally acceptable definition of quality. Each quality philosophy has its own working definition of quality. The question is, "if there are so many different definitions of quality, how do we know which one is correct?" Quality may not be as easy to define as we first believed as we began our journeys. It may be less important to agree on its definition than it is to learn to recognize it when we find it. The quest to find the quality in your organization and to channel it in the right direction may not always be easy and without problems or frustrations, but the search must go on and on in this important goal.

Understanding

Understanding — the word "understanding" implies a total knowledge of something or somebody. Imagine how much smoother your expedition to Remote Control would be if everyone was "on board" with a full understanding what the concept was all about and what their role in the process was supposed to be.

However, we live in the real world, not an ideal one. Again, many of the inherent problems we experience when starting on any new endeavor is that there is not often a clear understanding of what it will take to get there. It is like children in the family automobile who ask after the first 30 minutes of a 5-hour drive, "Are we there yet?" We still have our "journey" mentality in many ways, and it affects every aspect of the organization. For example, say that you are invited to join a group of people to visit someplace for the weekend. You are to travel there by some conventional means of transportation such as a car, bus, plane, or train. You expect to see some interesting sights along the way and maybe even get a chance to stop to do some sightseeing. How much preparation and information would you need? Of course you would spend some time ensuring that you brought the proper clothing and other personal articles that you may need, but your preparation would be somewhat minimal. You would likely do everything that a tourist would do getting ready to go on a vacation.

Now imagine that the invitation you received was to climb one of the tallest, most challenging mountains in the world. Assuming that you would still be interested in going, what would your preparation for this invitation be? Certainly, it would be different from that of the weekend visit. What kinds of information would you require, what questions would you ask, what training would you demand, what equipment would you insist you have? One thing is for sure, you would not casually set off to ascend the mountain without the proper preparation, equipment, or commitment to be successful.

Granted, so becoming a Remote Control Manager is not the same as climbing Mt. Everest, but the point is that you need to be prepared for both challenges. You can not expect to lead people on a mountain climbing adventure if all they are prepared for is a relaxing weekend of camping. Everyone must understand the challenges which lie ahead.

Empowerment

Empowerment goes beyond simply enabling those to be heard who have not been given a chance to share their ideas in the past. Empowerment can also have the ability to allow people's potential to be realized. Many Managers feel that empowerment is a great idea as long as it is two levels below them! Why? Because they don't want to have to change. They want to stay in control of those who work directly for them. They are comfortable with their authority and do not want to change the way they manage. They are supportive of change as long as it doesn't affect them. One of the problems with this thinking is that it grossly underutilizes an organization's most valuable resource — their people. It is like using your personal computer as a plant stand. It may do a darn nice job of holding up that plant but it has a great deal more potential if only given the opportunity.

Standards

In any organizational change effort, there are certain standards which must be established and maintained. Standards become benchmarks for excellence to be reached and exceeded. Sometimes it may appear that the establishment of standards takes away people's ability to set their own goals. However, there must be standards which are "givens" and not subject to debate. For instance, a customer's quality standards cannot be compromised and must be met. This carries over to everything the organization does.

For example, imagine that you were going to be taken by airplane into a remote forest in South America. As you prepare for this adventure you must pack your gear for the weeks you will spend hiking through this isolated part of the world. As there are no airports or landing areas where you are about to travel, you will have to parachute out of the airplane. The question you might ask is, "Do you need to meet all the established standards for packing a parachute as you prepare for this adventure or would you feel comfortable in just meeting some or even most of the standards for parachute packing?" How closely do you think you would listen to the instructions given to you on how to perform this task to the established accepted quality standards and how committed do you think you would be to mastering this skill? Obviously, you would be intensely interested and totally committed to learning how to perform this task to accepted standards. Standards must be met regardless of their purpose if you are going to do any job correctly, no matter if they are to pack your parachute or to meet the requirements of the job.

Teamwork

We hear a great deal about the need for teamwork in the workplace today. There is no question that a person can accomplish more working as a member of a team than as a single individual. By combining the efforts of individuals on a team, the end result is greater than those all the members could ever achieve working independently. In other words, teamwork is proof that the sum of the whole is greater than those of its parts.

Managing by Remote Control requires team effort as well. Working on a team at work is not unlike being part of a mountain climbing expedition. Each member of the team has specific jobs and responsibilities which support the group's overall or ultimate objective to reach the top of the mountain. Reaching the summit of the mountain is in every sense a team accomplishment, even if everyone on the expedition doesn't actually physically ascend to the top. The glory and the reward of conquering the mountain must be shared with every member of the team who helped make the accomplishment possible.

In the workplace, everyone on the team must also be recognized and rewarded for their contributions to the team's success. Regardless of their role or position, each team member needs to share in the pride of what they have accomplished working together.

Remote Control Coaching

The Remote Control Manager needs to be able to coach those who report to him or her as they learn to become more empowered and assume greater levels of responsibilities. Coaching is essentially helping to bring out the best in others. It is the most developmental aspect of leadership. It is in the role of a coach that the Remote Control Manager can perhaps have the greatest impact on the organization. Think about some of the best coaches you have had as you were growing up. How did they affect your life? What made them good coaches? What was it about their influence on your life that you still remember today? How can you influence those whom you will coach at work in a similar manner?

Coaches are typically associated with sports. In this role, coaches develop and guide their players to not only reach their own personal best as athletes, but also to work together as a team. The role of the Remote Control Manager as a coach is no different. The coach in the workplace must help each employee reach his or her greatest potential as a worker as well as contribute to the overall success of the organization. Once all the practices are over in preparation for the big game, all the coach can really do is sit on the sidelines and support his team. He may call some plays or make certain player substitutions, but success is now in the control of the players. This is similar to the role of the Remote Control Manager. He can do everything he knows how to do to prepare employees for their positions, but there will come a time when they need to perform on their own.

Coaching Skills

However, each person has different needs at different times during the learning process as they assume greater responsibilities. This will be determined by the level of expertise or task mastery that individual has as this transition process begins. To begin the process, effective communications in the form of **feedback** to the individual on his or her performance is essential. People need to know how they are doing. If it is a new assignment or job, people need to be shown the basics of the tasks or skills you want them to perform and need **development.** Others already have a certain degree of mastery of the task and require less instruction and more **direction.** Yet others may have already mastered the task and need **support** in the performance of those responsibilities. The Remote Control Coaching models shown in "Coaching Skills" below show how to begin the coaching process under four different learning scenarios. Once the process has been begun, the other stages of the Remote Control Coaching Model should subsequently be followed. People may have a need for their manager to provide all of these coaching skills — it is often the sequence in which they are presented that becomes most important to the individual.

Feedback

Feedback is essential for personal growth. Without feedback, people would have no idea how others, and in particular their supervisor, perceived how well they were performing their job. In any team environment, this information can be critical to the individual performer's success. The Remote Control Manager needs to ensure that feedback is provided to everyone for whom he or she is responsible. This feedback can come in many different forms. It may be directly from the Remote Control Manager or it could come from co-workers or even others outside the organization familiar with their work. Feedback is needed most frequently as someone is learning something new to help shape their performance and enable the next step in the coaching process — development — to take place.

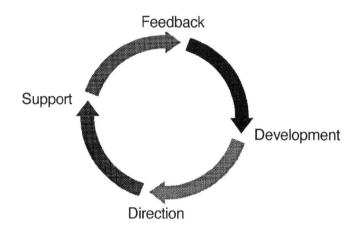

Development

Development is the key to establishing a culture of Remote Control Management. For this concept to become a reality, the development of the people for whom the Remote Control Manager is responsible is critically important. A major aspect of Remote Control Coaching is helping others develop their skills and grow both personally and professionally. This helps guide them in the direction in which they need to go in the future. Again, it is not fair to ask or expect people to perform tasks for which they have not been given the opportunity to develop the necessary skills required.

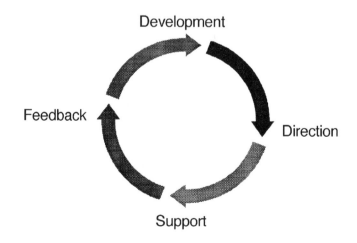

Direction

It is often in providing direction, that many managers seem to have the most difficulty. Giving feedback and providing developmental opportunities to employees is something that most managers are used to doing. However, providing direction is something far less familiar or even clear as to what is required to do this well. Regardless of how independent and capable employees may be, they still need direction. They need to know if they are going in the right direction and where they should be headed in the future. A Remote Control Manager must be careful not to distance himself too far from those for whom he is responsible. The Remote Control Manager needs to be at times like a beacon in the night guiding the way through times of uncertainty and confusion that his direct reports may experience on their jobs. The Remote Control Manager needs to provide this direction as well as support, as is seen in the last step of this coaching process.

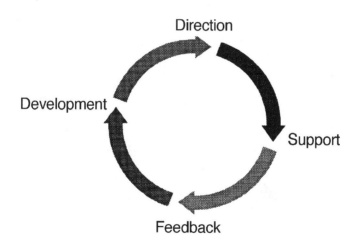

Support

Without support nothing can survive. The Remote Control process itself needs to have the support of the entire organization in order to thrive and be successful. Similarly, the Remote Control Manager must provide this support to the parts of the organization and people for which he or she is responsible. Support can come in many different forms. It may be providing resources, allowing others to take risks, in continuing to have faith in people

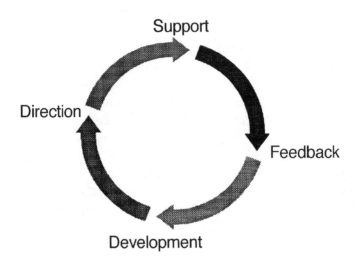

even during stressful or challenging times, or it might be just listening to what others have to say. Support, like direction, can sometimes be easily overlooked as being important. Of all the steps in the coaching process, support is perhaps the most important. It can drive the other three steps and make Remote Control Management possible even in those circumstances where common sense may tell you otherwise. Support gives people the confidence to perform to the best of their ability. Sports coaches have long understood its importance. The best coaches don't yell at their players when they make a mistake, but rather offer their support at those times when they need it the very most in order to help them have the confidence to perform to the best of their ability in the future.

2 Empowering Remote Control

Remote Control Management is truly a function of empowerment. Empowerment forms the basis for any remote control system that may ever exist. Empowerment involves entrusting others to make decisions and accept responsibilities that you would otherwise take on yourself. This can be a great leap of faith in others for most managers to make. What is most important is that a Remote Control Manager has an accurate understanding of what empowerment is and what it is not. Empowerment involves the changing of roles that people play at various levels of the organization. Empowerment also redefines the roles that employees play in an organization. Responsibilities not traditionally associated with certain roles in the organization now become part of the job. Empowerment moves decisions and responsibilities to the lowest level in the organization where they can be competently made. But empowerment is not an abdication of management responsibilities. The manager is just as accountable for the responsibilities he or she has been assigned by the organization in a Remote Control work environment as in a more traditional organization. What is different is the way in which these accountabilities are fulfilled.

Through empowerment, a Remote Control Manager enables everyone to make greater contributions to the organization and to reach their highest potential. Empowerment utilizes peoples' experience and expertise which may have been underutilized for years, even decades. Empowerment puts decisions in the hands of those who are the real experts in their area of expertise. It just makes sense that a person who has performed a job for a long period of time would know more about the problems that exist on that job than anyone else. Why not utilize this experience rather than ignoring it? Everyone will be more satisfied and productive as a result.

As can be seen in the following model of empowered management decision making, the manager sets him- or herself apart from most of the day-to-day decision making. The rationale for this approach is to give responsibility to those who work closest to the problems they face on their jobs, who are the "real experts" at finding their solutions, just as in the story that follows. In an empowered working environment, employees on all levels learn to more effectively utilize the resources that are available to continuously control and improve the processes at work.

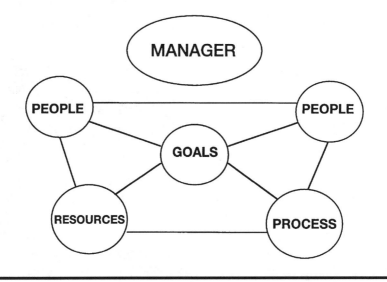

The Empowering Manager

In the following story, the expertise of those who work closest to where there is a problem with a recently installed computer system are finally given the opportunity to give their input into what they believe is the solution. As you read the story, think of how the concepts of Remote Control Management need to be built upon empowering others to accept more responsibility for the success of the organization. Think of this story as a "pilot" for a new show that might be appearing at your place of work. The story line and characters will be different but the concepts and lessons that can be learned may be very similar.

The Real Experts

John Green worked for the same company for the past 23 years. He began his career loading trucks on the shipping dock and progressed over the years through a number of positions in the shipping department. With a nationwide customer base, this part of the company's operation was a very important aspect of the business. As a Shipping Coordinator, John had responsibility for ensuring that all orders in a multi-state area were processed and sent out correctly. This job required interaction with a wide variety of other employees on many levels of the organization. John and the other Shipping Coordinators all reported to the Shipping Supervisor, Sam Kelly.

Sam gave the Shipping Coordinators very specific instructions and assignments each day. The Shipping Coordinators had little input concerning the way their department was operated. They had learned that it was best to simply do what they were told, even though they might not always feel that it was the right thing to do or that they had a better idea. Recently, a problem was discovered concerning the accuracy of the orders being shipped to customers. The problem began when a new computerized system was installed for processing orders and tracking shipping information. There were many, including John, who yearned for the "good old days" of not so long ago when this information was computed and calculated manually. At least then everyone had an understanding of how orders were processed and what needed to be done when a problem occurred.

"It's getting so bad I don't even want to go to work anymore," John told his wife at breakfast one morning. "That new computer system is completely disrupting everything in the department. The other Shipping Coordinators and I are spending more time trying to solve problems that the computer makes than doing our jobs anymore!"

"Why doesn't somebody do something to correct the problem?" John's wife, Sally asked, as she poured herself a cup of coffee.

"They brought in some expert from Headquarters who is supposed to know all about the system. He's been here for three weeks and still doesn't have a clue about what the problem is. All the big bosses have been in meetings all week trying to figure this thing out," replied John.

"What do you think is the problem?"

"What makes you think I would know the answer when all the experts don't seem to know what to do?"

"I know how smart you are, John Green, but obviously, even after all these years your company doesn't!"

"I'm not the only one in our department who has ideas about how to improve our operation. I only wish they would pay more attention to what we have to say. They might just find the answers to many of the problems we are dealing with today. Hey, its getting late. I have to go. See you tonight. I hope the kids will be home for dinner for a change, or do they have activities after school?"

"Believe it or not, everyone is going to be home for dinner!," Sally began to answer, but before she had a chance to finish, her husband had grabbed his lunch and was already out the door. "That problem at work must really be bothering John," she thought to herself as she cleared the breakfast dishes. "I only wish that they would listen to John's ideas and realize just how much he has to offer."

(*Later at work*) "So, are things any better today?" John asked several of the other Shipping Coordinators as they sat in the break room shortly before the start of their shift.

"Doesn't look like it," replied Dick Sanders, another Shipping Coordinator. "I heard Sam and that guy from HQ get into it again this morning. Sam said he's tired of having to put up with this problem day after day with no improvement in sight."

"So am I!," said John as he began to look at some of the order sheets for the day, "I wonder what problems await us in these orders and which customers we will upset today?" he continued as he shook his head in disgust. His thoughts were interrupted by Sam Kelly coming into the room looking very unhappy, as had been the case for the past several weeks, ever since the new computer had arrived. However, today he looked particularly upset. He asked to speak to the Shipping Coordinators in his office right away.

Once everyone was in the room, Sam began. "As you all know we're having a big problem with the new computer system that was recently installed. What was supposed to save us time, effort, and headaches has turned into a nightmare!"

"I wish we were dreaming this and we would all wake up and the new computer would be gone!" Herb Johnson interjected in his usual sarcastic manner, as several other of the Shipping Coordinators laughed in agreement.

"Let me finish," insisted Sam. "I know how you all feel about the new system, particularly you, Herb. The shipping schedules are all messed up; customers are getting the wrong orders or receiving them late. None of you have any confidence that the information you are receiving is accurate.It seems that, at best, there is only a 50/50 chance that the information is correct, which are not very good odds in our business! I know a number of you feel we should just get rid of the new system and go back to the old one, but its just not that simple. First of all, the old system was too slow and this caused many problems in itself. If you remember, many of us in this room complained so much about it that they bought the new computer. If we are to remain competitive, we must be able to respond in much less time to customer orders than we have in the past. Also, there has been a tremendous amount of money spent on this project and no one is going to allow the computer system to be abandoned, particularly after this short a period of time. Instead of talking about getting rid of it, we should be talking about how to make it work. We are all getting a lot of pressure to get this problem corrected. What I would like you as a group to do is to work together to develop some kind of plan to keep orders going out as accurately as possible until we get this problem straightened out. Why don't you meet again later on today to discuss this, say towards the end of the shift when things slow done at 3:00 p.m. Right now, I have to run to meet with Steve Andrews, the computer specialist from HQ. He keeps trying to tell me that all the tests he has conducted on the system show that it is working correctly, and I keep asking him, if that is the case then why does it keep sending orders to the wrong customers!"

"Sam, before you leave, can we talk to you now about this problem? I have some ideas about what we should do to correct it. Maybe you could share them with Steve Andrews during your meeting?" John asked.

"Sorry, John, I just don't have time. Maybe we can talk later," he replied as he rushed off to his meetings.

(*Later that morning*) Sam Kelly's boss asked to talk with him to review the problem and develop further plans to resolve it. "We don't seem to be making much progress so far," Sam told Frank Thompson. "I just met with Steve Andrews again this morning. We keep checking and rechecking they system and software programs and just haven't found the source of the problem yet. We're getting to the point where we're running out of possibilities to check. In the meantime, I've asked the Shipping Coordinators to try to come up with some kind of plan to keep orders being sent out as correctly as possible until we get the system working properly. The've got a pretty good idea from experience where orders should be sent despite the misinformation the system is providing them."

"Maybe the Shipping Coordinators could help solve the system problem?" Frank Thompson asked.

"But the Shipping Coordinators don't know anything about the computer system. How could they help?" Sam asked.

"I'm not sure I can answer that question, but I do know that they are more knowledgeable about their part of our operation than anyone else. I would like you to get together with our Human Resources Manager, Paul Martin, to learn more about something called empowerment that many companies like ours have begun with great success. I'll give him a call and let him know you'll be coming to see him today."

(*Early that afternoon, Sam went to meet with Paul Martin*) "Come on in, Sam," Paul said when Sam appeared at his office door. "Let's talk for a few minutes, and then I'd like you to come with me to a presentation this afternoon at the Community Center on the very subject you're here to talk about."

"I'm not sure I have time to do all this today. We're having some real serious problems in my area that I've got to get back to," replied Sam.

"Yes, I know. Frank filled me in on some of the background about what has been going on. I agree with him that the concepts and principles of empowerment may help your department out a great deal."

"What is empowerment all about, anyway?" Sam asked. "I've been hearing a lot about it lately, but I'm still not sure I understand how we can expect employees to be able to get their jobs done without supervision. After all that's why people like myself are employed, isn't it?"

"Well, first of all, empowerment doesn't mean that there is no longer a need for Supervisors in an organization. What is changing is the role that Supervisors and other management positions will play in the future. We're learning to allow employees, on all levels of the organization, greater authority and decision-making ability concerning their jobs and how our operation is run. We've learned that the people working on the jobs closest to where the problems exist are in the best positions to find solutions to the problems," explained Paul.

"I sure agree with that. We have good people working for us — the best, in fact. I can think of many times they have come up with ideas that have saved us a great deal of time and money. But I still don't understand where this leaves people in positions like mine?" Sam asked.

"I think I understand your concern, Sam. It's shared by virtually everyone in supervisory or even management positions in any organization where the concepts of empowerment are being introduced. Let me try to explain it this way. What would you do if you had the time that to do the things that could really move your department forward towards reaching its goals and be the best it could possibly be?" Paul asked.

"I guess there'd be a lot of things I'd do if I had the time," answered Sam.

"For instance?"

"Well, I'd do a lot more planning ahead, for one thing. Looking at what work is coming up and what we need to do to get prepared for it. I'd like to provide more training for the Shipping Coordinators as well as the other people in our department. I'm still not convinced that the root cause of our current problems with the new computer system doesn't have something to do with lack of training. I would have to give your question more thought, but those are a few things that come to mind that I would do," Sam replied.

"How much of your time do you presently spend doing these things?" asked Paul.

"Actually, when I stop to think about it, I hate to admit that I spend very little of my time on those types of things," answered Sam.

"Why not?"

"It seems like I spend most of my time chasing around trying to solve the everyday problems that constantly keep coming up. But someone has to take care of those kinds of details or our customers would take their business elsewhere," replied Joe.

"I'm not suggesting that we stop addressing problems. I *am* questioning who is in the best position to resolve these problems and accepting the responsibility to ensure that everything is done to prevent them from recurring," Paul replied. "It is clear that you and many others in our organization are not working up to your real potential for the benefit of both yourselves and the organization. We need to stop being restricted by our own perceptions of the roles we each traditionally have played in the past."

"Are you saying we need to allow our employees to have more responsibility for solving many of the problems concerning their jobs that supervisors have been trying to tackle all these years because they are in a better position to be able to resolve these problems?" asked Sam.

"That's exactly what I'm saying," said Paul. "Empowerment means just that. Employees are given more authority and ability to make a greater contribution to the organization. We will hear more about these concepts at the program. Say, it's getting late; we'd better be on our way. That's, if you are going to join me?"

"I guess I better find the time," said Sam. "I am beginning to see that we may have a greater chance of solving our problem through empowerment than by checking and rechecking that new computer system over and over again!"

At the workshop on Empowerment, a panel of several business executives in the community discuss the successes their companies were having in utilizing the concepts of employee involvement and participation in their decision making processes. The President of one of the area's largest firms explained,

"At our company we use the term 'Self-Managing Teams' to describe this new philosophy concerning the roles our employees now play in our organization, because that is what each person has become

— a manager of those aspects of our operation for which he or she is responsible. Our people today are more challenged and motivated and have a greater sense of accomplishment than ever before. They are now addressing many of the problems that have existed on their jobs for years that they previously didn't have the opportunity to correct. We are proving over and over again that the *real experts* concerning our operations are those working closest to where the problems exist. These people are more qualified than anyone else to create practical and cost-effective ways to improve their jobs and ultimately our business by becoming more involved. Listening is the most important key to being successful in developing self-managing workteams in any organization. All of us, on every level of our organizations, must do a better job of listening to what each other has to say In these communications is the answer to virtually every problem and challenge we face. By working together as a team and really listening to the ideas of others, there is no one we can't beat!"

"Empowerment," another business leader said during her presentation, "doesn't mean that you're giving up or losing your own authority. Empowerment actually means that you are expanding your authority by at least a number equal to or even greater than the number of people you have empowered with more responsibility to make a difference in their jobs. Your employees will have a greater sense of ownership of their jobs, becoming more satisfied and productive in their work. With empowerment, the more you give, the more you get back!"

It was beginning to rain lightly on the ride back. There was silence in the car except for the rhythmic beating of the windshield wipers going back and forth. "You seem deep in thought," Paul said to Sam, finally breaking the silence.

"I was just thing about what they were saying about empowerment. You know — that the more you give the more you get back and what that really means," replied Sam.

"What do you think it means?"

"I think it means many different things, but in our department it might mean the more authority and decision-making responsibility I give the people who work for me, the better they will be able to do their jobs and the more satisfied they will become concerning their work. I think it would eliminate a lot of the hassle and frustration they experience trying to get things changed through our present systems. That can only help everyone, including me, allowing me to do my job better, and so on up and down the lines of the organization. Like they said, the more you give the more you get back," explained Sam. "Is that the basic idea of the concept?" he asked.

"I think that you're beginning to get the idea!" said Paul.

It was nearly 3:00 p.m. when they returned. Sam didn't know exactly what he was going to say to the Shipping Coordinators at their meeting. However, he did know that as a result of the things he had learned that day there were changes that needed to be made. The first change was that Sam was not going to tell the Shipping Coordinators what the plan of action was going to be to deal with the systems problem; he was going to ask them what they thought should be done. "A small step for a Supervisor — a giant step for the employees and organization as a whole!" he thought to himself.

John Green and the other Shipping Coordinators came into the conference room a few minutes before 3:00 p.m. They looked tired and frustrated. It had been another particularly difficult day trying to correct the mistakes made by the computer. Also, more customers were beginning to complain about receiving wrong orders and wanted assurances that these mistakes would not happen again. Unfortunately, this was something that could not be guaranteed at this time with the problem still out of control. The situation was beginning to become a crisis, and if something did not happen soon there were going to be major consequences. The Shipping Coordinators were further frustrated by their expectation that this meeting would be no different or more productive than any of those on this problem in the past.

Sam began the meeting, "As we discussed this morning, we must do something about this problem before it puts us out of business. But before we talk about that, I'd like to begin with something else that I believe will help us solve our problem, something even more important to our future than the systems problem we are presently experiencing." The Shipping Coordinators looked at each other in astonishment. What could possibly be more important to discuss at this meeting than the systems problem that had their entire department in a tailspin and threatened their very existence?

Sensing their confusion, Sam continued, "Just today I began to learn about a new concept that I believe will help us solve this and other problems we have beeen experienceing in our department. When I think about it now, it seems so simple and logical I don't know why we never thought of it before or perhaps you had, and I wasn't listening. What I am talking about is something called empowerment."

"What do you mean by empowerment?" asked one of the Shipping Coordinators.

"Empowerment is something that many companies like ours are beginning to utilize in their organizations as a basic management philosophy. Empowerment involves allowing people in the organization to become more involved in the decision making process and to assume greater responsibility for the management of their jobs and the operation. The point is that no one knows more about their jobs and the impact they have on the rest of the organization than those who perform those duties on a daily basis. There is a huge amount of untapped resources in our organization that has not been allowed to be fully developed. Those working closest to where a problem exists are in the best position to find solutions to these problems. In turn, people find their jobs more satisfying and rewarding when they are given greater opportunities to share their experience and ability to improve not only their jobs, but ultimately the entire organization. People have far more ability to make decisions concerning their jobs than we have ever given them credit for in the past.

"Are you saying that we're going to become empowered?" John asked.

"Well, we certainly are going to begin taking the first steps towards becoming empowered," he replied. "As a matter of fact, if I'm not mistaken, you had a suggestion this morning concerning the computer system problem that I didn't have time to listen to. This is exactly what needs to change. What I'd like to do this afternoon is to allow you all as a group to discuss the problem and begin making recommendations concerning how it can be solved. Why don't you spend the rest of this meeting discussing this and continue on ti tomorrow if necessary? I'd like you to tell me how much time you feel you will need after that, so we can meet on a regular basis to discuss how to better operate our department and the roles each of you should play in making decisions concerning your jobs."

As Sam left the room, the Shipping Coordinators couldn't believe what had just happened. This was certainly totally different from anything they had ever heard in the past. Typically, they were told what to do and they did it, even though sometimes they disagreed that it was the right thing to do. No one had ever really wanted to know what they thought before!

"What do we do now?" asked Dick Summers. "I guess we should get busy solving this problem before we lose all of our customers," Jane Dover answered.

"And our jobs too!" stated Dave Reed. "But where do we start?"

"Let's begin by writing down all of the suggestions and ideas everyone has about how to solve this problem," suggested John.

Dick Summers began, "Well, one thing we know for sure is that our problems began when the new computer system was installed. Everyone has been focusing on the computer as the culprit and reason for the mess we are in, but I'm not so sure it is the cause," he questioned.

"Well isn't it? We didn't have any of these problems before they put in that wonderful machine that was supposed to make our jobs easier, our future brighter, and our lives more satisfying! You're beginning to sound like that expert from HQ who keeps trying to tell us that its not the computer's fault orders are all screwed up and we are about to lose just about every customer we have!" exclaimed Herb, with the agreement of several others in the group.

"Let me finish," Dick pleaded. "I think we all need to have open minds about this problem or we are never going to solve it. I've thought a lot about the events that led up to this problem, and I think by looking at these things we can get a better idea of the solution. Right now everyone is complaining about the new system, but like Sam said this morning, if you remember back about a year ago, everyone was complaining because we had to do this work manually."

"That's true," Jane Turner added. "As we got more and more customers and orders our old manual order-processing system became inefficient. We seem to be forgetting that we were the ones that wanted the new system. But we wanted one that made our jobs easier, not more difficult!" she added.

"Let's write down the sequence of events as they occurred," said Dick as he walked over to the padboard. "We first approached Sam about a year ago and presented to him the need for some kind of computerized order-processing system that could more efficiently allocate and schedule orders given to each Shipping Coordinator. We were seeing too many instances throughout the different shipping zones when we weren't able to take advantage of more favorable shipping rates by sending larger orders out. The problem was that it took too long to manually sort out all the order information that came in. We couldn't wait to begin filling orders until all this information was compiled. Once we had the information in a format that would be useful to us, it was too late to more efficiently allocate orders. The more orders that come in, the more time it takes to process them. This wasn't a problem when we had fewer orders, because we could process them in much less time. But now with our recent expansion this has become a real problem," Dick concluded.

"Dick, we already know all of this," remarked Herb. "We all realize that we need to do something about handling all the new orders. The question is how are we going to correct the mess we are in now?"

"Patience Herb, patience. That's what we're here to talk about," said John.

"Let's call those hotshots from HQ in here to come up with the answers. That's what they get paid the big bucks to supposedly be able to do. Why should we get involved in these problems. Its not our job, and even when we find the problem, they probably won't listen to us anyway. They never have in the past!" Herb snapped back.

"Wait a minute," said Dick. "I personally think that its a great idea to finally get us involved in solving problems in our operation. I think if a problem can have an effect on this department and our jobs, then it is our business to be involved in finding solutions to the problem. I believe that we have a much better chance of understanding and resolving the problems we face daily, because we are the ones most familiar with them. Anyway, who says all the brains are at the top?"

"Hear, hear!" said several others in the group.

"I'm just glad that someone is finally ready to listen to us. I think, over coffee in the break room each morning, we have many great ideas about what we should do to improve this department that never get implemented. What needs to be done is to make these ideas become reality, not just talk over coffee and a donut," offered Ken, who had been intently listening to the conversation.

"I think tha's exactly what we need to begin doing," said John. "We're almost out of time right now. Why don't we all think about possible solutions to this problem at home tonight, and instead of having our coffee in the break room, let's meet in here in the conference room in the morning and see if we can generate some more 'coffee breakthrough' ideas!"

"Coffee breakthrough ideas!" chuckled Ken. "We've got to write that one down."

On the ride home from work, John and Herb discussed the 3 o'clock meeting." John, you know that I'm not sure I'm convinced that they're really going to listen to us. We've worked together a long time, and you know as well as I do that we've heard these things before. Seems like every time a new vice president comes in, we start hearing about the importance of effective communications and how they are going to start listening to us. The problem is we are always listening to them instead of them listening to us."

"I think they are serious about it this time," replied John. "I really believe getting us involved in finding the solutions to problems rather than the way we typically approached problems in the past is really going to make a difference."

"We'll see," said Herb, "we'll see."

During dinner John told his family about what had happened at work that day. "I hope you are going to share your ideas with them about how to solve the problem," Sally Green said to her husband.

"Like I asked you this morning, what makes you think I know the answer to the problem?" John replied.

"You know the answer," both his teenage children said, and his wife nodded in agreement.

John explained to them what Sam told them about the concepts of empowerment and how they were going to begin utilizing these concepts in their department.

"That sounds like a great idea!" said John's daughter Cathy. "Why can't we become empowered around here? Kevin and I will make the decisions you and Mom now make — such as what time we have to be home at night on the weekends and how much we can spend on clothes!"

"And how often I can borrow the car," added Kevin.

"Somehow, I don't think those are necessarily the kinds of decisions that empowered teams make or what they are all about," replied John, as he thought about the answer he ad just given his children. "I think it would be more like becoming involved in helping remodel the new family room I'm planning to start in a few weeks. After all, the project is actually to give the two of you and your friends a place to watch television and listen to music," John explained.

"Are you sure you really aren't just trying to get the TV in our family room upstairs all to yourself during the football season?" Cathy asked.

"Well, that too! But seriously, I believe that our family could benefit from these concepts of empowerment. I think in our case, it would mean that the two of you would be involved in helping build the new room and in making decisions concerning how it should be designed, such as what color the carpet and the walls will be and any other details concerning the new room. When the project is completed you will feel a greater sense of accomplishment and pride in the new room."

"Sounds great, let's do it!" Cathy said. "I can't wait to start picking out everything for the new room. It's really going to look nice when we are finished."

"Well, you know along with decision making comes responsibility. If you are going to be involved in decisions concerning the new room you need to also accept the responsibilities and commitment which go along with making these plans. With all this help I feel like getting started as soon as possible!" said John.

"I think it sounds like fun," Cathy said.

"I'm all for it," said Kevin.

"Great. Maybe we can even get your mother to pound a few nails!" joked John.

"I'll be there!" replied Sally.

Most of the Shipping Coordinators came in earlier than usual the next morning and were in the conference room talking about the events of the previous afternoon. Several were discussing the reactions their families had to what they had told them about the concepts they had told about the day before.

Dick began the meeting, "Yesterday we started to talk about the sequence of events that got us into this problem. Last night I spent a lot of time reviewing in my mind what the chain of events had been. I thought it would be a good idea to begin by continuing to list these so we are sure we all understand how we got to where we are today. We already talked about why we needed the computer system in the first place. Now what happened once it was installed?"

"I think the problem was what didn't happen," said Ken Watson.

"What do you mean?" asked Dick.

"Do you remember when they had that big meeting to tell us that they were going to put in the new system?" Ken asked.

"Sure. The same guy, who made a big presentation about the capabilities of the new system and how much easier and more efficient it was going to make our jobs, is here again — trying to debug the system! What a joke! What is the name of the new computer — *The Genius System*. Some genius — it can't even send the right order to the right customer! I'm still waiting for it to make my job easier!" Herb added with his usual sarcasm.

"What I'm trying to get at," continued Ken, "is that I can remember thinking, even during that presentation, that several things were not included in the computer programming that should have been. I tried to tell that guy about this after the presentation, but he didn't seem very interested"

"What do you think should have been included in the program?" asked Dick.

"For one thing, the system was not categorizing orders by state — only by shipping codes. Even if the system ever does get to working properly, we will still have to sort out this information manually if a programming change isn't made. And judging by the interest they take in what we tell them about what we need the program to do, it'll never happen. Sorting out this data takes us as much time as the shipping codes, even more," Ken answered.

"Now that you mention it," said Jane, "I'm not very satisfied with the way the system identifies customers. Seems to me that the criteria that are used don't make a great deal of sense. Rather than the volume of business we do with each customer, it would be more useful to us to categorize the data by what product they purchase. How much they buy may be important to Headquarters, but what they buy is what we have to a greater need to know about in the Shipping Department. This is what tells us where we need to go to fill the orders. Once we have the product located, the rest of processing the order is easy. It is not that big a deal to enter the information concerning the amount ordered," Jane added.

"You know, there are a few things about the new system I *do* like," offered Dave Reed, who was the newest of the Shipping Coordinators and had recently been transferred from a different department. "I guess coming in new I'm not as used to the old system as most of you are, so I have nothing to compare it against. We had a similar computer system in the area I used to work in, and for the most part it worked quite well. Although I have to add, we didn't receive as much training on the system and how to operate it before it was installed as we did in this department. I've been trying a few things sort of on my own on my terminal and can do most of the same things we did on the other system."

"Like what?" asked Dick.

"For instance, the system will allow you to call up on the screen a customer's order history, and it has a place to enter your own comments concerning specific requirements that the customers has for processing their orders. This may include names of contact persons at the company who may not appear on their order sheet or an address that they want certain orders sent to. The system gives you a convenient way to get this information simply by pushing a button," Dave added.

"I'm sure glad we were told about all these features when they installed the system. It sure is nice to be *in* on things," Herb complained.

"As a matter of fact, I even found out we can do some things that we couldn't do on the other system I worked on. John suggested some things to do just a couple of days ago that have worked real well," continued Dave.

"Hey, wait a minute!" said Jane. "You know, come to think of it, John you've hardly said a word yet about this problem. We all know you better than that. In fact, you *did* start to say something to Sam the other morning. Now give us your ideas!" Jane demanded.

"Why does everybody think I know the answer to this problem?" John asked.

"Because you always have good ideas," replied Dave. "Just like the other day, when you asked me to try to enter that information into the computer. But I don't think you told me everything you were trying to find out. You were definitely leading up to some kind of theory about the root cause of this problem."

"All right, let's have it, John," demanded Jane with the rest of the group's support.

"OK, but it is just a theory I have that hasn't been proven yet," he began. "I've had the feeling all along that the problem wasn't really a systems problem, but a people problem."

"What do you mean, a people problem!" interrupted Herb. "It's not our fault the thing doesn't work like they thought it would. You keep saying things like that around here and they'll end up getting rid of us instead of the computer like they should!"

"But I'm not suggesting that its yours, mine, or anyone else's fault," John said calmly. "I just don't think that the initial data that was entered into the computer was correct. I keep thinking I can see some kind of pattern in the mistakes the computer has been making, but I can't seem to be able to identify what it is. That's why I asked you to do that switching around of information into the computer to see if we could fool it into giving us the right information and if the reports might come out more accurately," John said to Dave.

"Now that you mention it, the system has been consistently wrong," said Jane.

"That's for sure!" added Ken.

"No, I mean that John is right. There has been a pattern to when and where the system starts making mistakes. If we could just figure out the pattern, we would have the answer to the problem," Jane said.

"It may not even be that complicated," replied Herb, looking over a computer report summarizing the previous shift's shipping activity that the Shipping Coordinators had begun receiving each morning. "I've never paid that much attention to this report before, but we never really were told what it was supposed to be used for. It looks like the customer codes were mixed up when entered into the system. Take a look." Herb placed the report on the table for the group to review. "You know what?" he continued "I'll bet my last dollar that they used the old customer code book when this data was originally entered into the system!"

"Your last dollar? You probably have the first dollar you ever made, as cheap as you are!" John kidded, as everyone laughed. "But that's beside the point. I'll bet you're right as well. In fact, now that you mention it, I can recognize some of the old code assignments in wrong places, just looking at this report," said John. "Let's get hold of Steve Andrews, the systems guy, and tell him about this so he can make the corrections."

"What makes you think he'll listen to us now. He never has before?" asked Ken.

"We'll get Sam to sit in on the meeting — although I don't think that will be necessary. At this point, I think Steve will be willing to listen to just about anything that might solve this problem. Besides, I really believe that things are beginning to improve around here, and that the concepts of empowerment that Sam talked about are going to be a very good change for everyone. This is an excellent example of why these concepts can be successful. Neither Steven or anyone else from outside our department could have never known that the customer codes were changes since the system was installed and that the wrong ones were entered. And imagine, who would have ever dreamed it would be our own Herb who discovered the real cause of the computer problems!" added John, as everyone patted Herb on the back as they left the room.

A meeting was arranged for later that day for the Shipping Coordinators to meet with Steve Andrews, Sam Kelly, Frank Thompson, and Paul Martin to present their solution to the computer problems that had eluded all the experts. By unanimous choice, the Shipping Coordinators had appointed Herb as their spokesman to present their ideas at the meeting, as he was the one who had identified the true root cause of the problem. Obviously, Herb was an unlikely spokesperson for the group, but somehow for that reason everyone felt that he was the perfect choice. Herb, still surprising everyone, readily accepted the assignment. As the group came into the room and got seated, Herb finished drawing a chart on the board showing the sequence of events which had led up to the problem:

> *Decision to install new computer system → HQ's decides requirements for new system → Installation of new system → New system put on line → Old order-processing procedure eliminated → Present problem with incorrect orders being processed.*

"As we see it," Herb reported, "this problem began way back at the beginning of this sequence with the decision to install the new computer system. Despite our complaints and criticisms, we really do realize the need and potential benefits of putting in this system."

"I can't believe my ears!" said Sam in disbelief. "Are you sure that is you, Herb, or am I dreaming this? When is Rod Sterling going to walk in this room and tell us that us that we are now in the Twilight Zone? Somebody pinch me so I'll wake up!" Sam mockingly continued, as everyone laughed at the irony of hearing the greatest critic of the new computer making such an unlikely statement.

"You know, Sam, it really wasn't the system I was so critical of, but rather how we went about installing it. And by the way, I'm not done criticizing the system or most everything else around here, so you're not dreaming and Rod is not going to come walking in that door! Let me try to draw a flow chart of the sequences of events we think should have occurred, and what we feel could have prevented the problem from occurring in the first place."

"You are going to tell us what you found to be the problem with the system, aren't you!" interrupted Steve Andrews, rather impatiently.

"I'm getting to that," replied Herb as he began to draw the new flow chart on the board, obviously enjoying the moment and making Steve even more anxious to learn the answer to the problem that he had been working on unsuccessfully for weeks.

Meet with Shipping Coordinators to discuss requirements for new computer system → Explain the steps involved in installing the new system to coordinators and have us involved in the process → Train Coordinators on inputting data and using the new system → Ensure correct data is entered into the system → Ensure new computer operating correctly before old manual procedure discontinued → Run new computer system for processing orders.

"But what does all this have to do with the systems problem?" asked Steve, becoming more and more upset each minute that Herb delayed sharing the answer to the problem with him.

Herb pointed to the fourth section of the flow chart, which read, "ensure correct data entered into system."

"You mean to tell me that this whole problem was caused by incorrect data being entered into the system?" Steve said in disbelief. "How could this have happened?"

"We went back after our meeting this morning and reviewed the incorrect shipping reports for the past several weeks and found an exact pattern to these errors that we traced back to incorrect customer codes being entered in the system. They actually weren't incorrect — just outdated. All of the Shipping Coordinators received the new code book about a month ago. Any one of us could have given you a copy if only you had asked," explained Herb totally relishing the moment.

"Let's get those codes correctly entered in the system right away and get back in business before we lose all of our customers," ordered Frank Thompson. "I would like to compliment the Shipping Coordinators for discovering this problem before it caused us even more problems that it already has. This is another excellent example of the importance of teamwork and communications in an organization. I would like to thank all of you for your excellent work!"

"Let's get together first thing tomorrow morning," Sam said to the Coordinators. "We need to talk more about how we are going to continue moving towards the concept of empowerment and how I can continue to give you more decision making and problem solving responsibilities. I would also like to add my appreciation to all of you."

The next morning they all met in the conference room. Sam began the meeting. "I've asked Paul Martin from our Human Resources group to join us this morning to help get us started in the right direction. Paul, why don't you begin by telling the group more about empowerment, if that the right name to call it?"

"Thanks for inviting me here this morning. Actually there is no absolute right or wrong name to call these concepts. What is most important is that employees on all levels of the organization have the opportunity to become more involved by sharing their knowledge and experience. What has occurred here during the past few days with your group is an excellent example of just how effective and important these concepts can be. Without the involvement of all of you, the problem with the incorrect customer codes might not have been discovered for weeks, or even months. Imagine what could have been the result if that had been the case? We either would have had to do away with the new computer system or would have lost all of our customers!"

"Now I'm sorry that I ever got involved in solving this problem, if it saves the new computer from getting scrapped!" interrupted Herb.

"I guess I'm finally back from the Twilight Zone, and the real Herb has returned to earth!," laughed Sam. "The point is that no one knows more about their jobs and how to solve problems and improve them than the people who work in those jobs. All of you are the real experts when it comes to your work. What is needed for us to be successful as an organization is to have more effective communications on all levels. There needs to be a greater sharing of information and listening on everyone's part."

"We've been hearing about the need for more effective communications around here for many years now," Jane commented. "What's going to be different now?"

"That's a fair question," said Paul. "Trying to achieve more effective communications around here typically meant putting up more bulletin board announcements or having large group informational meetings. This is not to say that these methods of communications aren't important or necessary. However, what we are beginning to learn is that our communications efforts cannot end with these programs. These communications were only one-way — that is from the top of the organization downward. We need to have effective communications between all groups of employees and, most importantly, to listen to what each other has to say. In these communications are the answers to most of our problems, such as why a million dollar computer system like the one installed in your department doesn't work."

"What do we need to do now, and how do we start becoming more empowered?" asked John.

"There are really no absolute rules or format to follow to become empowered. It is more of a management philosophy of how decisions are to be made and the roles each employee plays in the organization. Actually in many ways, these are not entirely new concepts in our company. We have just called them different things over the years."

"Sure," said Ken. "We used to call them Quality Circles. I was even on one of them. We did a lot of good things on that team. It was too bad that most of the members either transferred to other departments or retired and the team eventually was abandoned."

"That's a good example of similar approaches we have used in the past. I feel that the biggest difference between programs such as Quality Circles and the concepts of empowerment is that Quality Circles addressed specific problems of the job rather than the entire job. The many benefits of empowerment are the permanent improvements that result in the ways that everyone does their jobs. The best way I know how to explain it is by asking the question: If given the opportunity, what would each of you do that could help move your department forward to being better able to meet the requirements of the customer?"

After a few moments of silence, Sam was the first to answer. "I've already thought a lot about this question, ever since the last time we talked about this concept. I know for one thing that I spend too much of my time giving instructions to the Shipping Coordinators that they really don't need to have. Most of them have been doing their jobs for many years now and know our procedures better than I do. I guess it is just the way I was taught to do my job years ago," answered Sam, "But I guess a lot has changed since then."

"That's a good point," said John. "There are many things we see you do that we could do more easily because we already have the information. For instance, everyday we see you rush around getting information from each of us for the report you complete at the end of the shift. Instead, you could simply ask us to complete this information ourselves for our area and give the report to you. We have time at the end of the shift because usually by then we have all the shipments on their way."

"Also, there are several ways I believe this information could be reported differently so that it would be better organized and more meaningful when the final summary report is developed. It seems to me that we are duplicating an awful lot of the information that just becomes confusing in the final report," added Ken. "Some of the information could be pre-printed, perhaps by the new computer system, since by the end of the shift when the report is completed this information already in the computer."

"These sound like great ideas," said Sam. "In fact, let's give them a try as soon as possible. Ken, would you talk to the systems department about having that information pre-printed on the report forms?"

"Sure, be glad to," replied Ken.

"I'm beginning to realize that we spend an awful lot of time either doing things that someone else closer to the actual work would be in a better position should do. I also am beginning to realize that as a supervisor, I do a lot of checking up on people who are very capable of accepting responsibility for completing their job assignments on their own," said Sam. "Instead of duplicating each other's efforts, we need to focus on ways to improve our operations and ability to better serve our customers. But how do we begin to operate this way?"

"I think you have gotten off to a very good start in the past couple of days," said Paul. "As we talked, the term we often hear today is 'empowerment.' Empowerment means exactly what the word sounds like — giving people the power to do their jobs to the best of their ability. Empowerment involves allowing people to have more decision-making ability and to accept increased responsibility concerning their jobs. Many of the ideas we have discussed this morning involve empowering people to be more effective on their jobs. Empowerment means letting go of many of our attitudes and perceptions of the past concerning how decisions should be made in an organization. Empowerment is a difficult concept for some people to accept, particularly from many supervisors and managers. Sometimes, they may feel their job security threatened or that they will lose their ability to perform their jobs as these concepts are introduced in their organizations."

"I also still believe that many Supervisors and Managers will feel that they are losing their authority as a result of these concepts and that their job security is being threatened," Sam added.

"Actually, just the opposite is true. In fact, empowerment can increase their value and effectiveness. Think about all that you can accomplish by allowing the people working for you to be involved in helping you solve the problems and meet the challenges you now are attempting to do all by yourself. Empowerment allows everyone to make their jobs more effective by getting more people involved in them," continued Paul. "Solving the computer problem yesterday is an excellent example of the power of empowerment. In that case, empowerment meant asking the right people to get involved in finding the root cause of the problem."

"I agree," said Sam. "If the Shipping Coordinators had not solved this problem we all could have been out of a job. What we need to do is allow each of us to have the ability to make the greatest contribution to the organization that we possibly can. I guess a good way to begin would be for us to start talking more about what responsibilities everyone should have and how decisions should be made in the future in our department, right? asked Sam.

"That would be an excellent way to begin!" replied Paul.

During the next several months there were many changes in the Shipping Department. Sam and the Shipping Coordinators met regularly to discuss the accountabilities and responsibilities of their jobs. Their roles were redefined, and the decision-making process improved to allow the individual in the position closest to where the problems existed to make the decisions concerning resolution of the problem. They began conducting a brief update meeting each morning in which the group reviewed events from the previous day, as well as upcoming assignments. As a result of a suggestion from Jane, the Shipping Coordinators were invited to the weekly operations planning meeting held by the Operations Manager, which in the past was only attended by Department Heads. The Shipping Coordinators started attending these meetings and each attendee would share the information with the others in their group. They also invited the Operations Manager and other department heads to attend their morning meetings so that they would have a better idea of the problems and successes they were having utilizing the concepts of empowerment. They began a series of training classes which covered a number of critical job-related areas, including the new computer system, as well as information relating to the needs of their customers. Also, a program was begun to provide the Shipping Coordinators the opportunity to visit customer's locations to gain a better understanding of how to meet their needs.

As a result of all these changes, the Shipping Coordinators were empowered with much more responsibility and decision-making ability, including planning their work and ensuring that the requirements of the customers were met. Sam no longer spent his time almost exclusively following up on the Shipping Coordinators' work. Instead, he now focused on planning for future orders and trends. This allowed the department to be much more proactive to customers needs, rather than reactive to problems that were created by lack of planning. These changes were very positively received by all the Shipping Coordinators, and customer complaints were reduced dramatically. Everyone was pleased with the changes in the department, even Herb!.

"Paul, I would like you to come to one of our morning meetings," Sam requested one day, after a few more months had passed since the changes had been implemented.

"Sure, I would be glad to. I haven't met with your group for some time now. I am looking forward to hearing more about your progress," replied Paul.

"That's just it," said Sam. "I'm concerned about our progress. Don't get me wrong — becoming more empowered has been a much better way to operate our department than the way we operated in the past. Our people have a greater sense of ownership for their work and the organization as a whole. I'm no longer running around in circles chasing problems and our overall efficiency has greatly increased," Sam explained.

"Then what's the problem?"

"I don't know for sure," answered Sam. "It just seems as if there is a lot more conflict among the group than I remember when we first implemented these changes."

"Well, some conflict is not necessarily bad and is actually to be expected as part of the team process. Out of conflict often comes progress," Paul advised.

"Do you mean to tell me we want our employees to argue among themselves?"

"No. Not exactly," laughed Paul. "What I am saying is that conflict is a natural part of the process of people working together and is always going to exist to some extent. What is important is that we don't let the conflict to get to the point that it stops the progress of the team. We need to manage conflict to allow it to help the work of the team."

"I'm still not sure I understand how this conflict is good for the team?" asked Sam.

"There are always some ideas that get challenged by other team members that do require closer examination. It is this challenging and testing of ideas that usually results in better decisions being made, even though it is not always easy getting to this point."

"I'm beginning to understand what you are talking about. Just the other day, several of the Coordinators were discussing a new procedure that had recently been implemented, and they didn't agree on several key points. When the discussion was over, they had developed an improved procedure that has proven to be very successful. But I just get concerned that this conflict will have a negative affect on the effectiveness of our team," said Sam.

"Why don't I sit in on your next team meeting. I know you meet each morning. I'll be there tomorrow," said Paul.

Dick Summers began the morning meeting by reviewing several problems that had occurred during the previous week. There were still some minor problems with the new computer system, even though the major problem with the customer codes had been long since resolved by the team. Everyone had now come to accept and even depend on the system to make their jobs and the Shipping Department more efficient. Several of the Shipping Coordinators had different ideas on proposed programming changes they felt would improve the system.

"I've talked to Steve Andrews in HQ about changing the program to give us hourly reports concerning the incoming orders so we can have more up-to-the-minute data concerning scheduling plans," said Dick. "He feels that he could make this change within a month."

"I'm still not convinced this is really such a good idea," said Ken. "We get awful busy during the day to be checking this report every hour. I don't know how we could possibly make these changes hourly."

"What happens if we don't look at this report for several hours? Are we going to mess up the whole scheduling system?" Jane asked. "One scheduler may be making decisions based on information received at the beginning of the shift as we presently do, and someone else, based on the hourly reports. I'm afraid we'll be going in too many different directions if we make this change," she continued.

"But that's the problem now," insisted Dick. "We are all making decisions based on old information by the time we are 2 to 3 hours into the shift."

"Wait a minute. We have been using the beginning of the shifts information to schedule orders for as long as I can remember and it has worked well all these years. Why should we go changing things now just for the sake of change?" argued Ken.

"That's just the point. If you look back, you will see that our present system doesn't work all that well. That's why they put in the new computer system in the first place. No one wanted that change when it was first installed, but now we have all come to accept it and even like it," answered Dick.

"I'm not sure you could say that I *like* the new system. Tolerate it, may be more accurate in my case!" interjected Herb.

"All right, let's just leave it that we have all come to accept it. But even Herb would have to admit that it has made our jobs better.

We are all just beginning to realize the many improvements that can be made in our operation by more fully utilizing this powerful resource we now have. In the past we never had the capability to receive hourly order updates and today we do. We need to take advantage of the system's capabilities to help us continue to improve," Dick added.

"The system does give us capabilities we never had before," said John. "All this information is now available to us just by calling it up on the computer screen. We really should take advantage of this information."

"So you are saying that we should go to hourly reports?" asked Jane.

"Not necessarily," answered John. "What I am saying is there are many times when you don't need the information to be updated as often as on an hourly basis. We obviously will always need to set up our schedules at the beginning of the shift to plan our shipments that day. If we didn't it would be mass confusion around here."

"What are you suggesting?" asked Ken.

"That we do just what we have been discussing this morning. We need to utilize the capabilities we now have with the new system," John said.

"I'm not still not sure that I follow you," said Jane.

"I think what John is saying," offered Herb, finally speaking up, "is that we utilize the up to hour data in the system when we find we have a need for up-to-the-minute current information. There are many times during any given day when this would be useful information to have. But this does not mean that we change our daily shipping plans every time we log onto the system for updated information. That would drive everyone crazy!" Herb continued.

"What about in your case when the person is already crazy?" Dick kidded.

"That's the one thing I think everyone can agree on this morning!" said John. "But seriously that's exactly what I was saying. Herb, as usual, has summarized what we need to do to continue to move us forward. Its just too bad that we have to listen to all his other criticisms along with his words of wisdom." John continued as everyone laughed.

"I think this meeting is beginning to go downhill!" interjected Sam enjoying the humor along with the others. "It sounds like we have come up with some very good ideas today. We are all still learning just how much the system can help us and how to more fully utilize this powerful tool. I asked Paul to sit in on our meeting today because I wanted him to see our progress, and I had some concerns that we were not working together as a team as well as we could. However, after talking to Paul yesterday and observing our meeting this morning, I think that it is obvious that we are moving forward and continuing to grow as individuals and as a team. I'm always amazed to come in here and hear Herb talk positively about the computer system or anything else for that matter! This is a sure sign we are making progress," Sam said. "Do you have anything to add, Paul?"

"First of all, I would like to compliment all of you on your progress as a team. I feel we have come a long way from where we were several months ago, desperately trying to figure out why our new million dollar computer wasn't working, without a clue as to the reason why. It wasn't until we finally asked for the involvement of your group that we were able to discover the cause of the problem. As you all are learning, the teamwork process does not always come easy and it has its ups and downs. Conflict is sometimes part of the team process as different ideas and approaches are discussed and reviewed. As I was sharing with Sam, conflict is not always necessarily a bad thing. Often, conflict can challenge the team to examine a problem more closely. Sometimes the best ideas come as a result of a team working through a problem after many frustration or unsuccessful attempts to find the solution. From what I heard today, I believe your group is working through these problems quite well and I look forward to hearing more about your progress in the future."

As time went on, the group learned more and more about how to work effectively as a team. They found ways to turn their conflict into positive problem-solving efforts which usually resulted in better solutions being discovered. The Shipping Coordinators developed a more efficient and satisfying work environment for everyone. Instead of their supervisor giving out assignments and following up to see that they were completed, they organized and distributed the work themselves. The Shipping Coordinators had a greater sense of ownership for their work and were more committed to the success of the organization. Sam was now able to focus his time and energy on activities that could result in making the entire department more effective and able to meet the needs of their customers. They had become a team in every sense, with everyone contributing to its success. They learned that trust and respect for one another is the real definition of teamwork and that there was no challenge they could not meet when working together.

"Your new basement really looks nice," said Ken as he relaxed on the sofa trying to catch the score of the game on television. John had invited the Shipping Coordinators to his home as a way of celebrating the changes which had occurred at work and the progress they had made as a team.

"Thanks, but I can't take all the credit. I had some real good help. Didn't I?" John replied proudly as he hugged his children sitting next to him on the sofa.

"I would just like to know just how much work your Dad did on this project and how much you two got stuck with," joked Herb, who was standing nearby. "It seems to me we kept hearing your father use the term "delegation" a lot when he talked about this project at work!"

"We heard that word a lot around here as well!" laughed Kevin. "But Dad said that if we really wanted this room to turn out the way we wanted, we needed to be involved in the project and accept the responsibility for seeing that it got completed."

"It was a lot of fun working together and sharing our ideas about how the room should look when it was finished," said Cathy. "And our room really turned out great!"

"Some of these ideas sound kind of familiar," remarked Sam.

John just smiled and nodded in agreement.

3 | **Before Remote Control**

I t is hard for most of us to imagine what it was like before Remote Control. "When I was a kid," parents tell their children today, "we had to get up off the couch and actually turn to the channels ourselves!" This would be the modern-day equivalent of the stories that parents today might have heard from their elders about trudging miles through the snow to go to school or to the outhouse in the middle of winter. No doubt, our children are as unimpressed and bored with these stories as we were with the ones that we had to endure. But this analogy is very telling of the advances that we as a society have made. One must wonder what stories our children will tell their children about how much tougher it was to live when they were young? It might sound something like this: "Son, you may not believe this, but we actually had to type words into our computers before digital voice recognition systems were perfected and became commonplace."

"Wow, Dad — I can't believe that's the way you had to operate your computers in the old days. That must have really hurt your fingers. You must have really lived in the dark ages!"

And so it goes — each generation feeling that the previous one had lived in some bygone era. Its hard to imagine that not that long ago it was a big deal to see the NBC peacock spread its feathers before a television show to indicate that it was being broadcast in color. Old black and white television shows look as archaic as a Model T Ford chugging down the road. Even the messages that were communicated in the early days of television were vastly different than those presented today. In many ways, these shows represented the traditional management styles that were more prevalent during the past several decades.

For example, think about the early television program, *Father Knows Best.* The show's very title is descriptive of the attitude that prevailed in most organizations in the post-World War II era in which the golden age of television was born. Robert Young was the driving force of this typical American family experiencing the growing pains of the great society that was beginning to emerge. We might reflect back to those days as simpler times. Robert Young as the symbol of truth and knowledge reinforced the concept of a top-down management approach. This benevolent, all-knowing provider could solve even the most seemingly serious of family emergencies by patiently listening and passing judgment.

Ward Cleaver, the father in the show, *Leave It to Beaver* from the same television era, also provided "all-knowing" direction and advice to those less experienced. While sitting in his study wearing a cardigan sweater, he shared his experiences from his own youth with his sons.

> "Gee Dad, I didn't know that girls were creeps when you were a kid." Beaver might say to his father.

> "Well son, you may feel differently about girls in a few years. You do realize that your mother was once a girl. You don't think she's a creep do you?" Ward would pose his questions to stimulate thought in his youngest son.

> "Heck no, I never realized that Mom used to be a girl!" Beaver replies, having learned his first lesson in sex education.

Ward would also receive counsel from his lovely wife who served as a sort of assistant manager of the family but certainly not a co-leader. June, even when preparing the family's breakfast, would listen with wide-eyed fascination to her husband's endless stories about experiences from his own youth.

> "Is that what it was like when you were a boy, Ward?" June would ask her husband, as she tried desperately to understand why something such as personal hygiene was so low on her youngest son's list of things to do each day.

The Traditional Manager

These images helped set the stage for the manufacturing revolution that was beginning during this period in American history. The "all-knowing" Senior Manager served in this same "father figure" capacity for the organization. All decisions were rightfully his to make. Although some youthful rebelliousness might be tolerated, everyone was expected to comply. This system worked fine, that is as long as *Father always did know best*. Unfortunately, this could not always be guaranteed. This style of management, relating to the organizational change model previously introduced, was a sort of one-man Sanctioning, Steering, and Design Team, all rolled into one. The vulnerabilities as well as advantages of this style of management, are shown in the following diagram. In this model we see the typical top-down approach to decision making and authority in an organization.

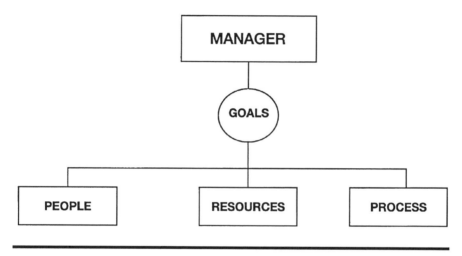

The Traditional Manager

The manager controlled the goals, resources, and process, and even the people in the organization. The manager was "Mr. Wizard." Everyone looked to him to perform his magic and lead the organization to success. The expanding economy and markets of the postwar era enabled even average top executives to seem to perform miraculous feats before the very eyes of their admiring employees. The CEO was indeed an icon representing truth, justice, and the American way — yes, even a Superman of sorts. These gladiators of the American executive boardrooms were fighting for our country's dominance in the economic battlefields of the world. For members of their workforce armies, the American dream was being fulfilled. The two car family, vacations at the beach, the ranch-style home, and, of course, the television set, became part of the new American frontier. The postwar expansion seemed unstoppable. President Eisenhower provided the ultimate father figure for the country. "I like Ike" was the new battle cry heard across the land. Americans settled down in their living rooms to watch their new magic box bring the world to them each evening. Those truly were Happy Days!

No one then would have thought it possible that the President would ever be a womanizer, a crook, or blatantly lie to the American public about his involvement in a break-in at a Washington apartment complex or an extra-marital affair with a young White House intern. History has taught us that these things are definitely possible, even probable.

This is not to say that the traditional style of management is wrong. A traditional style of management can be extremely effective. Command and control can get things done in a more expeditious manner than most of the other styles of management. If this is an important factor given the situation and circumstances in which an organization finds itself, then it may be the best way to manage. Too often, a certain style of management is envisioned and attempted to be implemented without consideration of what may be needed at that particular time for the organization. One size does not necessarily fit all. Management styles and philosophies need to be customized and adapted to meet the specific needs of each organization.

A continuum of management styles from Traditional to Remote Control Management styles is shown:

Traditional → *Team* → *Empowering* → *Remote Control*

Although a progression is implied in this continuum, it does not represent a scale of bad to good management styles or techniques. What is important is which one is most appropriate for the organization. This should be dictated by the circumstances, as well as the style of the organization. If, for example, the Sanctioning function of an organization can not be supportive of a Remote Control style of management in those who report to them, this obviously would not be an appropriate goal to try to achieve. If the Sanctioners can not tolerate hearing, "I don't know, Boss. I gave someone else the responsibility for knowing that," when asking a question of a subordinate, a more traditional style may be warranted and may more appropriately fit into the prevailing organizational culture. To try to impart Remote Control Management philosophies into this culture would be like trying to fit the proverbial round peg into a square hole. This would be like Hawkeye Pierce from the popular show of the 1970s and 1980s, *M*A*S*H,* appearing on the old black and white World War II drama *Combat.* It just wouldn't fit.

Another factor that needs to be considered when contemplating what management philosophy might be most appropriate for an organization, is the stability of the business at the present time. The question really comes down to: how much time does the organization have? The point is that the organizational cultural change required to transform a traditionally managed organization into a Team, whether an Empowering or Remote Controlled one, may take more time than a business in trouble may have. Cultural change is a long term process, measured in years, not months. This can be a very disconcerting fact to many decision makers in organizations. If the response is, "We can't wait years to go through a cultural change, we need it now!" then a different plan other than achieving cultural change needs to be developed. To establish a goal to truly change the management philosophies and practices organization would only frustrate and disappoint everyone and could actually be destructive. More realistically, the organization needs to look at what are the most appropriate goals and objectives given the current situation in which the business finds itself and develop a plan to achieve them.

The Team Manager

A model of how decisions might be made in a Team-Managed work environment is shown. As seen in this model, the Manager shares the responsibility with others who may work for him or her. Everyone is focused on the goals of the organization from virtually the same perspective. Thus, decisions

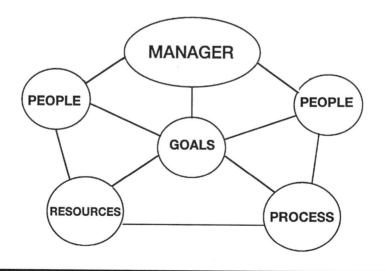

Team Manager Work Environment

concerning how these goals are to be met are arrived at by reaching consensus among the team members. How resources and the process are affected are also team functions, subject to the same decision-making process involving the entire team. Again, this may or may not fit the current needs and objectives of an organization.

For example, if an organization is in a position where profitability must be increased within a certain period of time or their existence might be threatened, the focus of that entire organization needs to be that goal. In this scenario, a Traditional style of management may indeed be the best and most effective way of achieving this objective. Changing the culture of an organization to that of one that is Team Managed, as seen in this model, requires long-term investments that may not show a return for many years to come. This obviously would not be the appropriate focus or vision for an organization in a "do or die" situation.

However, decisions often are made in this type of crisis situation to make changes in the way the organization is managed. Problem solving and decision making are moved to lower levels in the organization and the business is saved from extinction or some other undesirable event. Everyone rallies together and they work as a team, perhaps for the first time in their existence together. They are successful in reaching their goals and meet the challenge. At some point, the pressure is off and the threat of closure or the undesirable event is over. Most likely, the organization will go back to its original management style and the cycle may begin to perpetuate itself over some period of time. Why? Because the culture of the organization was not changed — just some of its short-term goals and procedures. And in this situation, it was just what was needed.

An important factor to be aware of concerning traditional styles of management is that success is usually leader-driven. The very nature of this style dictates this to be true. Everything emanates from the leader, the vision, direction, resource allocation, and process decisions, as well as the actions of those who follow him. Again, this style may work perfectly, that is as long as there is a good leader in place. The flip side is seen if there is not an effective leader in this powerful position. An ineffective leader could be in a position to do a great deal of harm to the organization. Poor decisions are still carried out despite the better sense that subordinates may have. There may be no checks and balances in the organization to ensure that bad decisions are not carried out with "blind obedience." The culture of the organization may not support the expression of disagreement, even in appropriate ways. Perhaps it was this vulnerability that created the need for alternate ways to manage an organization. The reality of the situation is that we will not always have great leaders in positions of power. Organizations have learned through experience that ultimately the management systems must be designed to be successful, despite the leadership that may be in office at any given time. Philosophies such as teamwork, empowerment, and remote control, are "fail-safe" devices of sorts, providing that needed check and balance of the decision making process in the organization.

Identifying the *"Real"* Experts

Identifying who the real experts are for any given problem may not always be so easy to understand. As in the previous story, common sense may not always direct the leadership of the organization to ask the right people to become involved in the problem-solving process. After all, as was asked in the story, "What do Shipping Coordinators know about correcting a major problem with a computer system?"

However, as it was discovered, the solutions to problems are not always where you would expect them to be found. But how do you begin to identify the real experts on a problem? Think of a problem that has been identified in your workplace and describe it in the center of the circle below.

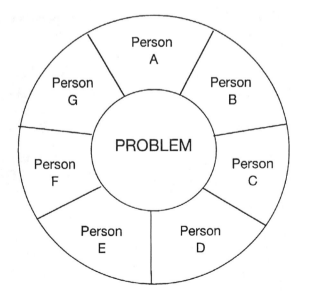

Now identify those people who are affected in some way by this problem. Fill in their names or positions from the various vantage points from which they may perceive this problem. You may need to add additional spaces in this "wheel." Now, ask yourself, "Have all of these people been given the opportunity to provide input into the root cause and possible solutions of this problem?" If not, you may need to go back and solicit this input and factor it into the problem-solving process.

However — a word of caution. There may be certain aspects of the business in which you do not want to empower people to be involved or even provide input. This is fair and legitimate and doesn't necessarily negate the principles or concepts you may be trying to introduce. There is always going to be certain information that must be kept confidential and which would not be an appropriate topic for general discussion. People will understand and respect this fact. But there also may be other areas, perhaps not confidential in their nature, but still not any more appropriate for discussion. These may be certain policies that for legal reasons cannot be altered, even though everyone would like to. And other policies might just be "givens" that are not open to debate for whatever reason by the management of the organization. People will generally accept this fact as well if it is clearly communicated.

You also to have to ensure that people are being empowered on a problem for which they at least have the potential of being able to provide knowledgeable and reasonable input. Perhaps, even though someone may be very knowledgeable about one aspect of the business or operation, he/she may have zero knowledge in another area. For instance, you might have a great deal of respect for your accountant's understanding of the latest federal tax laws, but you wouldn't want him to remove your gall bladder! You instead would go to a qualified surgeon who specializes in this type of medical procedure.

Similarly, this principle needs to apply to those whom you ultimately empower at work. Again, this can be one of the most important factors in achieving the success you desire in the organizational change process. You want to be neither too traditional nor irresponsible in choosing whom you give certain responsibilities to, to solve problems and make decisions in your organization.

Making clear up front into what areas you are encouraging employees to provide input as part of your Remote Control Process is critically important. This way, there should be less misunderstanding and disillusionment about what this process is really intended to accomplish. For example, if you have no intention of changing your policies on certain topics, even though they may be of interest to employees, you need to make this clear in the beginning of the process. A common misconception about empowerment is that it is sometimes believed that if you ask for people's recommendation on certain aspects of your operation, you have to accept their opinions on everything. This simply isn't true, and in fact, might be irresponsible if they are not qualified to make decisions in certain areas. People understand where their strengths and weaknesses exist and respect the expert opinions of others more qualified than they to make certain decisions. They will always want strong and effective leadership that is willing to make the difficult and unpopular decisions as the situation dictates and warrants.

Conditions for Success

Are there then, certain conditions and circumstances that need to exist for philosophies such as teamwork, empowerment, or remote control to exist in an organization? Conversely, are there those where these concepts definitely should not be introduced? Again, these questions can only be answered by the organization itself and will be determined by a multitude of factors, not the least of which is the support that is given by the sanctioning function of the business. If something is truly supported by the right people in the organization, almost anything is possible. However, this may not always be the case. Following are some of the factors that should be present to optimize the possibility of success of organizational change shown to the right of the Continuum of Management Styles.

- **Stability of the business** — If a business is in trouble or the organization's financial health and stability is threatened, changing the style of management should not be its primary objective. As mentioned, organizational change takes time. An organization in trouble may not even have the time that is necessary for organizational change to be successful. Shorter-term goals would be more critical at this point, such as increasing productivity, lowering costs, or improving quality. This is not to say that in order to accomplish these goals, the organization may not get its employees on all levels more involved in the decision-making and problem-solving processes to achieve these goals. But this is different than fundamentally changing the culture and management style of the organization.

- **Willingness of the organization to accept short-term losses to achieve longer-term gains** — Any organizational change requires adjustments and time to get established. Learning something different can require resources to be invested and even expended. If the sanctioning function of organization expects immediate gains from the process, they will quickly become disappointed and their support soon start to wane. There are few, if any, permanent quick fixes for changing the culture and management style of an organization.

- **A vision for the future** — An organization must have a clear picture or vision of where it wants to go in the future. It is not enough to say that you want to become something: you must understand what that something is, and what it will take to achieve your goals. Many organizations say they want to have a team or empowered management style but don't have a clear understanding of what that means. It you don't know what it means, you can't very well become it!

- **Leadership that has confidence in its employees** — If the top management is convinced that only they can make the good decisions and must maintain control of all critical functions of the organization, trying to move towards the right of the continuum would turn out to be disastrous. The leadership of the organization must have confidence in its employees and their ability to make good decisions and accept greater levels of responsibility and accountability. Without this faith and trust in their employees, concepts such as teamwork and empowerment, not to mention remote control, would never truly get off the ground. Instead, the organization will fall into the syndrome of deceiving itself that these management philosophies are being practiced when in reality they don't exist. This can be a frustrating experience for employees. They hear their managers talk a good story when it comes to sharing responsibilities, but never get a chance to experience it for themselves.

- **Management that is willing to change** — Organizational change always needs to start with the top. Change is not really possible without the support of the top management of the organization. There are those who believe that a "grass roots" initiative is desirable because it proves to upper management that the change is not only necessary but possible. However, the success of these initiatives is more likely the exception rather than the rule. It assumes that upper management will "see the light" once everyone else has adapted to the new way. This may be a difficult and long process if it happens at all. It is more likely that the changes will not get very far without the support of upper management. It is even far more likely that upper management will resist what they don't understand and have not been included in from the very beginning. A more desirable situation is one in which the Sanctioning function of the organization is willing to listen to new ideas and act upon them in the absence of a critical change event. In other words, "fix it before it is broke!" Inertia or conservatism can make this a very difficult concept for organizations to embrace. It is easy to get people's attention and commitment to change during crisis. Convincing people they need to change is quite different in the absence of a compelling reason to change.

- **Management that is willing to stay involved** — The management of an organization can not simply delegate the responsibility for organizational change to a lower level and then become detached from the process. The Sanctioners may play a less active role than those of the Steering Team or Design Team, but still are critical to the success of any desired organizational change. The top management must be willing and available to be actively be involved when needed. Even though much of this involvement may be only in an approval capacity, it is critical that this support be provided. Often top managers fail to realize just how important it is for them to simply show interest in what is going on in the organization. They need to make those who report to them accountable for the change process in the organization. This can be the most powerful driving force for organizational change and development to occur

Management Style Matrix

An important point to keep in mind as we look at organizational change on the continuum is that it doesn't always occur concurrently everywhere in an organization. In other words, one part of an organization may be progressing on the continuum, while others are lagging behind. You might find entire departments of an organization operating at one level and others much farther to the right of this scale. This may occur for any number of reasons, including the leadership style of those in charge of these segments of the organization, the nature of that particular part of the operation or business, or possibly the attention and effort that have been spent on that aspect of the operation. Even looking at more specific functions of an organization, there may be those that develop at different paces than others. It is not as if you can turn a switch and "voila," the entire organization has passed completely from one level to the next on the management style continuum.

Obviously, you will always have "pockets" of change as an organization progresses through these various levels. One particular area may become a strength for an organization and propel it several levels ahead of where the rest of the organization may be. In other areas, the organization may be behind in their progression. The following table expands the Continuum of Management Styles into a matrix which includes ten important organizational factors that could be tracked as part of this progression. Each of these factors may be affected differently by the changes occurring in the transition from an organization's current management style to where their vision is taking them.

For example, an organization may have progressed in the second area listed on the matrix, "operating methods," to a level of a Team or even Remote Control Management style. However, at the same time they may still be at a traditional style of compensation which is totally controlled by management. These inconsistencies can cause the confusion of a "mixed message" from the management to those being directly affected. In one aspect, the organization has become very progressive and innovative, and in another, it retains traditional philosophies which may not fully support these other changes. These types of alignment issues must be explored and addressed by any organization undergoing changes in its management style.

The point that should be kept in mind as the Steering and Design teams map out their plan to reach the organization's vision for the future is that all of these areas need to be considered and plans developed to progress in each one. This matrix can help organizations to set goals for reaching their vision and enable measurement of the progress being made in each of these areas.

Conscious decisions may be made as to where the organization may want to focus its energies and resources and in which of these areas it is willing to lag behind. Goals and timetables could be established for each of these elements of organizational change. This could serve as the basis for the organization's "Strategic Change Plan," which maps out where you are today and where you would like to be in the future.

However, an organization may make a conscious decision not to progress or focus its energies on certain factors in this matrix. Again, this may best fit the overall philosophies, goals, and even style of the organization. There

Continuum of Management Styles Matrix

Traditional ————————————————————————————————→ **Remote Control**				
1. Organizational structure: Many layers; decisions top down	Input after decision made	Employees (EE's) involved in certain decisions	Teams provide input into decisions	Flat organization EE's make own job-related decisions
2. Operating methods: Determined by management	Limited input	Certain idea of EE's accepted	Teams make work process decisions	EE's empowered to make process and methods
3. Workforce competencies: Management decides what training needed	EE's provide input	EE's involved in design and implementation	Teams develop training criteria	EE's develop own training needs and initiate them
4. Productivity: Management sets expectations and goals	EE's give input concerning goals	EE's involved in setting goals	Teams work together to reach goals	EE's set own goals, commit to obtain
5. Compensation/benefits: Compensation solely management issue	EE's given information on compensation and financial performance	Compensation affected by performance	Team goals affect compensation	Compensation directly affected by performance
6. Measurement: Management establishes all measurement, communicating results	EE's involved in communicating measurement	EE's involved in estimation and communicating measurements	Teams develop own measurement and criteria	EE's develop own measurement and criteria

Continuum of Management Styles Matrix *(Continued)*

Traditional →				→ Remote Control
7. Safety/environment	Management establishes all safety and environmental policies	EE's given feedback on safety and environmental policies	EE's involved in establishing and communicating measurements	Teams develop own measurements and criteria	EE's responsible for safety and environmental compliance
8. Management philosophy	Management philosophy established at top	EE's have opportunity to comment on management philosophy	EE's provide input into management philosophy	Teams have influence on management philosophy	Teams help develop management philosophy
9. Business strategy	Strategy established at top	EE's receive information about business strategy	EE's provide input on business strategy	Teams given opportunity to impact business strategy	EE's help establish business strategy
10. External forces	Concern of top management	EE's receive information concerning external forces	EE's provide input concerning external forces	Teams given opportunity to impact external forces	EE's directly impact external forces

are no absolutely right or wrong ways to approach organizational change and moving toward Remote Control Management.

The Strategic Role of Remote Control

An important key to developing this strategic focus is to look at the roles that people play in the organization. Do they perform their jobs with a focus on the present or on the future? To illustrate this distinction, think about a typical manufacturing work environment and the roles that various people in this organization might play. Let's categorize these functions as either **today** focused or **tomorrow** focused. Functions that are considered to be today focused would be those things that are necessary to produce the product and ship it to the customer — that is, what needs to be done to meet the demands and requirements of the customer today and stay in business. Obviously, these functions are critical to the continued success of the organization. Now, let us focus on the tomorrow things. This is what needs to be done to be better able to serve the customer tomorrow.

The distinction between **Today** and **Tomorrow** responsibilities can be developed into an interesting and insightful exercise with managers and supervisors in your organization. The Today and Tomorrow Exercise is easy to play. To begin, write the word "Today" on the top left of a padboard and the word "Tomorrow" on the top right. Draw a line down the middle of the padboard paper. Next ask the group the following question: "What needs to be done in order to operate our business today?" The point that you need to make clear is that on this list are the "today" things that must be done to operate the process or run the business. For example, in a manufacturing process, this would be everything associated with the actual production of the product. As can be seen in the example in the following table, this "Today" list would likely include such things as: run the equipment, bring in raw materials, assign jobs, give breaks, perform quality checks, record production data, perform packaging and shipping, fix equipment, keep production records, and so on. Continue this list on additional padboard sheets if necessary until everyone's input has been recorded. Be sure that the suggestions relate to "Today" things. You may need to restate several times what type of input you are looking for at this point in the exercise. Again, the question at this time is, "What things do we need to do to operate our business today?" If a suggestion is made that is more future focused, for example you get a

Today and Tomorrow Responsibilities

"What do we need to do to operate our business:"

TODAY	TOMORROW
Operate equipment	Production planning
Bring in raw materials	Training
Assign jobs	Process improvements
Give breaks	Customer contacts
Perform quality checks	Quality assurance
Record production data	Employee development
Packaging	Counseling
Shipping	Communications
Fix equipment	Preventative maintenance
Production records	Continuous improvement

response such as "planning or training," ask the person to hold that thought until you get to the "Tomorrow" list.

The next step in the exercise is to ask participants to complete the "Tomorrow" list. The question you should now ask is, "What will we need to do to operate our business better tomorrow?" Again, using our manufacturing example, you might hear responses such as, production planning, training, process improvements, customer contacts, quality assurance, employee development, counseling, improved communications, preventative maintenance, continuous improvement, and so on. Again, after each participant has had a chance to share all of their ideas, you should ask, "Which of these two lists is most important?" You may hear a variety of responses to this question but you should emphasize that both of these types of activities are critically important. The "Today" list keeps you operating, while the "Tomorrow" list allows you to improve in the future. The next question to ask is, "Which list are you working on?" In most traditionally managed workplaces the answer to this question is that the supervisor or manager is working primarily on the "Today" list.

Today things focus on the present. Tomorrow's focus is on the future. What focus would you want various people in your organization to have? This is what is changing as organizations are moving along the Continuum of Management Styles. As you move to the right on the continuum, you find more managers and supervisors becoming tomorrow focused. Perhaps the greatest challenges of these new management styles are found in supervisory positions. The role of the supervisor can become the most telling sign of the true management style of the organization. It is the supervisor who has always played the most pivotal role in linking the various levels of an organization together. Often, as organizational change is introduced, it is the supervisors who must make the greatest adjustments. Let's examine in more detail how the strategic focus of these key positions is affected by these changes in management style and philosophies.

The Supervisor's Challenge

Supervising in today's workplace brings with it many challenges. Concepts such as empowerment, teamwork, and remote control are changing the traditional roles of many jobs. Possibly the most dramatically affected job is that of the supervisor. It used to be that an effective supervisor was someone who was skilled at telling workers what they were to do and ensuring that the work got done. Control and compliance was what this supervisor/employee relationship was based upon. There was little or no opportunity for the employee to provide any input or suggestions to anyone in management, despite their years of experience and knowledge of their job, no matter how logical their argument. They simply were hired to perform the labor and the supervisor was to do all the thinking.

Fortunately, much of this has changed in many of the new work environments of today. It is becoming more and more clear to organizations that for years they have been under-utilizing a very important and valuable resource — their employees. But just how do you go about fully utilizing the experiences of your employees without changing the role of the supervisor? The answer is simply that you can not.

Many supervisors, as well as managers, feel threatened by the introduction of these new concepts. They may wonder, like those supervisors at that manufacturing plant in the Midwest, where the young engineer began introducing the concepts of empowerment, "If we begin having our subordinates assume many of the responsibilities that we have always performed, what will we do?" These new management styles should not be viewed as simply a means to reduce or even eliminate supervisors from your organization. If this is all you accomplish, then you may indeed have reduced your head count costs but will find that you will accomplish little else. Even if the same amount of work gets done with fewer people, you are really no better off than you were before in the traditional supervisory organizational structure.

The point here is that the real potential benefit of Remote Control Managed organization goes beyond just giving your employees more decision-making and problem-solving capability and accountability. Remote Control also provides supervisors with growth opportunities not previously afforded to them in traditional organizations. This is a totally different perspective than is typically experienced in many organizations where supervisors view the introduction of concepts such as empowerment as the "beginning of the end" for them. Quite the contrary, it is really just the beginning.

Typically as the concepts of empowerment are implemented in an organization, the focus is almost entirely on the jobs and roles of the hourly workforce. The supervisors sit back and watch their responsibilities being delegated to those who work for them. It doesn't take long before they begin to ask, "What will be my new role in the organization?" This is a legitimate question that deserves an answer. Unfortunately, supervisors may not always get a clear answer to this important career-determining question. Typically they may hear something that sounds like, "We're not just sure yet what your new role will be in the organization but *trust* us, you'll like it once we figure out what it is!" Yeah, right. What's the one word that doesn't belong in this last statement? The answer is *trust*. The supervisor in this case isn't being given any real basis for trust to be established.

Before any organizational change can be implemented, it is critically important that everyone's new responsibilities and roles in the new organization are as clearly defined as possible. This will help create the trust needed as everyone's jobs are dramatically changed from what they have been used to doing for years to their new roles in the future. To accomplish this goal for both supervisors and employees when introducing the concepts of empowerment, utilize the Today and Tomorrow Exercise. It can help put into perspective what the new role of the supervisor needs to be in the future.

You will find it most beneficial if you have those supervisors directly affected by changes in your organization participate in this exercise. As an outcome of the exercise, supervisors will be better able to understand where their future focus needs to be, and even help begin to develop their new roles and responsibilities.

But you also need to ask, "What list is the people who work for the supervisors focused on?" The answer most likely will again be the "Today" list. What is actually happening is that both the supervisors and those who work for them are working on the same *lists*. This results in duplication of efforts and under utilization of resources. Do both the employees and their supervisor need to be focused on the same things? Under this arrangement is anyone focusing on the "Tomorrow" list? Is it possible to eliminate this redundancy and have the employees focus on the "Today" list and their supervisors on the "Tomorrow" list? Under which system would the organization operate most efficiently? Under which system would everyone feel most fulfilled and be a contributing member of the team? Under which system will the organization have the greatest chance of reaching its goals?

This is essentially what Remote Control Management is all about. In many workplaces, employees have been performing their jobs for many years or even decades. They are very capable of accepting more responsibility. They may need additional training to be able to accept more of these responsibilities, and this becomes an essential part of the empowerment process. It is unfair to ask someone to do something that he or she has not been given the necessary training to be able to perform. This will end people's interest and enthusiasm for Remote Control Management faster than anything else! This same principle also applies to the changing role of the manager or supervisor. They, too, must be given the opportunity to develop the skills necessary to accept the challenges of tomorrow.

It is not the existence of supervisors or managers in our organizations that should be questioned but rather the traditional roles they have played in the past. They need to become **tomorrow** focused. They bring to their jobs a wealth of knowledge and experience that, like the hourly workforce, has yet to be fully utilized. They can add value not only to their jobs but to the entire organization in their new roles by becoming more strategic in focus of their responsibilities and focused on tomorrow.

Remote Control Management gives the manager the opportunity to focus on tomorrow issues. This is its greatest benefit and advantage. Remote Control Management can help reduce many redundant and wasted efforts by both managers and those they manage. Instead of working on essentially the same things, both can focus on their own areas of expertise and be better able to accomplish their goals and objectives. Remote Control Management creates a much more efficient and productive working environment for everyone. Contrary to what may have been formerly believed by managers for many years, you don't always have to be there watching over those that you supervise in order to for things to run smoothly.

What is needed is to trust the people who work for you and that, provided the necessary resources, they will make the best decisions for the operation and ultimately the business. Remote Control Management nurtures this environment, focusing everyone on those tasks that can make them most productive and contributing to the success of the organization. Again, it is important to understand that Remote Control Management does not diminish anyone's responsibilities, but rather the ways in which these responsibilities are met.

What type of manager are you? The Management Matrix presented in the next chapter can help you identify your present management style and what you believe would be most effective and supportive of your organization's goals. You need to make the decision for yourself as to which would be the best management style for both you and the organization.

Identifying Management Styles

Before any change is even contemplated in the way your organization is managed, it is important to have a clear understanding of under what management style your organization is presently operating. The Management Style Matrix describes some of the differences between the four styles of management described earlier in the management continuum.

It might be interesting to look at each of these management styles as they relate to various television personalities over the years. Let's begin with the **Traditional** style of management. Who do you think would best represent this style? How about Ben Cartwright from the early television show *Bonanza*. When you think about it, Ben was a very traditional manager of the both the Ponderosa and his three sons, Adam, Hoss, and Little Joe. Like Robert Young and Hugh Beaumont (Ward Cleaver), he was in complete control of everyone's lives, most all those of his family. "I had better ask Pa first, don't you think, Hoss?" Little Joe might ask his enormous brother, trying to decide if he should try to sneak a kiss from one of the young ladies in town who would have given anything to catch one of the rich Cartwright boys, preferably one of the good-looking ones. Fortunately Ben was wise to the desires of young people, and made sure that none of his sons strayed too far from the ranch.

An example of a **Team** manager might be Rob Petrie in the classic *Dick Van Dyke Show*. As head writer for the fictional *Alan Brady Show*, he shared his responsibility for creating a script that would meet the demanding standards of their eccentric boss each week. His was a team approach to managing this function of the variety comedy show. He brought out the best in everyone

Management Style Matrix

	Communications	Accountability	Support	Strategy
Traditional	Leader tells employees	Leader accountable	Top down	Management has all knowledge
Team	Leader shares information	Leader accountable	Top down	Leader has the knowledge
Empowering	Team has access to needed information	Leader and team	From team	Team has the knowledge concerning their jobs
Remote Control	Information is shared in creative ways using new technologies	Accountabilities shared, with focus on self-management	From entire organization	Leader and team both have knowledge essential to the team's success

in his life's team, including his beautiful wife Laura, played by Mary Tyler Moore, and even the next door neighbors Millie and Jerry Halpern. Mary Tyler Moore took this same concept to her ever-popular comedy about a single woman learning the television news business in Minneapolis in the 1970s. Her boss, Lou Grant, was seemingly a tyrant, with his gruff manner and authoritarian style. "You got spunk, Mary," he said to her in one of their first meetings together in his tiny office where he often sulked away to, "I hate spunk!" However, Lou was also a very good communicator, sharing whatever strategy may have existed from the main offices of their Minneapolis television station. He pulled his subordinates together as a team and became part of them. He accepted whatever responsibility he had to protect those in his charge and almost always supported the actions of his employees, even when it was difficult to do so. However, the price they had to pay for this support was often another long and boring lecture from Lou about his personal experiences as a newsman that usually had nothing to do with the current situation.

The enormously popular and frequently rerun show *M*A*S*H* provides another excellent example of an **Empowering** management style. McLean Stevenson, as the mostly inept Colonel in charge of a Mobile Army Surgical Hospital during the Korean conflict, empowered his unruly surgical staff to perform their jobs without his personal direction, just about all the time. In fact, the Colonel even went a little too far in his empowering style of management, allowing Hawkeye Pierce and Trapper more freedom than they could handle. They defied all convention and military rule but could get away with it, due to their brilliant surgical skills. The Colonel did have at least some understanding of the meaning of allowing subordinates the freedom to do their jobs to the best of their ability. In *M*A*S*H*, as long as the job got done, the methods for reaching these objectives became far less important, even meaningless. Empowerment breaks the rules of Traditional Management in many ways. *M*A*S*H* was all about getting the job done under the most adverse circumstances possible. Its universal appeal was in watching tradition being thrown out the window as those talented surgeons "thumbed their noses" in the face of authority, while saving the lives of soldiers in the battlefields of Korea. Ability became more important than authority or rank. What was most important was that the job got done by those most qualified to perform the operation. In the end, nothing else was important.

The *Cosby Show* was a great example of a **Remote Control** manager. Bill Cosby as Dr. Huxtable, seemed to manage a thriving medical practice without ever going to the office! In fact, Cosby never seemed to leave his home. All of life seemed to occur either in the kitchen or the family room couch. Even Phylicia Rashad who played his on-screen wife and was also a practicing attorney, seemed to spend most of her time as well in these same two rooms. Cosby helped his children learn life's lessons for themselves. At times he could have easily solved their problems for them as did his predecessors Robert Young and Hugh Beamount. But he resisted the easy way and looked more strategically instead. We may never know if there was a long-term return on his investment in his children's development, unless there is a reunion show someday, which is a likely prediction. For now, we will need to have faith that Dr. Huxtable did know the best way to raise children in the 1990s in contrast to the ways of the 1950s when we were first invited into the lives of families growing up before our eyes in our living rooms.

What kind of management style do you think that Jerry Seinfeld in his popular sitcom about "nothing" would utilize if he were running a Fortune 100 company? Even more intriguing would be the roles that George, Kramer, and Elaine would play in the organization? Of course, reporting directly to Jerry would be George as vice-president of operations, Kramer the Director of Marketing and Elaine in charge of Human Resources. Jerry would never actually go to the office but rather run the business from his apartment. His staff would show up there for work each day as well. Actually this is not that much different than what happens in the lives of these characters on the show in each episode! As a Remote Control Manager, can't you just envision Jerry standing next to his kitchen counter in his apartment buzzing up important business contacts and customers? That certainly would be Remote Control "worthy."

Management Style Profiles

Read each of the following profiles of managers at work and identify which of the four Management Styles is being described. Refer to the Management Style Matrix in Table 4.1 to help you in identifying these styles.

Profile   4.1

Charlie was known as a no-nonsense manager. Little, if anything, went on in his department that he didn't know about or personally control. He had built the business from being a money loser to one of the corporation's most profitable. He knew almost all of the business's customers personally and would frequently have direct contact with them, often to the displeasure of his salespeople.

> "How I am supposed to know what's going on in my accounts if Charlie is making deals and commitments to them on the side?" was not an unusual comment to be heard from almost any member of the salesforce. Almost no one was foolish enough to challenge or even complain to Charlie about his doing this for fear of getting on the "wrong side" of him. This was paramount to career suicide. If Charlie wasn't happy with you, you might as well start sending out your resume because you were going nowhere with this company.

But Charlie had another side to him. If he believed in you, he would support you even beyond the point that might normally be expected. As long as he felt you were giving him and the company an "honest effort" he would back you even if he didn't always agree with you. People who worked for Charlie had the greatest respect for him and felt comfortable taking their problems to him. They always knew that he would listen with an open mind and give them sincere and honest feedback.

As Charlie's career began to enter the last stretch, there was a great deal of speculation about who would replace him. Few people would dare present themselves as Charlie's equal, at least not in this particular aspect of the business. Replacing Charlie would involve more than just filling a single, albeit very important, position in the organization. Replacing Charlie would mean redesigning and restructuring the entire organization that he had built and ran so effectively.

Identifying Charlie's management style is an easy one. He was strictly a **Traditional Style Manager** in that he was unwilling to release authority or decision making to others who worked for him. It is important to stress that this does not mean that Charlie was not an effective manager. He obviously got results and was singlehandedly responsible for building the business into the success it was today. It is also quite possible that this was the most appropriate and effective style of management in this given situation. Certainly Charlie was the right manager for the job at the time when the business was floundering and needed strong leadership to save it from extinction.

But what are some of the long term consequences of Charlie's management and leadership style? Where will the business be when he retires? Has anyone else been "groomed" to take the helm when Charlie is gone? What effect might this have on the business in the future? How strategic was Charlies's style of management in terms of the long term growth and health of the business?

Let's look at a second scenario that might not be quite as easy to identify:

Profile   4.2

Alice Fredricks had been a Supervisor at the facility for many years. She started her career with the company as an hourly employee and had worked her way through the ranks to her present position as part of the management of the organization. She was proud of what she had accomplished in her career and always worked hard to achieve the goals of the organization as well as her own. Recently, Alice was put in charge of a new production area and crew of employees. As this was a new area that was just beginning production, there were many critical decisions to be made. Alice was given the responsibility for establishing almost all of the process and policy decisions that needed to be made in order to get this new production unit up and running as quickly as possible.

This of course, was a huge responsibility. Alice had never had to make these types of critical decisions before in her career. She sat down and began to think about how these decisions could best be made. She thought about the employees that were to be assigned to this new area. It occurred to her that the best way to set up the procedures and policies for this new area was to utilize all of the expertise and experience of her new team. She arranged for a meeting of her new production team and told them that for the next few weeks they were going to develop these procedures and policies for operating this new production area. She would then take their suggestions and present them to the upper management of the organization for approval. The employees were quite surprised by this announcement as they had never been asked for their input before concerning operational matters, even though they had many years of production experience.

What style of management was Alice utilizing? This is really an example of a **Team-Based Management Style.** Although the distinction between these various styles may often become blurred and will overlap, in this case, Alice is utilizing the ability and experience of the employees, but is still the focal point for driving this process. She will be the one to take their recommendations to the appropriate approval levels before implementation. Given the history of the organization from what we know, this is good plan. Moving toward the concepts of Remote Control must be taken in small steps or at least one at a time. Trying to move too fast can be destructive to the process as well as becoming a formula for failure. Both the people and the culture of an organization must be ready to accept greater "handoffs" of responsibility. To rush into this process would be unfair to those involved. This could be termed "reckless empowerment." Reckless empowerment involves giving employees responsibilities that they are not yet prepared to accept. Reckless empowerment leads to certain failure of the concepts being introduced. "This crap doesn't work," would be a likely evaluation after experiencing the frustrations of an ill conceived and hurried empowerment initiative. The aftermath of such a failure can often take the organization farther back in their organizational development to even a more "command and control" environment than previously existed.

Empowerment involves sharing of responsibilities with others, especially subordinates. The following is short story of a manager learning to utilize empowerment to achieve goals previously unobtainable.

Profile   4.3

Ken Meyerson was extremely frustrated with his department's lack of ability to reach the company's productivity goals for the third consecutive year. This was particularly troublesome, given the fact that the company's home office had identified this particular measure as the most important goal for the performance improvement in the upcoming year. Ken was getting enormous pressure to improve in this area from his supervisor. His future with this company would very well be determined by his ability to improve in this area of performance next year.

As he sat in his office looking out its glass-windowed walls and watched his department at work, he wondered what else he could do to try to improve their productivity. He had already tried giving his people ultimatums to improve or else — but what was that "or else" going to be? He tried watching over them to try to make sure that everything they did was done correctly and most efficiently. That seemed to result only in his working 80 plus hours a week and nearly causing him to get divorced. All of this sacrifice, and productivity still didn't improve. In fact, it even got worse. It was almost like his employees sabotaged productivity to get him out of their faces all the time and allow them to do their jobs. As Ken sat and thought about it, he became more and more convinced that was exactly what had happened. One of the worst things that had occurred as he tried to be more in control of the work being performed was a sort of malicious obedience that began to emerge from his employees. They would follow whatever directions he gave, regardless of how they felt about the reasonableness of his ideas. When problems occurred, the only response he ever got was, "I just did what you told me to do, Boss."

Clearly that approach was not the answer to the problems his department was experiencing. He thought about why his employees responded so negatively to his attempts to improve productivity. Was it that they didn't want the department to be successful? No, these people were just as dedicated and concerned about their jobs and security as anyone and realized that their performance was important to their future. Then why were they so uncooperative in helping him improve their performance? He had made it very clear to them the challenge that they were faced and the possible consequences for not improving their performance. Given this, how could they be so self-destructive? They had become like a band of real life "Hogan's Heroes," cleverly sabotaging everything that Colonel Klink tried to do while in command of a prisoner of war camp in Germany during World War II. If only they would channel as much of their energies and imagination into improving production as they did in trying to prove that they were capable of making decisions for themselves, they would certainly be able to meet the productively goals that presently seemly so elusive. Then it finally dawned on him. "Maybe that's exactly what I need to do — let them make more decisions for themselves concerning productivity improvements."

Before he went charging out his office to tell everyone his new plan, Ken caught himself and thought about how successful his previous attempts to change the workplace had been. Part of the problem was that he tried to implement change without having a well-thought out and developed plan to follow. He also didn't have the buy-in or support he needed from his boss to make organizational change work. He remembered one particular change that he tried to implement that had great potential, except that it never was truly accepted by his boss. Despite progress that the new procedure was achieving it ultimately had to be abandoned. Ken was finally beginning to learn his lessons from failures in the past.

He sat down and developed a plan to give his employees more decision-making and problem-solving responsibility on their jobs. The plan involved removing many of the approval steps that had been required in their jobs. He also had the foresight to think about what training and information they would need to operate in this new work environment. He developed an extensive plan to provide these resources as timetables for achieving each step. He went to his boss with this plan, and asked for the support and approval to move forward. He was somewhat surprised at how receptive his boss was of these ideas. He just hoped that this support would continue, even if there were problems and even decreases in productivity during the implementation of this plan. There were certain inherent risks that would need to be accepted as part of this new approach to managing his department. Ken and his boss discussed these particular points in a fair amount of detail, and again he was pleasantly surprised by his boss's understanding and apparent support of this concept. With this support from his boss and plan in hand, it was time to talk to his employees. They were about to become empowered — like it or not!

Again, to his surprise, Ken found that his employees were very receptive to the introduction of these concepts. This support came despite what would certainly require more work and effort of them under this new system. "It's about time somebody asked us what we thought!" was their collective response. During the next several weeks, Ken and his department determined the new responsibilities that everyone would assume in the reorganization. They discussed what training and information people needed in order to meet these objectives and developed plans for implementation. In this new plan, the employees in the department were given more authority to make operational decisions and resolve problems without having to go through the former cumbersome approval chain of command. This enabled the work to get done in a much more expedient manner, resulting in significant productivity improvements. Without being consumed by being involved in all the day-to-day operational decisions of the department, Ken was able to focus on more strategic issues that allowed the department to become even more efficient by focusing on those areas that potentially could cause production delays in the future. Ken was becoming an empowering supervisor and finding that those from whom he might have expected resistance became the strongest supporters of giving employees more decision-making and problem-solving responsibility.

The **Remote Control Manager** is a bit more distinctive in style and identity. By definition, the Remote Control Manager is easily identified by his/her absence. The following story is about a Remote Control Manager.

Profile   4.4

Helen was recently put in charge of sales for a major product line with distribution centers across the U.S. As part of her new responsibilities, she had seventeen salespersons located in eight offices strategically located across the country. Although she had been with the company for a number of years, she had worked in a different product area and was not yet very knowledgeable with this particular line or its customers. Helen had a history of successful performance in her career and everyone's expectations about her ability to achieve positive results in this new position were very high.

"With all these locations that I am now responsible for, I am going to be spending all my time on the road," Helen thought to herself, as she contemplated how to go about starting the new job. And that is just what she began to do. Her life became one airplane trip after another to the various sales offices across the country that she was now responsible for managing. Although these visits helped make her much more knowledgeable about the product line as well as the salespeople who reported to her, Helen felt that she was getting off to a disappointing start in her new assignment. There were expectations that she would have a more immediate positive impact on the sales in this particular business. After she had been in the job for over 6 months, there was no improvement in the performance of this sales group, and even some decline in sales in certain products.

David Kimble was the National Sales Manager for the company and Helen's boss. It was David who had personally recommended Helen for this challenging assignment and had a keen interest in how she was performing so far. Because of the confidence he had, he was not worried about Helen's performance or ability to be successful. He had been working in sales management positions long enough to realize that to achieve results takes time. He arranged for a meeting with Helen to review her first 6 months in the new position and discuss how he might be able to help her.

"How do you think you are doing in the new job so far?" David asked as he began the meeting with Helen. He had arranged for the meeting to be held in Helen's office, as he knew her well enough to know that she might want to have access to certain data that would be more readily available to her there.

"As you can see from this quarterly sales report, we have made some slight progress in these particular product lines but overall the numbers aren't where either of us would like them to be," Helen replied, showing David the latest sales report that she had just compiled. David had anticipated correctly that Helen would want to show him a great deal of data to try to explain why sales had not improved as hoped and even expected under her management. The data presentation continued as Helen showed him printout after printout of numbers relating to the sales of the products for which she was responsible. Besides being very analytical, Helen also had the talent and determination to be very a very effective leader. She was considered to be tough but fair with others and was a good listener. She had high standards for both herself and those who worked for her. Helen worked hard to be successful and had earned the position to which she had aspired.

David was somewhat concerned about Helen's performance to date in the new position, not so much because of the lack of improvement in the sales numbers, but in Helen's concern about her performance and the effect it appeared to having on her confidence. This was not so much about Helen's confidence in herself but in the people who reported to her. Helen's back-up management style, what she would do when under pressure, was to become more directive and involved in the work of her subordinates. This was exactly what David thought he was beginning to see, and he knew from experience that it would be the worst possible approach to improving sales in these product lines.

After Helen had finished reviewing the sales numbers, David commented, "There are several things that come to mind as I hear these numbers and where they seem to indicate the business is going. First of all, I think you are doing a good job getting yourself established in this new product area, and as always you have worked hard to learn this business. Even though I realize that we both had high expectations as you began this job, you really have only been in this position a short period of time to be expecting significant improvements in these numbers. We need to be realistic about how long it takes to see improvements or even trends in the direction we want to go. To be honest with you, I am less concerned with what the numbers are today than in what you are doing to develop your salespeople and organization to perform better in the future."

"I'm not sure I understand what you mean?" Helen replied. "I thought you charged me with the responsibility to improve these sales numbers when you gave me this job 6 months ago? I understand that it is important for me to help my employees develop into better salespeople, but I never thought of that as my primary goal or responsibility in this job."

"I think that these two objectives are one and the same," David replied. "It's getting close to noon; let's go to lunch, and I will tell you a story about a time earlier in my career when I was going through a struggle similar to yours today and what helped me achieve the goals that were expected of me."

Helen was uncharacteristically quiet as they drove to the restaurant. Her thoughts were on what David had said about what her main objective should be in her new assignment. She had fully expected that their discussion earlier that morning would have been centered on developing a new sales and marketing strategy for her product lines, not talking about her management style. Now, to make things even worse, she had to listen to David tell "war stories" from his past! "How did I get myself into this mess?" she thought to herself, as they pulled into the parking lot of the restaurant.

As they were being seated at their table, David began the conversation, "I know what it is like to have to listen to a lot advice that others give you at different times in your career about what it was like when I was in a job like yours. So I will make this brief. But I did want to share one experience I had that I think could be helpful to you in this job."

"I appreciate your sharing these things with me. Hopefully it can help me learn from your experiences and avoid future problems for my group," Helen lied.

"Well, I'll make this as brief as possible. I'm going to take this back about 7 years ago. I was put in charge of a product line similar to yours today. I had sales offices across the country and a number of products that we were responsible for marketing. As this was my first assignment as a Sales and Marketing Manager, I was determined to be highly successful. I literally threw myself at the job. I was working 60 to 70 hours a week. I lived in airports and on the peanuts they serve you on airplanes. But the thing that was most frustrating to me was not the effort that I was putting into the job, but the lack of results that I was achieving. In fact, after a few months it seemed that the numbers were looking worse than when I had begun the job. To top it all off, you can imagine what my work and travel schedule was doing to my homelife. Obviously, it was a very difficult and frustrating time in my life."

"What did you do about it?" Helen asked, becoming more interested in what David was telling her. "I don't remember your having a bad experience in that job. In fact, if I remember correctly, weren't you promoted into your current role from that job several years ago?"

"Yes, you are correct but I don't believe that would have ever happened if I hadn't changed the way I was trying to manage that job and the people who worked for me. What I learned was that working harder doesn't always achieve the results you want. Sometimes you can be counterproductive in your efforts if you are not doing the right things. There is a difference between doing things right and doing the right things."

There was a pause in the conversation as Helen seemed to mull over what David had just said. "Are you saying that I am not doing the right things?" she asked.

"I don't know. That is for you to decide. What I wanted to share with you is what I did in the my last job that helped me become more effective as a manager that may be useful to you," David replied.

"I'm all ears!" Helen said, by now very interested in hearing the rest of David's story.

"Well, like I was saying, I starting out trying to get everything done myself or at least be involved in just about everything that happened in the business. The problem was that I couldn't be everywhere, all the time. There were always decisions and actions that needed to taken when I wasn't available. What I unknowingly had created was a system that required my approval before anything could be done. Ultimately that took away the ability of the people who reported to me to perform their jobs properly. I was turning them into order clerks instead of salespeople."

"So I assume that you stopped becoming so involved in all of their decisions and allowed them more freedom to perform their jobs?" Helen asked.

"That's exactly what I did, but it isn't as easy as it sounds. Its not like you can just flip a switch and all the problems that your management style created will go away," David explained.

"What were some of the things that you had to do?" quizzed Helen.

"I guess the first thing that I did was to arrange for a meeting with all of my people at some central location. Instead of doing what we typically did at these kinds of meetings, which was to review each office's sales numbers and projections for the upcoming year, I decided to do something different. I asked the group what they thought we should do to improve our sales, and then I did something really radical!" David said with a bit a sarcasm.

"What did you do?" Helen asked, becoming more and more intrigued with David's story as he went on with it.

"I actually listened to what they had to say," David replied.

"What were some of their suggestions," Helen asked, already projecting in her mind what some of her new direct reports might say to her under similar circumstances.

"Actually, there were no great surprises. They said all the things that I already knew or should have known that we could have been doing better. There were also a few surprises. I guess, thinking back, the most significant change that they suggested was what my role should be," David said.

"What did they say that your role should have been?" Helen asked.

"Well, basically they wanted me to take a much less active role in the day-to-day activities of their businesses. I found that what was most important to the success of the entire business was for me to better understand what the people who worked for me really needed in order to be successful. Once I had a better vision of what that role needed to be, we began to really make some progress," he explained.

"I don't understand how your taking a less active role in the business could actually improve it? If that's all it takes, why don't you just eliminate the Sales and Marketing Manager's position?" Helen responded, getting a bit upset at what David was saying.

"It is not that simple. I didn't mean to imply that. I *did* need to play a role in managing the sales and marketing functions of the business, but it was just that my role needed to dramatically change. I had to learn to manage this function from a distance. This provided a number of benefits. First, it allowed me not to ruin my family and personal life. Doing that does not make you a better manager. It only makes you unhappy. Second, it allowed the people that we put into important positions at the various sales offices across the country the opportunity to run their businesses the way they saw fit. This didn't always agree with the way I would have done things, but that was the very point and benefit of this strategy. By allowing these people to make their own decisions, they also had ownership for the outcome. This creates a completely different mindset and motivation for people."

"I still don't think I understand what your new role was?" queried Helen.

"Don't get me wrong. I was still ultimately responsible for the bottom line sales results of the business. I just wasn't trying to make all the decisions about what needed to be done on every detail anymore. What I did was share with each of the managers of the sales offices what my overall objectives and directions were for the business and asked them to develop plans of their own that would support them. I made it clear what the parameters of their decision-making authority would be, and what I would hold them accountable for achieving. I made it clear what type of information I wanted from them and how often I expected it. I told each of them how I would measure their performance and what the rewards would be achieving their goals. We set up a regular communication plan to bring everyone up-to-date on the latest developments in the business. I also stopped setting up systems that pitted one office against the other in a win/lose scenario. That ultimately only became self-destructive. What we need to have is win/win scenarios." David explained.

"What would you consider to be a win/win scenario, as you call it?" Helen asked.

"For instance, what do you presently do to encourage your salespeople to support one another in providing better service to their customers?" David replied.

"Well, the system is not set up that way. Each salesperson has their own customers. Occasionally they may help each other out by covering for one another when they are gone or on vacation or something like that. I guess that's what I consider to be part of my job — to see those situations when we need to have someone get involved in helping out with a customer problem."

"That's my point exactly. How much synergy and efficiency do you think we lose in your present system, not to mention customer satisfaction?" asked David.

"I'm sure we lose a great deal of both," answered Helen. "What did you do to address this issue?"

"I changed the reinforcement system. The problem as I saw it was that we always talked a good game but didn't play it. For instance, we give speech after speech about how important teamwork is in our organization, but we don't really support it," he replied.

"We don't support teamwork in our organization?" Helen said, somewhat perplexed at his statement.

"No, I don't think we do. Let me ask you this. What do your salespeople get bonuses for? David asked.

"Obviously, for their sales," Helen answered.

"Whose sales?" asked David.

"For their own accounts," Helen retorted, getting impatient for David to make his point.

"And what incentive is there for them to help one another or be of service to someone else's customer?" asked David.

"I guess there really isn't any, except to do one another a favor," she said.

"That's one of the first things that I decided to change in the offices that I was responsible for. I set up a reward system that reinforced the entire salesforce for achieving goals as a group. This way they had an incentive to help one another. They were happier in this new setup, our customers got better service, and I didn't need to get involved in making sure that we were not missing any opportunity to help one another out when necessary. It was a win/win for everyone!"

"What else did you do to make your employees more independent?" asked Helen.

"I significantly changed their spending approval limits. Instead of my having to approve any expenses more than two thousand dollars, I changed their approval requirement to twenty-five thousand dollars. I gave them control over pricing for our customers, and allowed them to develop their own marketing plans. I let them set their own sales goals and recommend how they would be rewarded for reaching them. I guess those were some of the most significant — but there were other things as well."

"OK, if your subordinates were doing all these things, what did you do?" Helen asked.

"Instead of dealing with all of these details associated with selling the product, I let my salespeople focus on them. I began looking more strategically at the business."

"What does looking at the business more strategically mean?" Helen questioned.

"To me, it means that I focus more on those things in our business that can add value to the business. For example, I began to spend more time with our customers and learning more about their requirements. I worked with our research and development groups to design products that better met these needs of the customers. I spent time looking at the entire process from the time we get an order from a customer to delivery of our product. I developed follow-up procedures to ensure that the customer is satisfied with our service. I could go on and on. It was really great fun."

"Yes, it certainly sounds like more fun than I am having right now!" observed Helen.

"One thing that you have to remember is that changes like this take time. You didn't get to where you are today in a day or two; it will take time for things to improve," David advised.

"It also sounds like a huge challenge, with lots of potential obstacles in the way," observed Helen.

"You're right about that. You will need the support of a number of people on all levels of the organization to make these kinds of changes. Obviously, you know that you already have my support, but there are others that need to understand the changes you want to make and how they will be affected. If you don't get everybody on board from the very beginning, they can become those road-blocks that you just mentioned. What you begin to do in this style of management is create a system for getting things done, as opposed to simply making sure it gets done. In this new system, you don't always have to be there. In the old one, you do. When you begin to manage from a distance like this, you dramatically begin to change many of the roles that people in your organization will play. They need to understand what their new roles and responsibilities will be and be prepared to accept them," David summarized.

"This Is Only a Test"

"This is a test of the your management style. It is only a test. If this were an actual emergency, you would be required to contact a number of people that work in various roles all around you for detailed feedback on your management style. At this time, this information is for your use only and will be shared with no one. Again, this is only a test."

Your Management Style Profile

Directions   Answer the following multiple-choice questions concerning how you might react in each of the following situations. Your responses will help to identify your personal management style:

1. You begin noticing a downward trend in the quality of the work that is being performed in the department that you manage. It has reached the point that several of your most important customers have complained about these types of problems. You realize that something must be done immediately to address this problem. Which of the following actions would you take:
    a. Personally investigate what is causing this quality problem to occur and ensure that it is corrected.
    b. Hold a departmental meeting and share with everyone the seriousness of the problem and ask for their input concerning how to correct it.
    c. Review the situation with the supervision in your department and asked them to develop a plan to correct the problem.

d. Stay in touch with those in your department who have responsibility for ensuring that the quality of your products meets the customer's requirements concerning their actions to correct this problem.

2. There has developed a disciplinary problem with one of the employees in your department. It has gotten to the point that other employees have been complaining that nothing is being done to address this issue. You realize that some action needs to taken right away. Would you:
   a. Call the employee into your office and issue the appropriate level of discipline.
   b. Ask the team what they think should be done to discipline this employee.
   c. Assign responsibility for this discipline to whoever is most familiar with this situation, most likely the employee's immediate supervisor or team leader.
   d. Try to understand why nothing has been done to date to address this problem through the normal channels and disciplinary procedures before taking any other action.

3. As manager of an important segment of the company's business, you have been given the challenge to improve efficiencies by 6% over the next few months. How would you go about accomplishing this goal:
   a. Establish new productivity goals for everyone in your organization and ensure that they were met.
   b. Meet with the top managers in your organization to develop a plan to reach this aggressive goal.
   c. Ask your top managers to develop a plan to reach the 6% efficiency goal by the targeted date.
   d. Communicate the challenge to your organization and offer any support they need to meet this objective.

4. You have to fill an important position in your organization. This person will ultimately be in change of several of the key functions in your operation. Which of the following approaches might you take to find this individual:
   a. Conduct a candidate search in much the same way as you always have in the past, utilizing executive search firms to screen candidates and then personally interview the three most qualified for the position.
   b. Have a group of your key managers also interview the candidates and provide input into the selection decision.
   c. Ask those who will work most closely with the person selected to develop their own interview criteria and selection process and bring a hiring recommendation to you.

    d. Give this responsibility for filling this position to those who will work directly with this individual.

5. There appears to be a serious morale problem in your organization that is beginning to affect the ability of employees to get their work done in a timely and quality manner. How would you address this problem:

    a. Communicate to everyone that regardless of how they may be feeling about issues that may be occurring at the time, they still have a job to do and requirements that must be met.

    b. Meet with as many people in the organization as possible to try to get a better understanding of why they are upset and to "brainstorm" ways to improve the problem.

    c. Commission a group to study the problem and develop a plan for improving morale.

    d. Encourage those in positions that have the greatest impact on employee moral to continue working on identifying and addressing the issues that are driving this problem.

6. The competition has introduced a new product that has the potential to take a significant amount of market share from your company. What actions would you take:

    a. Lead a task force to begin developing your own product to compete against the other company's.

    b. Establish a team to investigate how you could develop a competitive product.

    c. Ask your research and development people to develop a competitive product.

    d. Have those in key positions in your organization look at the situation from a number of aspects and allow this group to decide what should be done to address this problem.

7. Lately, there seems to be a problem in keeping confidential information confidential in your organization. Which of the following actions would you take:

    a. Send a memo to everyone in the organization telling them that if anyone is caught violating the company's confidentiality policies, under no uncertain terms, they will receive discipline up to and including termination.

    b. Ask a select group of individuals study the problem and determine when and where this problem is occurring.

    c. Call the appropriate manager who is responsible for ensuring that these policies are adhered to and enforced and ask him/her to investigate the problem.

    d. Allow those in the positions that are responsible for the areas where the problem is occurring to deal with the problem in the manner they feel is best.

8. As the General Manager of the business, you want to reward employees for an outstanding performance during the past year. You decide to:

    a. Give everyone a bonus in recognition of their outstanding work.

    b. Establish a team to make recommendations concerning what would be the best way to provide additional compensation to everyone in the organization.

    c. Ask your compensation committee to develop a bonus program to reward good performance.

    d. Allow the managers that report to you to decide what would be the best way to recognize and reward their employees.

9. You want to share more financial and business information with employees on all levels of your organization. You decide that the best way to do this would be to:

    a. Set up a series of meetings for all employees to present the current financial and competitive information concerning the business.

    b. Have a team of top managers in the organization conduct a series of informational meetings to share this data.

    c. Ask the Human Resource Managers in your organization to develop a plan to communicate this type of information to everyone.

    d. Share your commitment that everyone in the organization understands the financial and competitive aspects of the business and encourage your managers in the organization to develop ways to broadly disseminate this type of information.

10. At a recent business symposium, you learned a great deal about new management philosophies that many of the more progressive companies are implementing with impressive results. As president of your company, would you:

    a. Make a directive that the entire business adapt these new management philosophies as soon as possible.

    b. Create a committee to investigate the feasibility of implementing these new management philosophies and techniques into the organization.

    c. Ensure that the managers in the organization understand that they have your support in implementing these new concepts and philosophies in their areas of responsibility.

    d. Give the managers in the company the opportunity to learn more about these concepts and decide if they would be able to be implemented in their parts of the organization.

A successful manager quickly realizes that regardless of what philosophical objectives may be currently embraced by the organization, there will always be the need for a body of leadership skills and characteristics to be utilized. Even a Remote Control Manager needs to become directly involved at times. Managing by remote control doesn't mean that you never show up. The Remote Control Manager must appear live and in person once in awhile! It may be that the most important management skill that is needed to be a successful manager is knowing when to manage outside the box and when to let the system work through a problem for itself. Even the most sophisticated television sets today need an adjustment once in a while that can not be performed on the remote control device, and we are forced out of our recliners on a journey to the actual set itself. But what the heck, we need to get some exercise once in awhile!

Your Organizational Style

Another slightly different variation of management style is your organizational style. By organizational style, it is not meant those descriptions mentioned earlier such as Traditional, Team, Empowering, or Remote Control, but rather how you organize yourself.

    Each of us has certain organization traits that affect how we perform our jobs. These traits are neither necessarily right nor wrong but more descriptive of our own individual styles. However, in their extremes, any of these traits can be counterproductive. These traits can often be readily recognizable by simply entering a person's office or work area! However, sometimes it may not be so easy to categorize people without some more information than casual observation might provide. By understanding a person's organization style, you can have a better insight into what they might do with certain information that you need or might provide to them. It may also be helpful for you to have a better understanding of your own organizational style. As we may have a tendency to overuse our natural propensities, it is often useful to work on skills outside of our comfort zones. In this case, it may be to develop skills outside of our natural organization styles.

    The organizational styles are:

Management Style Grid

A TRADITIONAL (controlling)	B EMPOWERING (delegating)
C TEAM (sharing)	D REMOTE CONTROL (allowing)

Scoring: Count the number of a's, b's, c's, and d's that you selected as answers. Whichever one you selected the most frequently would be indicative of your management style.

Interpreting your score: Notice the descriptions corresponding to each of the management styles. The Traditional style is more *controlling* and the Empowering is the most *delegating*. The Team style is characterized by *sharing* and the Remote Control style is more *allowing*. Whatever your management style, there are always times when it may be more appropriate and effective to utilize a different management style than what comes most naturally to you. It is important to understand that any of the answers in the Management Style Test may have been effective in dealing with each of the situations described.

Thinking outside the box: The more versatile and flexible you can become in your management style, the more effectively you will be able to deal with the many different situations that you will undoubtedly face as a manager. Perhaps this is what truly is meant by the popular business cliche today — *thinking outside the box.*

- Throwers
- Savers
- Filers
- Pilers

- **Throwers** are those people who have a tendency to get rid of any unnecessary material or items that might come into their lives.
- **Savers** are on the opposite side of the spectrum of throwers. They tend to save the things that come into their possession.
- **Filers** tend to put everything away in its place. This could be in a filing system or some other storage and retrieval system. Note that filers could be either Throwers or Savers.
- **Pilers** use a pile system of organizing things. There may or may not be a categorization system employed, and if one does exist, it probably would not be obvious to anyone else trying to find anything. Pilers can also be either Throwers or Savers.

The following is a brief questionnaire to help you identify your organizational style, just in case it is not already apparent to you! You could also use this tool to profile someone else you work with to better understand their particular organizational style. This understanding can help you work more effectively with others by knowing what types of organizational behaviors to expect from them in the future.

Based on the responses you give, you can then plot your organizational style on the Organization Style Matrix. If you have profiled other people, plot what you found to be their profiles on this matrix as well to see how they compare to yours. Instructions on how to plot your answers on the matrix are provided following the questionnaire.

Your Organization Style Profile

Directions: Circle number 1 through 5 which best corresponds to your work habits and behaviors.

A. When you go through your mail at work do you:
  1. Look at what requires immediate action and put the rest aside to look some other time.

2. Reroute any mail that someone else needs to see and leave the rest on your desk.
3. Decide what is "junk" and ignore it, taking action on the rest of the mail.
4. Review each piece of mail first before doing anything else.
5. Separate each piece of mail and put in its proper place or send to its proper destination.

B. How would you describe the neatness of your office or workspace:
1. Cluttered, disorganized, unable to see the top of your desk.
2. In need of more storage and filing space.
3. Outward appearances would make one believe that everything is well organized but this is not necessarily true beneath the "surface."
4. Desk always looks as if you have nothing that hasn't been taken care of, even if not necessarily the case.
5. Neat and orderly, everything in its place; plenty of filing and storage space available.

C. How readily available are the records of documents that you need to perform your job:
1. You can usually find something if given enough time to sort through everything in your office.
2. Some things get lost and are not retrievable, particularly if some period of time has passed since you last used them.
3. You can usually easily find what you need, but someone else might have trouble understanding your filing system.
4. Can usually be found in a reasonable period of time.
5. Always readily available to anyone who might look for them.

D. How long do you think you need to save a document, assuming it isn't something that you are required by someone else to keep:
1. Forever and a day!
2. Until you feel comfortable that you will not have a need for it again.
3. As long as you have someplace convenient to store it.
4. For a brief period of time after you have completed using it.
5. Just as long as there is an immediate need for it.

Directions for Plotting Organization Profile on Matrix: Add the numbers of your answers for questions A and C and mark on the vertical axis (Filer/Piler). Next, add the number of your answers for questions B and D and mark on the horizontal axis (Thrower/Saver). Find the quadrant in which these two scores intersect. This represents your Organization Profile according to the two dimensions of the matrix for which you seem to have a propensity.

Organization Style Profiler Matrix

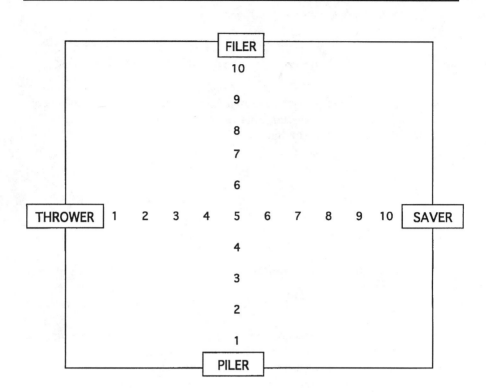

The Marriage of Throwers and Savers

The concept of Throwers and Savers is also important in our personal lives, particularly in marriage. For instance, in every marriage there is one spouse who is the *Thrower* and one that is the *Saver*. This creates the natural balance needed for a couple to be able to live in relative harmony concerning this issue without either saving everything that they acquire during their years together or throwing everything out! Interestingly, which spouse is the Thrower or the Saver in the family does not follow any gender lines. The likelihood of the husband being either the Thrower or the Saver is equal to either of these roles being played by the wife. If two Throwers or two Savers happen to marry one another, then one of them will eventually take on the opposite role and balance in this aspect of marriage will be restored.

5 | The Remote Control Manager's Programming Guide

One of the most popular weekly magazines on the market today is *TV Guide,* and there are countless variations of this format printed in newspapers across the country each day. Millions of viewers depend on these programming guides to tell them what will be on television as well as to receive recommendations on what the critics suggest we watch.

What if there were a similar guide to help you better understand what to expect in your management future? This guide would allow you to "tune into" what opportunities may exist in your workplace to utilize these concepts to support the objectives and goals of the organization.

The following is the first edition of the *Remote Control Manager's Programming Guide.* It is designed to not only help you better understand the concept but to see how it may be applied in a variety of different situations. In keeping with the format of many of its prototypes, the *Remote Control Manager's Guide* is presented in the following categories:

- Educational Programs
- Television Evangelists
- Daytime Dramas
- Cops/Detective Shows
- Sitcoms
- Late Night
- Sports

As with television programming, there are certain hours of the week that are considered to be "Prime Time." For purposes of the *Remote Control Manager's Guide,* you need to think about when prime time would be in your organization. When are people most receptive to hearing and learning about change? When do you have the most people's attention? How can you get the largest audience for what you want to say? Who are you focusing your communications on and what is it that you would like them to do differently? Whom do you need to support and where will your advertising dollars come from? As you read the *Remote Control Manager's Guide,* think about these and other related questions to ensure that your ratings as an effective Remote Control Manager stay as high as they can be and your *show* is renewed for another season.

Educational Programs

Some of the best television viewing each week is in the form of educational programs designed for all ages of the family. These include children's shows, documentaries, public television programs, specials, and a variety of other programs intended to help us learn more about our world. They are both educational and entertaining, utilizing the television medium to its best use and potential.

Remote Control Management also needs to focus on the educational needs of the organization as well. If people are going to be expected to make more decisions for themselves than before this concept was introduced, they must also be given the opportunity to improve the skills they need to accept this greater responsibility.

An important part of any organizational change initiative needs to be an educational plan designed to provide the skills that people need throughout the organization to perform their new roles and responsibilities. To expect employees to be able accept new responsibilities without this training would be grossly unfair. Sometimes, this training may need to be fairly basic. Again, you can not always assume that everyone knows what you may expect them to. Taking yet another lesson from television, let's look once again at how this medium approaches teaching the basics to its fastest growing audience — children!

Now don't get offended by this analogy of children's educational TV programs and preparing employees for organizational change. There are many good lessons to learned here. For instance, our friend Mister Rogers might ask, "Can you say productivity and job efficiency leads to customer satisfaction?" Maybe you are not ready to put on a cardigan sweater and sneakers to make those who report to you more comfortable with the changes that will be occurring in the organization, but Fred does make many good points. Being patient and supportive of others, particularly during these highly stressful times of organizational change can't do any harm. If fact, it just may make the difference for some in being able to cope and eventually adapt to the new work environment being introduced. Just imagine calling a meeting of your employees one morning in the near future and serving them cookies and milk. Suddenly you break into song: "*Won't you be my, won't you be my, won't you be my neighbor?*"

Once the astonished looks on their faces go away, what effect do you think this might have on your relationship with those who report to you? Assuming that you are not sent to the company physician or for psychiatric evaluation, don't you think that everyone would feel better and more trusting of you? Don't you think that they would feel more comfortable being given greater responsibility and decision-making ability by this display of warmth and sincerity? You obviously wouldn't sing Fred Rogers' song to your employees (or would you?), but it is the concept that is most important. What effect would changing your relationship with those who report to you have on their overall performance? How much better might they be able to perform their jobs if they felt that they had the kind of unconditional support that Mister Rogers tries to convey to the children who watch his show each day? Confidence and trust can be a tremendous performance enhancer. Remote Control Management similarly builds on these very same principles. In many ways, Mister Rogers is a Remote Control Manager, sending his message of trust and support to millions of young viewers across the world with each program.

Remote Control Competencies

There is a great deal of focus today on developing competency based programs in organizations. Competencies are the skills and knowledge that employees need to perform their jobs. The first step in evaluating the training and educational needs of an organization is to determine the competencies that currently exist, and then to identify those that are needed to meet future goals. There typically will be core competencies that are important for every individual in an organization to have or develop. These are the universal business drivers for the organization. Although they may be universal in the sense that everyone in a given organization may need to have them, these core competencies may be different for another organization. Competencies for an organization are determined by the norms and goals that exist within its culture.

Going beyond these core competencies, different levels of the organization may need somewhat different competencies to be successful on their jobs. For example, an executive vice president of a corporation would need different competencies than of a front line supervisor. But there may also be shared competencies as well. A core competency for both of these roles might be: effective communications. In other words, no matter what level in the organization that you manage, it will always be important for you to be an effective communicator. However, there are specific competencies that would be unique to of each of these positions. The executive vice president might need to be very strong in leading change in a certain organization. This would be determined by the direction and overall objectives of the organization at the time. However, the front-line supervisor may not be required to lead change in his/her position as much as to help others adapt to change. Thus helping others adapt to change would become the needed competency for the front-line supervisor. Obviously, you can see how these competencies begin to relate to and support one another.

Competencies specific to your organization can be determined by conducting your own research. This can be accomplished by interviewing the incumbents in a variety of positions in your organization that have been identified as being highly successful in their jobs. In these interviews, ask them what competencies they possessed or acquired that allowed them to reach this level of success. They will describe to you in as much detail as you want, what competencies were important in their success as well as what competencies they felt they lacked. It is important to get both of these perspectives.

What are the competencies that a Remote Control Manager needs to have? Again, these will be determined by needs and objectives of each organization. However, there are certain competencies that can be described that would likely by identified in most workplaces as being important to the organization's overall success. For example, given the nature and overall objectives of a Remote Control Manager, the following are presented as possible Core Remote Control Competencies:

- Trusting others
- Sharing information
- Developing others
- Providing resources
- Managing change
- Helping people adapt to change
- Dealing with uncertainty
- Having confidence
- Reassuring others
- Mentioning
- Giving people accountabilities
- Coaching

- Creating strong working relationships
- Flexibility
- Showing empathy
- Commitment to quality
- Concern for people
- Building partnerships
- Empowering others
- Accepting responsibility
- Courageousness
- Modeling ethical behaviors
- Results driven
- Thinking strategically
- Listening

When assessing an organization's training and educational needs, it is necessary to look at both the competencies that are technical in nature as well as those that are managerial or administrative. The technical competencies might be described as the hardware of the learning process and the managerial/administrative as the software. Both of these aspects of employee development are critically important and are interrelated. A good analogy is found when shopping for a personal computer. The computer equipment itself is the hardware component of the system that you seek to buy. This, of course, is very important to your ultimate satisfaction with the computer system that you ultimately purchase after researching all of the options currently available to you on the market today. However, the software is what ultimately enables your new computer to perform whatever functions and operations you expected. The software would be useless without the hardware and vice versa. To focus exclusively on only the technical competencies that an organization believes it needs in the future would be like spending thousands and thousands of dollars on computer hardware and not buying any software to run on it. The reverse situation could also be true, if an organization focused only on the software side of training but little on technical development. It would be like having the latest computer programs available, but not the computer capability to run them.

Organizations whose business depends on technology to maintain a competitive advantage, need to address the technical competencies to maintain this edge. They could not operate successfully in the long term without this focus on the hard side of development. But the question still remains how much better they could perform if both the soft and hard aspects of training were more adequately addressed. Conversely, organizations that are not in technical businesses may have a similar tendency to ignore this holistic approach to training and development and focus more on the softer areas of education.

Perhaps the greatest obstacle to the development of a comprehensive training plan addressing both the hard and soft aspects of development is the following two factors:

- Lack of insight on the part of the Sanctioning or Steering functions of the organization concerning the importance of both the technical and managerial/administrative aspects of training and development.
- The assumption on the part of many managers, particularly those in higher levels of the organization, that there is not the need for additional development (either hard or soft) for experienced and seasoned managers and professionals.

One way to overcome these obstacles is by conducting a training needs analysis within the organization. This analysis should address both the soft and hard aspects of the organization's developmental needs. This does not necessarily have to be a complicated exercise. The following is an example of how this analysis might be designed (more lines may be added if required).

Training and Development Needs Analysis

Hardware — Technical/Job Specific	Software — Managerial/Administrative

The question is what is the appropriate mix of these soft and hard training experiences. What is most important is what meets the needs of the organization and its employees. One way to begin to determine this appropriate ratio would be to first develop these lists from a historical perspective. In other words, list the training that has been completed in the past few years as part of this assessment. Then take a look at the balance of the technical vs. managerial/administrative training that has been provided. This may make more apparent any deficiencies that might exist in either side of the training and development balance most appropriate for your organization.

Back to Basics

As indicated, there may also be problems getting decision-makers in an organization to realize that sometimes people need basic level training even if they have performed their jobs for a long time. Again, let's look for lessons we might learn from another television program that utilizes creative teaching techniques and approaches — *Sesame Street*. This timeless and enormously successful children's program provides an excellent learning model, even for adults. When you think about it, even in workplaces where people have worked together for years, maybe decades, in the most sophisticated organizational systems, we still see some very childish behavior at times!

Sesame Street can take what may seem like complex concepts, such a language, mathematics, and reading, and presents them in clear and understandable terms. This is done in a comfortable and entertaining manner that permits the viewer to learn, often without realizing that he/she *is* learning. They present the materials in extraordinarily creative ways. Humor and satire are used in their teaching approach, giving the show its universal appeal to both young and old. Children learn mathematical concepts presented by a character called the Count. Most children have no idea this character is based on the blood-sucking star of the story of Dracula. They may not appreciate this level of the humor, but do enjoy seeing this strange-looking character who loves to count things — anything in fact. Imagine if the Count gave your company's next financial report your annual Shareholders' Meeting? Maybe that would get everyone interested in the numbers!

The point is that learning, even in a sophisticated corporate organization, needs to be both interesting and educational to be effective. There is no reason that even technical training can't be presented in an interesting format. The computer offers unlimited teaching options, with interactive programs, touch screens, 3D graphics, sound, video teleconferencing, Internet access, and many other new applications constantly being developed. The more creative the approach, the more receptive employees will typically be and the more they will learn. Just imagine, if your training and development programming was presented by *Sesame Street* ...

> "Good morning ladies and gentlemen. I hope you are having a wonderful day," the very pleasant voice says over the company intercom system. "Today's word is CUSTOMER SERVICE. There will be a seminar in the Sunshine conference room on the ABCs of meeting the customer's requirements at 2:30 p.m., immediately after everyone has awakened from their afternoon nap. Of course, we will be serving cookies and milk. Mr. Smith, the Vice President of Sales, a very important and busy man, will be available to answer any questions you might have on this subject. I want all of you to put on your thinking caps about what you might want to ask him. I am sure that everyone will be very good listeners today, isn't that right? Thank you for your attention and we will see you this afternoon."

Now does that really sound like it would be such a bad way to announce a seminar that will be held? This approach might just get more people interested in attending.

Different Perceptions of the Job

Training and education play a critical role in changing the culture of an organization. Again, it is grossly unfair to ask people to accept accountability if they have not been given the training to perform competently. This would be like giving a student a geometry test before he/she has taken the course. Similarly, it is also unfair to expect employees to perform their jobs in a manner that has not been clearly defined or explained to them. A clear vision and understanding must be established on the part of the manager and his/her direct reports concerning what they expected to do.

However, peoples' perceptions of this vision can be radically different. This is well illustrated by tastes in television viewing. One person may enjoy detective shows and another situation comedies. Who is right? Which is the best program to watch? Obviously viewers have different perspectives on this question as they fight over who controls the remote control in the home. Even if two viewers are watching the same program, one may be hysterical with laughter and the other may not amused at all. Does this mean that the show is funny or not? Like beauty, the answer to this question is in the eye of the beholder. Viewers can also have vastly different perceptions of the value of television programs. Some people prefer to only watch documentaries, others are only interested in sports programs, while for still others, daytime soap operas may represent the epitome of what television has to offer. It is all a matter of perspective.

The eye of the beholder is given no greater test than in viewing any one of the many beauty pageants frequenting television programming throughout the year — Miss Universe, Miss America, Miss Teen U.S.A., Mrs. America, even Mr. Universe. Most include a number of different settings and challenges for the contestants. There is certain to be disagreement in many households on who should be the finalist, and ultimately, the winner. Everyone sees the contestants in a different way and by varying standards. One person's preference may be influenced by the talent that a contestant displays, while the swimsuit competition may the deciding factor for another. It really is a function of personal taste, attitude, sensitivities, preferences, and a multitude of other factors that influence how we see and feel about different things.

It's like the old question, "Is the glass half full or half empty? If you see it as half full you are the type of person who has the most positive perspectives on life. This same principle could be utilized in your workplace should you fall behind schedule in completing an important project. The next time a deadline looms ominously on your work horizon, and your boss wants to know the status of a project or assignment, instead of explaining what remains to be done describe all the things that have already been completed. Your boss might just walk away with a more positive impression and feeling better about the status of the project. However, beware if this technique is being tried out on you when you are in the boss's role!

The problem is that the perceptions of what the key responsibilities are supposed to be can be dramatically different for both the employee and the supervisor. This may go beyond just seeing the glass as half full or half empty. There can be significant perceptual differences concerning the job between the boss and the employee. These differences are illustrated in the following figure. On the left is what is perceived by the supervisor as being most important; on the right is what is perceived to be most important by the employee. The overlapping shaded area is commonly agreed to be most important to both. It is only in this common area of overlap that there is any agreement. But what about the other areas of the job in which there is disagreement on what is important? Obviously the employee's and the super-

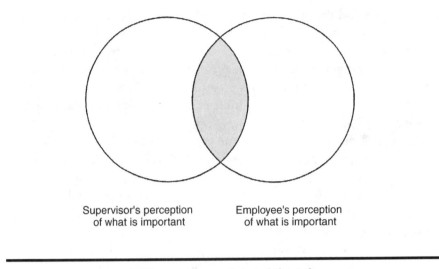

Supervisor's perception
of what is important

Employee's perception
of what is important

Different Perceptions of the Job

visor's perceptions are very different concerning how the job is to be performed and what is most important.

To become a truly Remote Control Manager, there needs to be a much
better understanding of what is important and what are the priorities of the
subordinate's job. Lack of this common understanding is most likely the basis
of much misunderstanding that might exist between managers and those
they manage concerning job performance. This may need to be part of the
overall training and educational process of the organization to ensure that
everyone has a better understanding of what is expected of them and what
is most important.

Future Roles

Preparing employees for their future roles in the organization should be a
major objective of any training and development function. In Chapter 3, the
concept of "Today and Tomorrow" tasks was introduced. This focused on
changing the responsibilities of employees from being focused on Today
issues to a more strategic focus, looking more towards how the work process
could be improved in the future. Another exercise called "Changing Roles"
again looks at the responsibilities that certain key employees may have at the
present time as well are what these roles should be in the future. In this
analysis, we look at the present, intermediate and future goals. Table 5.2
shows an example of this exercise for a Customer Service Representative.

Table 5.2   Exercise for a Customer Service Rep

Current Responsibility	Transitional Responsibility	Future Responsibility
Calling customers on telephone	Creating sales leads	Account development
Responding to customer's complaints	Troubleshooting problems	Product improvement
Expediting orders	Computerizing accounts	E-Mail capabilities
New product	Internet access	Create home page
Order processing	Computer compatibility	Automated order processing

In each of these steps, there needs to be training and development to make these changes become a reality. You need to go back to your Training Needs Analysis to develop both the technical (hard) and managerial/administrative (soft) training that employees need to achieve these future responsibilities.

A major responsibility of a Remote Control Manager is developing others to be able accept these future responsibilities. This plays a major part in developing the systems and support that are needed to create this type of work environment.

The Organizational Change Evangelist

Among the many life-style changes that television has created, the advent of the television evangelist stands out as one of the most unique. Through the miracle of television, a clergyman's congregation on any given Sunday morning *knoweth no bounds*. Literally millions of viewers and, hopefully, worshipers could participate in the religious service in the comfort of their own living rooms. This provided a wonderful opportunity to be part of a religious worship service for many people who, for any number of reasons, may not have been able to visit a church or synagogue during the week. It also offered the opportunity to commercialize the concept of the collection plate.

Pleas for donations from these Television Evangelists reach the hearts and pocketbooks of millions of devoted viewers each week. And their message is heard, as millions of dollars flow in from people both rich and poor, in hopes that it might help them buy whatever it is that is being promised. Sometimes they are hoping for a miracle like the ones they see on television as they watch the crippled suddenly healed and able to walk once again; or they may hear about families that are reunited in love and devotion as a result of the work of the TV Evangelist. Whatever their cross is to bear, the TV Evangelist offers the one thing that they desperately need the most — hope.

Unfortunately, the hard-earned money of the faithful viewers does occasionally fall into the hands of the unscrupulous. The well-publicized escapades of Jim Baker and his then-mascara-laden wife Tammy, are testament to the temptations of mortal man. In the name of the religion, they lavished upon themselves material riches that befit a king and queen (perhaps how they viewed themselves).

There is a lesson to be learned for the aspiring Remote Control Manager from these TV Evangelists. Beware of those who promise you miracles that they might not be able to deliver. Providing guidance and hope for something better in the future is one thing. Deception is quite something else. Fully realizing that there may indeed be miracles through the power of prayer and religious devotion, there are no instant cures when it comes to organizational change. Organizational change is something that must be approached in a systematic manner utilizing some kind of structure such as described in the model presented in Chapter 1. Beware of the Organizational Change Evangelist who promises you miracles with no sacrifice. It doesn't happen that easily. Be particularly cautious when you see the "collection plate" coming around a little too fast and frequently in order to achieve the organizational "miracle" that is being promised.

If you hear the words, "Let me place my hands on your expense accounts and pronounce you a Remote Control Organization," you might want to be a little suspicious of this Organizational Evangelist's credentials!

The Remote Control Covenant

It may not qualify as a religious experience, but there is a covenant that needs to exist within an organization for Remote Control to truly become a management practice. With Remote Control Management comes the imperative to develop others. In a real sense, everyone must become a manager of his/her own work area, regardless of the relative importance of their position or role in the organization. As part of this covenant, employees have an obligation to speak up, to give their opinions, to share their experience and knowledge.

Remote Control Management creates a partnership between the boss and the employee. Believe it or not, they are on the same side, even though at times it may not seem like it! They share the same ultimate goals for success for both the organization as well as personally. Both of these objectives are connected, although this relationship at times might be difficult to see.

Look again at the gap between Organizational Capability and Individual Competency found in Chapter 2. It is in this gap that the greatest potential gains of Remote Control Management are found. This where the covenant begins.

There are no quick fixes to create an organizational culture that not only supports but nurtures the concepts of Remote Control Management. To achieve this goal requires hard work, patience, understanding, and time. To try to rush the process would only serve to circumvent some of the basic developmental needs essential to its success. Goals are typically reached by taking things one step at a time and as the result of the hard work and dedication of everyone involved in the process.

Daytime Dramas

The television daytime drama, or "soap opera" as they are popularly known, is a curious phenomenon. For some strange reason, we enjoy watching stories of other people's lives that are so full of bizarre problems that you wonder how they could ever cope with life. Perhaps the universal appeal of these shows is that compared to the problems that these soap opera characters face each afternoon on television, our own problems may not seem so serious.

Imagine that your workplace was more like one of these soap operas that you see on television. You may be thinking that it already is! However, after you finish reading the following story, you may look at the problems that you must deal with at work as being merely trivial in comparison!

"As The Organization Turns"

As part of a recent promotion, Scott Preston was put in charge of five Service Centers located across the country. This seemed like a perfectly natural transition for Scott as he had *grown up* in his career in the Customer Service system in the company. He started as a Customer Service Trainee 12 years ago and had worked his way up through a series of increasingly responsible positions. Scott was a handsome young man, even more youthful in his appearance than his age might reveal, with a strong desire to succeed and get what he wanted. He seemed destined for future corporate greatness — that is unless *she* ruins his promising career, but more about that part of the story later.

Scott sat in his office looking out the window as he contemplated what he should do. The business that he was suddenly in charge of, was now in serious trouble. Sales were down by over 10% over the past year, and they were losing more and more customers everyday. There was nothing but distrust among the various managers of the Service Centers who all seemed to be working against one another. And then there was *her*. His thoughts were distracted by what she had told him last night. He wasn't sure that he would ever see her again, or if he even wanted to. But for now he had to try to concentrate on the situation he now faced in his new job. His personal problems would jut have to be put on hold for now. He just hoped that she would still be there, he thought.

Things got even more complicated in the Service Centers. Scott's first instinct was to call each of the centers and make it clear what he expected from each of them. If the center didn't reach the goals that Scott would set for them, then he would just have to find someone else who could. It was clear to him what needed to be done to improve the performance of each of the centers. He had been a Service Center Manager himself in his last position, so he knew what he was talking about when it came to dealing with the problems and challenges they faced. In fact, that is exactly what he started out to do in the first few months of his new job. Unfortunately, this strategy didn't work very well. The biggest problem was that Scott couldn't be everywhere all the time. He was like the proverbial Dutch boy, putting his finger in the dike to stop one leak only to have to abandon it to try to plug another someplace else.

Within just a few months on his new job, he was nearly completely exhausted and with little positive result. He spent all of his time flying from one office to the next, trying to turn the business around through his own expertise and efforts. This was made even a greater challenge by the fact that the offices were spread across the country. Two of the offices were located in the east, one in the midwest, and one in the west. Scott would no sooner get off a airplane from the East Coast and stop and visit the midwest office, than he was on another plane to the West Coast. This was not only extremely frustrating to Scott, but to the managers of the Service Centers as well.

"I thought things were going to be better when I heard Scott was taking over the National Service Center Manager job a few months ago," Pat Newton, Manager of the midwest office said into the telephone. "I've known him for many years and he really does know this business from the inside out. But he needs to give us more space. He is driving us crazy, over-managing everything that is going on in my office."

"I know exactly what you mean," replied Stan Henderson, the manager of the office in California. "He's doing the same thing when he comes and visits us, which has been more often than we would like! At first, I appreciated what he was trying to do. There is no doubt that we can use all the help that we can get with all the problems we are facing in this business. But I don't think the way that Scott is approaching things is the right way. We all have a lot of experience. What we need is support and direction, not someone trying to make all of our decisions for us."

"Exactly. Scott can't possibly stay on top of everything that we are doing all the time. He spent most of his last visit going through our budget in so much detail that none of us could get anything else done during the 3 days he was here. We all had to work over the weekend to get caught up on the work we couldn't get done because he was here. I really would not mind so much if I thought what he was doing was productive. But all we accomplished was to go over numbers that I had already reviewed myself. Maybe it made Scott feel better about knowing what we were doing in this office, but it didn't help me or my staff out at all," Pat commented.

"What do you think we should do?" asked Stan.

"I don't know. But I don't want to get on Scott's bad side over this. We have always gotten along pretty well in the past and I sure don't want that to change now, especially with him as our new boss!" Pat replied.

"Yeah, I think that he's getting pretty frustrated. No doubt he's feeling the heat from his boss to improve the numbers. I agree with you. This probably isn't the best time to be critical of him, not when he's feeling the way he does right now. What he is doing is definitely not helping anyone. I've talked to the managers at the other two Service Centers and he is doing the same things there. But what can we do about it?" Stan asked again.

"I don't know. I guess nothing for now. Let's just wait and see what happens," replied Pat in frustration.

"By the way, I've heard some rumors about Scott and a certain woman. Have you heard these same things?" Stan cautiously asked.

"Yes I have. I think there is a lot more to this story than we know!" replied Pat replied before hanging up the phone.

We will return to "As the Organization Turns" in just one moment. But first, let's ask these questions (imagine the organ music getting louder as we pause for this break):

- *Will Scott turn the business around without driving everyone crazy?*
- *Will he realize just how much he is screwing up by being so involved in everyone else's jobs?*
- *Who is this mystery woman that Scott is allegedly having an affair with?*
- *Are Stan and Pat having an affair?*
- *Will this show be renewed for another season?*
- *Does anybody care?*
- *Does anyone deserve a Daytime Emmy for their role so far?*

As time went on, the problems in the Customer Service Centers only got worse. As the pressure mounted, Scott's dominating management style only intensified. The situation was beginning to get the attention of the upper management of the company. One morning, after a few more months had passed without any improvement in the situation, Scott was called into his boss's office.

Alice Holstrom was on the phone when he arrived at her office door. She motioned for him to sit down and gestured that her call would only be a minute more. Alice was very attractive woman in her early to mid-thirties, with long, reddish-brown hair pulled back in bow. Her long slender legs were intertwined under her desk and were in full view, due to the open style of her desk and office furniture. She wore a dark business suit, but had on a silky blouse revealing just a suggestion of the her ample breasts below its open third button. She motioned for Scott to close the door as he entered the room. "Damn it, Henry, I want those numbers on my desk by 2 o'clock this afternoon, and they better look good!" she sternly spoke into the telephone. "No, I don't care what you have to do, just get them to me," she concluded, as she ended the telephone conversation and now turned her attention to Scott. This wasn't exactly the tone on which he wanted this meeting to begin.

"Hello," she said somewhat softly, suddenly seeming in a much different mood than she appeared to be just seconds ago in her telephone conversation. This made Scott perspire even more, as he tried unsuccessfully to get comfortable in one of Alice's oversized leather visitor's chairs. "I've been looking over the numbers from the Service Centers since you began this job. How long has it been now?" she asked, although she probably already knew the answer.

"About 6 months," Scott answered, knowing that she already knew the answer.

"Yes, that's right. I remember now. As I remember we had quite a long talk before you began this job didn't we?" she almost purred to him, as she thrust back in her chair and smiled as if reliving that time.

"Yes, well things are much different now. I see things much differently now than I did then. The only thing I care about is getting this business back on its feet. Nothing else!" Scott blurted out.

"Just remember, Scott, that I put you into this job and I can take you out of it just as easily," Alice shot back, returning to the demeanor that she had displayed a few minutes ago on the telephone.

"I'm sure you won't let me ever forget that," Scott replied. "What are you going to do?"

"I'm going to help you," she said, again changing her mood again in what seemed like microseconds.

Scott got even more uncomfortable and he began squirming in his chair. Alice, of course, saw this and capitalized on his uneasiness.

"Now, Scott, you know that I wouldn't do anything to hurt you, would I?" she asked in an almost mocking tone.

"No, of course not," Scott replied sarcastically, beginning to feel that he didn't have much to lose at this point.

"No, I am serious about wanting to help you. I think I do understand some of the problems you are having in this job. I made many of these same mistakes in one of my first managerial jobs. It really is a fairly common problem. I think that together we can do something to get things turned around in the Service Centers. You know, I'm in this, too. I've been getting even more pressure than you to improve those numbers. When you have the Executive Committee on your back, you really have troubles!" Alice replied.

"I'll just bet that you have the Executive Committee on your back" Scott thought to himself, slightly smiling. Alice saw the smile but misinterpreted it to mean that he was pleased to have her support.

"This is what I think we need to do. Let's discuss this over dinner tonight and develop a plan to address this problem head on," Alice suggested.

"Well, I sure would appreciate your help, but I'm afraid that I have plans tonight," Scott timidly replied.

"Cancel them," Alice said. "Now, I have an important meeting right now. What I want you to do is to think about what you think has been the problem since you took over the Service Centers and what needs to be done to improve this situation. We will discuss it tonight. Pick me up at 7 and we will go to Rizzo's. As I remember that was always your favorite restaurant, wasn't it?" Alice didn't wait for his reply but instead turned to her telephone and waved Scott good-bye. As he waved back he saw that certain look in her eye that made him even more apprehensive. Alice in her unique style had just put him on notice that he had better do what she said or else. It was clear to Scott that now Alice was going to take control of the situation and of him. This was clearly not what he wanted to happen when he began his new job 6 months ago, after a similar meeting with Alice. He wondered how everything could get so screwed up in just a few months.

"With all the bosses in the world that I might have, why did I have to end up with her?" he thought to himself, and he tried to focus on something else for the rest of the work day.

Are Alice and Scott having an affair?

Or, is Alice using her position to force Scott to do something he doesn't really want to?

Does Scott really want to?

If something wasn't going on between Scott and Alice, then how would Scott know where Alice lives to pick her up this evening?

What kind of business does Alice really want to talk about tonight?

As Scott pulled in front of Alice's expensive apartment building, the door-man greeted him, "Good evening Mr. Preston. Ms. Holstrom is expecting you. I'll park your car for you, sir." Scott pulled the collar of his overcoat up, hoping that no one else would recognize him going into the building.

"Why hello, Mr. Preston," an older woman said to Scott, as he got into the elevator and pushed the button to Alice's floor, nodding his head in reluctant recognition.

Alice answered the door still trying to put on one of her earrings. "Come on in and fix yourself a drink. I'll be ready in just a minute," she said.

Alice looked fantastic. She had on a little black dress with a pearl necklace and matching earrings. She had on sheer black stockings and spiked black heels. Her hair was pulled into a bun on top of her head. She asked him to fix the catch on her necklace as she turned her back to Scott and held it together with her hands behind her neck. Her perfume filled his nostrils and sent chills up and down. She was wearing his favorite fragrance, and she knew it. His was afraid that before this evening was over that he would be completely helpless and at the mercy of Alice. Alice, on the other hand, was certain of this outcome.

"I'm so glad you could make it tonight, Scott. I think that this will be a very good time for both of us," she said softly as Scott finished connecting the clasp.

"Like I really had any choice in the matter," he mumbled.

"I didn't quite understand what you just said?" replied Alice.

"Oh, I just said that I hope that we will be able to get some of the problems that I am having with the Service Centers straightened out," he recovered.

"Yes, that's what I thought you said," Alice replied, knowingly. It was clear to her the game that Scott was trying to play tonight. "We'll see about that," she thought to herself, as they left her apartment.

Rizzo's was a dimly light but very elegant restaurant. Scott was glad that Alice had picked it as he hoped that he would find cover in the dark surroundings. As they checked their coats, he thought he saw several other managers in the company having dinner with a customer. He asked to be seated in another section of the restaurant giving the waiter 20 dollars to honor his request. Alice seemed to be oblivious of all of this. Of course, unlike Scott, she really didn't have anything to lose.

"OK, now let's talk about the Service Centers and what I need to do to improve this situation," Scott insisted, trying to establish the tone and agenda for the dinner.

"Is that what is really on your mind right now?" Alice asked softly.

Scott swallowed hard before answering, "You know what I have to do, Alice. You are not making things any easier for me!" he replied somewhat emotionally.

"All right, we will do it your way, at least for now. I think that the problem you are having with the Service Centers is that you are actually trying too hard," she replied.

"I don't understand?" said Scott. "How could I be trying too hard?"

"I don't think that you are allowing the Service Center managers to do their jobs. You are trying to do them for them. There is no doubt that you personally know more about running a Service Center than anyone in the company and that you did it better than anyone else. That's why you are in the job you are in now," she replied. "That fact and a few other abilities of yours that we won't mention right now," Alice added with a rather wickedly sexy smile.

"If everyone agrees that I know so much about running the Service Centers, then why don't they listen to me. I get the distinct feeling that they are resisting what I am trying to do more than cooperate most of the time," Scott said, desperately trying to keep the subject of the dinner meeting on business and his problems on the new job.

"Your job is not to do the job for others just because you may know how or even could do it better. Your job is to help develop the other managers to do their jobs to the best of their abilities," Alice replied.

"I'm not sure that I know how to do that," Scott admitted.

"Okay, that's fair. Sometimes I think that we too often expect that just because you have acquired strong skills in one job that you naturally have all the knowledge that you need for the next. Unfortunately, these types of managerial skills are usually learned from experience rather than education, although a combination of both is most effective," Alice explained. "Do you remember when I first was in a job similar to the one you are in today?" she asked.

"Yeah, I guess I do, that was about 6 years ago," answered Scott.

"Yes, that's right. And do you remember what it was like, at least in the early days?" Alice probed.

Scott thought back to those days and began to smile. "If I remember, you didn't get off to such a great start yourself. All of the Service Center Managers were getting pretty frustrated. We really wanted to get old George McLeary back in that job. George really knew how to handle the Service Center Managers. When you showed up with all your new ideas, we all were a bit taken back!"

"Exactly what was it about George that you all liked so much?" Alice questioned.

"Well, let me think. I guess it was that we all felt that George was fair with us. If we did our jobs well, he left us alone and allowed us to do our thing. But if we screwed up, he would let us know that as well. We always knew where we stood with George," Scott replied.

"How do you think the Service Center Managers feel about you compared to George, at those who are still around? Wouldn't that be Stan and Pat?" Alice asked.

"Yes, that's right we all started with the company at about the same time. I don't know, I never really thought about it like that. I guess they feel about me much the same as we did about you back in those days," Scott answered still thinking about the question.

"If Stan feels that way about you, we have another problem that we didn't even know!" Alice teased.

Scott, clearly embarrassed, valiantly tried again to focus the conversation on his problems in his job. "You make an excellent comparison," he said.

Alice let out her naughty laugh that he had heard so many times before and instantly knew what she was thinking.

"No, not that comparison. What I meant was the point you made about how the managers felt about you when you first took this job and how they probably feel about me," he clarified.

"I knew what you meant. Let me share with you what I learned at that time and some advice I received that really helped me," Alice continued. "The first thing I did was to meet with each of the managers and ask you what I was doing wrong in the job. But before I did that, I made sure that I had the understanding and support of my boss at the time to make some pretty significant changes. Do you remember?"

"Yeah, now that you mention it, I do," Scott replied.

"My boss and I discussed in great detail the changes I wanted to make. George had done a good job, but his management style was not going to allow us to achieve our goals in the future," she explained.

"What do you mean, I thought George did a great job?" Scott asked.

"He did. There is no question about it. But what kind of management style did he use? You just alluded to it a minute ago." Alice replied.

"Well, I guess he was a control kind of manager. He wanted to know everything that was going on and be involved in just about every decision. He was very detailed oriented. But I don't understand why that is bad? It seemed to work very well for him?" Scott said in confusion.

"I am not saying that style is necessarily wrong. It did work for George for many years. The problem was that the business was changing and George's style of managing didn't necessarily meet the new requirements of the job. Think about the major changes that occurred that directly affected the Service Centers about that time," Alice explained.

"Well, I guess it was about that time that we suddenly had several new competitors on the scene that we never had before. We had to get better at what we did or lose even more of our customers to these other companies. In fact, as I remember it, there was some real concern that we could even survive as an organization. There were rumors that we could go out of business or even be bought out by one of these new "upstart" companies," Scott recalled.

"Yes, that was the time that we finally realized that we couldn't keep doing business the same way that we always did. As you are well aware, our service is the backbone of our business. We needed to make quantum leaps in our ability to provide this customer service to our customers. George's style worked well before we had these new challenges, but now that we needed to change it was difficult for everyone, particularly George," Alice explained.

"What specifically did George do that was the problem? He certainly had all the knowledge that anyone could have about the part of the business that he was responsible for. Like I said, he really knew what to do and he did it!" Scott said.

"That was the problem, just as you stated it — he knew what to do and he did it," Alice countered back. "George never really gave anyone else a chance to learn to accept responsibility. He always was there doing it. What was happening was that no one else at the Service Centers was learning about the business. They were all just following George's orders and doing what they were told. Think about your own situation. You really didn't begin to grow and develop as a Service Center Manager until after George left. There are others that were in the same boat as you. You know who they are; we both do. George's style of management may have served us well in the short term but did it help us in the long term?" Alice further inquired.

"I never really though of it in that way, but you are right. I didn't really feel challenged when I worked for George. Unless he was giving me hell for something that he thought that I did wrong, which happened pretty frequently!" Scott remembered, smiling.

"And how would you compare how you are approaching this to George's style?" Alice asked.

"Again, I never really thought about it, but it is obvious to me now that I am really trying to run the Service Centers the way that George did. The only difference is that George was successful and I'm not!" Scott lamented.

"Don't be so hard on yourself. Believe me, even old George had his problems and critics as well and often for good reason. But even more than all of those factors, as I said, the demands of the business are much different than when George was in charge. We need to manage our business and people differently," Alice explained.

"I'm still not sure I understand what I need to do?" Scott replied.

"You have good people working for you at your Service Centers. Let them do their jobs," Alice simply replied.

"I guess you mean I need to back off and be less controlling, don't you?" he asked.

"That would be a good start!" Alice replied as she removed her high-heeled shoe and began rubbing her stocking foot inside the bottom of Scott's leg underneath the table.

As Scott tried to ignore this under-the-table activity, he continued, "Do you mean that I should show up less often as well?"

"Definitely," Alice firmly replied, "I think that your role is to ensure that the Service Centers have the resources, direction, and support they need to operate. You need to evaluate how ready each of the Centers is to accept the freedom to operate that I am suggesting. If they need more training or whatever may be an obstacle to achieving this level of independence, then I see it as your role to ensure that it is provided. I am not saying that you are no longer an important part of the operation of the Service Centers, but your role needs to be more of a resource and support person than that of a decision maker of their day-to-day activities. They are they ones who are there all the time and know their customers best. It just makes sense that they should be the ones to make the decisions about how to best serve them."

"I'm not sure I understand what I am supposed to do if I leave all the operational decisions up to the Service Centers?" Scott candidly admitted.

"That's where your real contributions can be made. Like I said, we have experienced and talented people at our Service Centers. They for the most part are able to make the decisions necessary to run a successful center. What I would like to see you focus your time on is more strategic issues that can help us grow and develop the business, not so much on the operational issues. I know this is a big change from what you are used to. You have spent your whole career learning about our operations. It is what you are good at doing. This is the ability that got you your present job. But now you have got to use that knowledge to provide guidance and support for the Service Centers that you are in charge of running, but not allow it to consume your entire time. Of course, there may be times when you do need to become more involved in what is going on at the centers, depending on the problems or even crises that they may be dealing with at the time. But these will be the exceptions rather than the rule. What I want you to be focused on are those things that will help us achieve our business goals in the future. You need to spend your time working on what I call the *drivers* of the business. In other words, you need to look more towards how we can run our Service Centers better tomorrow than what we need to do today to operate," Alice further explained, becoming more aggressive in her "footsie" game.

By this time Scott was fighting unsuccessfully to maintain his composure. Between the seduction game that Alice was playing under the table and the direction that she was suggesting that he needed to take in his new position, it was more than he could handle.

"Would you *please* stop playing with my leg for a moment so I can understand what it is that you are trying to tell me!" he exclaimed. "This is all too much for me. How am I supposed to lead the Service Centers to tomorrow, as you refer to it, if I don't know what is going on today in the business?"

"Scott, I'm not saying that you ignore the daily activities of the centers, just that you entrust this part of the business to the managers. You need to have trust and confidence in their abilities, or need to do something about it if you don't. That is what managing is all about. I need you to be looking at the longer term aspects of the business, the things that can really give us a competitive advantage in the future. If all you focus on is on today-type issues, we may never get any better than we are today," Alice said removing her toes from the front on his shin.

"I'm not sure that I know where to begin to manage in this way. You are right, I'm much more comfortable being involved in the day-to-day aspects of the Service Centers. After all, that is what I know best. I need to learn more about the overall business itself. I think I need to spend more time at our Headquarters talking to our the General Managers of the businesses that the Service Centers serve. They could give me a better idea of their overall vision and strategies for the business and how it will affect the Service Centers. I also need to spend more time with our Salespeople to better understand the needs of our customers. If I understood the trends and anticipated needs of our customers maybe the Service Centers would be able to begin to find ways today to meet their needs tomorrow. Is this the kind of things that you think that I should be doing?" he asked.

"Yes, that is exactly what I had in mind. Why don't you develop a plan to help you address the things that you would like to do to meet this objective and let's review it together. It doesn't have to be formal or complicated, just so it lets us both know what direction you would like to go in this job and how I can support you. How does that sound?" she asked.

"That sounds like a great idea. I want to make sure that I am going in the right direction, particularly at first. I would appreciate any ideas or suggestions that you might have that should be included on the list. I'll start working on the plan right away and should have it for you in about a week."

"Well, now that we have that settled, there is something else that I want to discuss with you," Alice said. "I have some news to tell you."

"Well, what is it?"

"Maybe you had better have another drink first."

"No, I don't want another drink. Just tell me whatever it is!" Scott said, becoming a little anxious as well as irritated. "Just tell me what it is!"

"OK, here it is. I'm pregnant."

"Who's baby is it?"

"You mean, babies."

"I don't understand?"

"I'm pregnant with twins."

"OK, who's twins are they?"

"I think you already know the answer to that question."

"Well, I got news for you as well. I'm in love with someone else"

"Who is it?"

"I think you already know the answer to that question."

Is Scott the father of Alice's unborn twins?

Who is Scott in love with? Could it be Pat? How about Stan?

Will Alice keep the babies? Will she keep Scott in his present job? Should she?

How will the business be affected by all these problems? Will anybody be able to get any work done?

Does anybody really care?

And so … *"the organization turns."*

Murder Mysteries/Cops and Robbers

We never seem to get our fill of variations of the "cops and robbers" television show. Even from the early days of television, we have been fascinated with watching in the safety and comfort of our living rooms, the most hideous of crimes being committed and ultimately solved by clever detectives at work. Perhaps these shows provide a stark contrast with our relatively mostly boring jobs to the excitement of tracking down murders and high-speed chase scenes. Perhaps we project ourselves in these situations trying to solve the mysteries of our jobs. But what if your job really was more like a murder mystery? What if trying to become a Remote Control Manager was like trying to solve a murder mystery? Your work life might be more like this:

"A Murder Mystery"

"Seventh Street and Elm, yeah I got it. We'll be right there. Don't touch a thing until we have our accounting boys look over the numbers. 10–4; that means good-bye," you say into the telephone after you get the urgent call about a problem with one of your major accounts. It looks like the entire deal may have been killed by one stupid act of someone who was obviously very desperate to get ahead in the organization. "You just can't trust anyone anymore," you mumble to yourself as you reach for your double-breasted trench coat and fasten the belt in front. "We better get some coffee, Joe, it looks like its going to be another long night," you say to your partner.

"Right," Joe says, "I'll call my wife and tell her not to hold dinner."

The two of you race to the scene as fast as the company car can go. You have called in on your cellular phone to the best experts in the company to meet you there. You have also faxed the facts as you know them to the company's research lab on your laptop personal computer, paged two other associates traveling in other cities, E-mailed your boss, downloaded information from the company Intranet that you think might be pertinent to the case, surfed the internet for other related information, and set up a teleconference to review all the available facts in this case with the West Coast office for later in the day. You are nearly exhausted before you even get there!

When you and your partner arrive on the scene, it looks pretty grim. Everyone is walking around almost in shock. It appears that the company is about to lose one of its largest and most important customers. As you take notes on your initial observations, you notice several very curious things. The upper managers are all scurrying around, running to answer telephones, chasing after faxes, huddling in small groups trying to share and compare bits of information about the situation as it slowly trickled in. Surprisingly, everyone else looked relatively calm. It was as if you drew two triangles inverted from one another and labeled one as the hierarchy of the organization from top to bottom and the other as the stress level of the people from the highest to lowest positions. The higher the position, the greater the stress level. This was somewhat understandable. Of course, the top management positions carried with them the ultimate responsibility for the success of the organization. Regardless of how empowered any organization may consider itself, this ultimate accountability can not be delegated or subordinated. After all, that is the job of top management, to successfully run the business. That can and never should change. To do otherwise would be an abdication of management's responsibilities. Instead, what often needs to change is the way these responsibilities are fulfilled. This is where management style and philosophies come into play. Organizations need to make conscious decisions about where they want to be on the management continuum. A Traditional style of management may indeed be the most effective and appropriate style for an organization given the current business and prevailing culture. However, it is beginning to become painfully clear that this "command and control" style of management has not proven to be effective in this circumstance. In fact, it has become destructive and counterproductive.

"What do you think, Joe?" you ask.

"I'm not paid to think, I'm not a member of upper management!" Joe replies, possibly joking.

"Very funny, Joe. You *are* joking, aren't you?"

"Yeah, of course I am," Joe replies, as still stonefaced as usual. "Yeah, right. And the problem is that they aren't. Joking that is."

"Who's that, Joe?"

"Just about everybody who works here."

"And the biggest problem is that upper management doesn't even have a clue that this is the problem," you observe.

"Looks pretty grim, doesn't it?"

"Yea, it sure does."

"What should we do?" asks Joe.

"Get the facts, just the facts," you reply.

The two of you spend the rest of the day doing just that — getting the facts. You begin your fact finding by interviewing as many employees at the scene as possible.

"No one ever asks us what we think," said Sally Winston, a long-time employee in the customer service department. "I've just learned to do what I'm told and mind my own business."

"But what if you see something being done that you know is wrong?" Joe asked.

"I still keep my mouth shut. The last thing the boss wants to hear is that she is wrong — even when she is. The best advice anyone ever gave me was 'you have two ears but only one mouth.' Somebody must be trying to tell you something!"

"Hmmmmm. sounds pretty bad," said Joe. Joe was very fond of saying things like that.

"What should we do now?" he asks and then answers his own question. "I think we need to get some more facts."

"Right," you reply.

"More interviews?" Joe asks.

"Yep, more interviews," you answer.

As the two of you spend the rest of the day talking to people about their jobs and the roles they play in the decision making process in the organization, you are the same story over and over again.

"Seems like a pattern is emerging here," Joe finally observes, after the twelfth person you interview.

"You think so?" you ask in jest.

"Yeah, I definitely think we are on to something," Joe astutely observes. "What do you think we should do now?"

"There's only one person left to talk to," you say.

"Who's that?"

"The boss."

You arrange for a meeting with Christine Murphy, the manager of the operation for 4 o'clock. She reluctantly agreed to the meeting because of her hectic schedule. It is only after you drop the name of her boss in Headquarters and his interest in this situation that she agrees to give you any time at all.

"Is this going to take very long?" she asks, before you and Joe even get a chance to sit down in her office.

"We won't take up any more of your time than is necessary to get to the bottom of this problem. We appreciate how busy you are," you try to assure her, but it is clear from the expression on her face that she is not satisfied with your answer. Christine was used to having people answer her questions directly and if they didn't, she certainly would do something about it. However, she felt that she had a little less leverage at the moment with the mention of her boss as the sponsor of this investigation. She was smart enough to know that whatever she said or did would be reported to her boss and his boss's boss. She was already in enough trouble with them without making matters worse. So she decided to cooperate or at least give her version of cooperation, which wasn't going to be very much!

Her desk was cluttered with papers, reports, books, files, and unopened mail, as well as a pile of "While You Were Out" pink telephone messages that she was obviously ignoring as well. You wondered what important messages might be in that pile. Somehow she ignores the frequent ringing of her telephone as if she had become somewhat practiced in this skill. You wonder where her secretary is, and them remember that you interviewed her earlier that day. It seems that the secretary, probably more as a survival skill than anything else, has learned to make herself as scarce as possible during Christine's bad days at the office. This was definitely one of those.

Christine appeared to be in her late thirties or maybe early forties. She was very attractive, and had chestnut brown hair worn to her shoulders, a pretty face, and beautiful eyes. She was tall and lean, and one would suspect that she was still very athletic from the tone and muscles in her long slim legs. She was dressed in a black blazer with a gray pleated skirt with a white silk blouse. On the lapel of her blazer was a pin with the company's logo which was bestowed upon a special few in the organization as recognition usually for outstanding performance or a significant accomplishment. Her neat and tailored appearance were in stark contrast to the disorganized surroundings in which she was working, as well as to the polyester suits that you and Joe are wearing.

It was very difficult for Christine to be in a situation in which she was not succeeding and in which people were beginning to question her abilities and methods. Her whole career up to this point had been a pattern of successes. She had progressed through a number of lower-level managerial positions at what some thought to be break neck speed. She had a way of taking control of a situation as well as the people involved. She had learned when to use her considerable charms, but also wasn't afraid to work hard to get the job done. She was very bright and had a good business sense and instincts. She realized that to get ahead in a business predominately run by men that she would have to prove herself to be worthy of notice. And notice her everyone did! She was always known to be someone you had better get out of the way of when she decided she wanted to get something done. However, this aggressiveness and drive to succeed appeared to be becoming a double-edged sword that she was in the process of falling upon. In her previous roles in the company, these traits and abilities served her very well. Her fierce drive to succeed propelled her ahead, as everyone dived to get out of her way. Unfortunately, the more difficult the current situation became and more the pressure mounted, the more Christine tried to control everything and everyone.

> "I really do only have a few minutes to talk to you," she reiterated. "As you know, we are experiencing a major problem with one of our biggest customers. I need to get back to trying to salvage this situation. But tell me again who you guys are and what it is that you want? I've been told by my boss to give you whatever you wanted. Now don't get me wrong. I want to cooperate but, like I said, we're in the middle of a crisis right now and ..."

> "We understand," you say, interrupting her about to tell you again how busy she is. "We'll try to take up only a few moments of your time. We do appreciate the seriousness of the situation."

"What do you want to know?"

"Just the facts, Ma'am," says Joe.

"You need to understand what I am dealing with here," Christine offered. "I've got to watch what everybody does every minute. If I don't, they get everything all screwed up. The whole reason we are in this mess right now is because I was away too much on other business and didn't pay enough attention to what they were doing. Its just like the old saying, you know what I'm saying don't you?"

"No I'm not sure that I do," you reply.

"When the cat is away the mice will play!" she answered. "And if you want something done right you have to do it yourself. You just can't seem to rely on anybody anymore," she further elaborated, glancing slightly in Joe's direction and then back to you. "I'm sure you get my drift."

"Yeah," you reply.

"Well, gentlemen, I would love to spend more time talking to you," she dryly replied, "but I'm afraid I need to attend to more pressing matters. With that she stood up and opened the office door inviting the two of you to leave.

"Now what?," asked Joe.

"Let's talk to some others and get their side of the story."

"Sounds good. We can get some more facts."

You arranged for several other interviews. the next person you talk to is Sam Gregory, who was Christine's Assistant Manager. He was a young man who was considered to have a promising future with the company. That is, unless this problem should somehow derail his progression.

"Thanks for taking time to talk to us today. We know how busy you must be today."

"Why's that?" Sam asked.

"Because of the big problem with the major customer we just lost," you explain, feeling kind of stupid by stating the obvious and remembering how abruptly the previous meeting ended.

"Oh that. Well I'm not really all that involved in that problem, to be perfectly honest with you. I guess there really isn't anything left to talk about or do at this point, is there?" he asked, rather perplexed.

"Weren't you deeply involved in dealing with the customer before this problem occurred?" you ask.

"No, none of us were, except Christine of course. She handles all of that type of thing," he added.

"What type of thing is that?" you ask, appreciating Joe's momentary silence.

"You know, calling on the customer, following up on service provided, complaints, troubleshooting, things like that."

"Christine did all those things herself?"

"Yes"

"Everything?"

"Just about."

"Then what did you and the rest of the people in this office do?"

"Exactly what Christine told us to!" he replied.

"Didn't you ever have contact with the customer?"

"Almost never."

"When did you have any contact?"

"Only when Christine gave us very specific instructions. As long as we said or did exactly what she told us to do there wasn't any problem. But if we didn't — watch out!"

"How do you think this approach worked," Joe asked, speaking up for the first time during the interview.

"We lost the account. What does that tell you?" Sam replied.

"Yeah, right," said Joe.

There was really only one other player in this scenario that you wanted to talk to — the customer. "Shouldn't we ask Christine before we contact the customer?" Joe asked.

"It isn't her customer anymore, remember?"

"Yeah, right," said Joe.

You and Joe make the 4-hour drive to the customer's main office. Being cooped up in a car with Joe for half a day make the trip seem to go much slower. When you finally do arrive, you are able to arrange a meeting with their Purchasing Manager, Ed Brown.

"Thank you for meeting with us, Mr. Brown. We won't take up too much of your time."

"No problem. What can I do for you?"

"We would like to get a better idea of why you chose to stop doing business with our company."

"Well that decision has already been made. I'm afraid that there is no going back on it now. We've already made commitments to other suppliers," warned Mr. Brown.

"That's not why we are here today. We just want to try to have a better understanding of what we may have done wrong to cause your company to take their business elsewhere and how we can prevent that from happening again in the future," you explain.

"Well OK — I guess then, that is a fair question. There may have been a number of reasons, but I believe the primary one was the service that you provided to us."

"What was wrong with it?" Joe interjected.

"Well it wasn't that there was anything wrong with it when it was provided."

"How's that?"

"The key contact that we had with your company, Christine Murphy was her name. She wasn't always very responsive to our needs. We are in a business that changes quickly, so we need suppliers that are willing to partner with us to meet the challenges we face. It just seemed to us that you have your Ms. Murphy spread a little too thin. She seemed to be carrying the burden of servicing our company all by herself. Why didn't you get her some help instead of making her do everything herself? We really thought that we were an important enough customer for you to invest some more of your resources in ensuring that we were kept happy. She was certainly competent enough and really understood our business. But we just couldn't get enough of her attention or time or whatever."

"I guess that solves this one," Joe said as your were leaving to return home. "It's just a shame. It just didn't need to turn out this way."

"How's that?" you ask.

"If only Christine Murphy had managed her time a little better maybe we wouldn't have lost their business."

You just shake your head wondering if you should try to explain to your partner the concepts of empowerment, delegation and remote control management, but wisely decide it probably wouldn't be worth the effort.

Postscript: The story you have just read is true; the names have been changed to protect the innocent. The following is a result of the investigation:

Christine Murphy was found by the corporation to be guilty of trying to do everything herself and not fully utilizing their potential to the valuable resources assigned to her. She has been reassigned to a lower-level administrative position for a period not less than 1 year.

Sam Greg was promoted to Christine's old job, and has delegated many responsibilities to his staff. The company was eventually able to get the customer's business back, with the provision that Joe is never assigned to their account.

Late Night Talk Shows

Always a favorite of insomniacs, Late Night Talk Shows provide something to watch while you think about how tired you're going to be tomorrow at work. Because supposedly younger viewers are in bed at the time they are broadcast, these shows can deal with subjects and jokes not appropriate for prime time. Imagine that one night you can't sleep and surfing the channels trying to find something decent to watch. After you switch from one infomercial to another, you are about to settle on watching Cher talk about how to avoid the aging process, when you come across something that really catches your interest.

"Late Night Talk Show"

You see the comedian host of a Late Night Talk Show being introduced to the live studio audience. You hear the band strike up the theme song and watch the host come bouncing out from behind the curtain to the roaring applause of those in the studio audience. After the greeting finally quiets down, the host makes several jokes about the latest scandal in the news that day and then introduces his guests. "We have a great show for you tonight, folks," he explains. "We have a beautiful young actress who starred in her first major picture ...." He goes on to mention two other actors who will also be appearing in tonight's program. Finally, he adds, "and we have something really unique tonight that we think you will enjoy, a Remote Control Manager who will talk about his experiences at work. Now doesn't that sound really exciting! I just can't wait to find out what the heck a Remote Control Manager does all day at work. Do you think he just sits around watching television surfing the dial with a Remote Control? Hey, that would be OK with me as long as he watches our show! "he adds, with as much enthusiasm as he can muster up, trying to get the TV audience interested in his last guest. "We'll be right back after a word from our sponsor with all of this and more. Now, don't change that the channel while we are gone with that remote control!"

The show goes on in its typical format. Each guest comes out and chats with the host about his or her latest project, trying to top one another with the funniest or most unusual stories from their lives and experiences. The host helps each one by adding punch lines or commentary to help the guest be entertaining. As the show begins to wind down, the director gives the host a signal that there is indeed going to be enough time remaining in the show to interview the last guest. The host isn't sure if this is good news or not. Up to now, it had been a pretty funny show. Bringing out someone called a Remote Control Manager could bring the momentum of the show to a virtual standstill and cause the viewers at home to click to another channel. The sponsor doesn't appreciate that very much when it happens. But the decision is out of his hands and after another commercial he begins the brief introduction.

> "As you know, from time to time our staff likes to find usual and different kinds guests for our show, and I think that they have been working overtime to find this next person. Either that or they have been having too many martinis at lunch again, I don't know! Anyway, our next guest is something that is called a *Remote Control Manager:* To tell you the truth, I'm not quite sure what a Remote Control Manager does so why don't we just bring him out and learn more about this unusual job and why he is on our show tonight!"

The audience gives the last guest some polite applause as he walks out on stage and shakes hands with the host and the other guests who are still sitting on the couch after their interviews. Of course, only the most famous and successful are allowed to leave after their turn in the interview chair has been completed. The host is glad that at least two of them are still there to offer at least some comic relief that will surely be needed with this last guest. He regains a little more faith in his staff for at least arranging to have them remain on the set to prevent a complete disaster from occurring. "Why would anyone be interested in listening to someone called a Remote Control Manager," he thought, as his last guest walks was about to sit in the big chair to the right of his interview desk.

> *Host:* Its a pleasure to have you with us tonight. I am told you are what's called a Remote Control Manager. Your certainly have a very interesting sounding job. What is it that you do anyway — settle disputes that people have over who gets control of the TV remote control in their homes? I would think that job could get to be pretty dangerous at times!

There is laughter from the studio audience as they also struggle to understand what the heck a Remote Control Manager's responsibilities could possible include. The host picks up on their response to his joke and continues with another one.

> *Host:* I would think that there would be a great demand for your services. There certainly would be in my home. I hope you make people click on to our show at night! In fact, maybe that would be a way to get my wife to watch the show!

Remote Control Manager: No, I'm afraid that's not quite what a Remote Control Manager does. Although at times it seems that I might be more successful if that was my main responsibility in life! Actually, being a Remote Control Manager involves utilizing a different kind of management style and philosophy than may have traditionally been the case in the past.

Host: What does a Remote Control Manager do?

Remote Control Manager: Being a Remote Control Managers involves many things, and each person might approach the job differently. Basically, the concept involves empowering others that work for you to accept greater levels of responsibility and decision making as part of their jobs.

Host: You used the term "empowerment." Does that mean as you indicated, that you give others greater levels of responsibility and authority? Maybe I should let the band do more around here. That is, if I can ever get them to stay awake throughout an entire show! Hey, how 'bout you guys taking my suits to the dry cleaners on your way home from work tonight?

The band strikes up the theme song from the old "Three Stooges" movies that sounds like mock laughter.

Host: Are you sure this stuff really works? As you can see, I'm obviously not getting much respect around here!

Remote Control Manager: Maybe you should empower them to tell some of the jokes. Maybe then they would get some laughs!

The audience laughs loudly at the Remote Control Manager's joke and then begin all saying "oooohhhhhh," when they see the expression of mock anger on the host's face.

Host: Listen, buddy. I tell all the jokes around here. You got that!

Bandleader: Yeah, funny or not!

The audience again laughs loudly, not having expected so much humor from this last interview, clearly enjoying the "roasting" that the host is experiencing.

Host: Maybe I need to empower the cameraman to lead the band. Maybe then we would be able to keep in tune for once!

"Ooooohhhhhhhhh," the audience collectively responds.

Remote Control Manager: Well, I need to say that wouldn't be what a Remote Control Manager would do.

Host: What do you mean? Wouldn't that be giving people more responsibility and decision making ability? I thought that was what it was all about?

Remote Control Manager: In part it is. But, the point that is important to keep in mind is that a Remote Control Manager must act responsibly concerning what he or she empowers others to do. It wouldn't be fair to empower someone to perform a job or task that they haven't been given any training or opportunity to learn how to do. That is what we call "reckless empowerment."

Host: I guess judging by the way we do things on the show, we have a whole lot of reckless empowerment going on around here!

Remote Control Manager: The question you should ask yourself is "Does the Cameraman have the training or skills necessary to lead the band," before you empower him to perform that job.

Host: I would say that his skills would be about up to par with what we are used to in that position!

Bandleader: Hey, watch it or you might just have the Cameraman leading the band before this show is over!

Host: Well tell me then, how do you decide who should be empowered?

Remote Control Manager: First of all, you need to empower people to do things for which they have expertise and experience. Again, your Cameraman would probably not have any expertise in leading the band. Thus, it wouldn't be appropriate or even fair to expect him to be able to perform this job with any level of competence.

Host: OK, then let's assume that is true. Then what would be appropriate for the Cameraman to be empowered to do that he is not doing now?

Remote Control Manager: Well, what kind of things would you like a Cameraman to be able to do that could make him more effective on his job?

Host: It would be helpful if he would come to work sober for once!

The audience laughs as the camera shows the Cameraman pretending to be drunk behind his camera.

Remote Control Manager: OK, let's assume that he is sober when he comes to work. What would you like him to take responsibility to do that he doesn't do now?

Host: Well, I guess, now that I think about it, he could do some of the things that our director does.

Remote Control Manager: What might that include?

Host: I guess make more decisions concerning what the camera shots should be or from what angle, things like that.

Remote Control Manager: What do you think might be the benefits of the Cameraman being empowered to do these types of things?

Host: Well, I guess it would allow the Director to do other things, like making sure that I have guests to talk to!

Remote Control Manager: I guess that would be important to you!

Host: If you don't mind, could I ask you a few questions now? I think that is the way this is supposed to work.

Remote Control Manager: Sure, fire away.

Host: How do you manage by Remote Control and what does that really mean?

Remote Control Manager: What is means is that you empower the people who work for you to do their jobs.

Host: What do you mean, empower them to do their jobs; isn't that what they are getting paid to do?

Remote Control Manager: Yes, of course. But often we don't let people really perform the jobs we give to them. Instead, we micromanage them and try to make all the important decisions for them. Often, the best thing we can do is to get out of the way. Being a Remote Control Manager involves trusting others to make the right decisions. Of course, as we discussed earlier, we need to give them the training and opportunity to make these decisions.

Host: What do you do then in your job if you are delegating all of your responsibilities to others?

Remote Control Manager: Empowering others to truly do their jobs gives the Remote Control Manager the opportunity to move away from the day-to-day functions of the operations and focus on more strategic issues instead. Ultimately this makes everyone more productive and satisfied with their jobs.

Host: So you don't feel that you are working yourself out of a job by empowering the people who work for you to do the jobs that you traditionally have done?

Remote Control Manager: That's really just the point. I've got plenty of things that I could and should be doing that can help move our organization forward towards our ultimate business goals. Empowering others gives me the opportunity to do these things.

Host: One thing I've been meaning to ask you, why are you called a Remote Control Manager?

Remote Control Manager: Because that term really does describe how we manage others — remotely. Being responsible for managing part of an organization doesn't necessarily mean that you have to physically be there, at least not all the time. The concept of empowerment makes this style of management possible, even desirable. Those who work in the jobs closest to where problems exist are in the best positions to make decisions concerning how things should be done. They can make better decisions and have a greater sense of ownership for the results.

His comments were interrupted by the band beginning to play the show's theme, indicating that it was time for another station break before the show ended.

Host: Well, I would like to thank you for being on our show tonight and telling us what a Remote Control Manager does. I'm very glad to hear that it isn't someone who spends their career clicking our show off of people's television sets in their homes! I do think that the concepts that you described to us do make a great deal of sense and I'm sure they will become more and more commonplace in the workplace in the future. Good night everyone and thanks for watching.

The show ends with the band playing the theme song once again as the credits scroll across the TV screens of the million of viewers watching at home in their beds.

Situation Comedy

You may be thinking that your workplace already resembles a situation comedy a little more than you would care to admit. However, what if your work was *really* a situational comedy and you were the star of the show? The cast of characters is described below. You might find them to be curiously and frighteningly similar to the people you work with every day. Of course, similarities which might exist are purely coincidental as these characters are fictitious and not based on anyone either living or dead.

"An Un-Named Sitcom"

Gordon plays the leading role in the show and is the only relatively sane person in the cast. He is the manager of a small company that provides a undescribed service to obviously very patient customers for putting up with all of these antics. All of the other characters report to him either directly or indirectly. Gordon is desperately trying to become a Remote Control Manager and get others involved in resolving at least some of the chaos that surrounds him at work. Unfortunately, none of these efforts have proven even the least bit effective, and he just can never seem to get things turned around. There always seems to be one disaster after another to deal with and he never seems to have the time to work on developing the type of organization that could really be productive and meet all of its goals.

Carol has the supporting role in the show. Carol is Gordon's assistant, who attempts to keep everyone else in order. The problem is that Carol is not in control of herself, which makes it much harder to be a role model to the others. However, she works hard and has good intentions, which is more than can be said for most of the other characters. She is also very sexy and dresses quite provocatively.

Karl is definitely the most neurotic of the group. He has a severe inferiority complex which manifests itself in almost everything he does. You have to wonder how he ever successfully interviewed for this job, or any job, for that manner. He is the Chief Accountant for the organization and could be very good at his job if only he didn't keep checking and rechecking the numbers all the time to make sure he added things correctly. Karl can talk himself out of success in almost everything he does. It seems that if given a 50/50 chance of making the right decision on something, Karl would be wrong 50 times out of 50. That is, if he counted correctly. Karl is also a hypochondriac and deathly afraid of germs of any kind.

Cooper or "Coop," as he prefers to be called, is the overconfident one of the group. Coop thinks he is irresistible to the opposite sex, which he isn't. He believes that he could manage the business better than Gordon, which he could not. And he thinks that he is headed for a big promotion in the company someday, which he isn't. As you might imagine, there will be a great deal of sexual tension between Coop and Carol.

The opening scene is in Gordon's office, where, incidentally, most the show's action occurs for some reason. As usual, Gordon is in the middle of another crisis in the workplace due to poor planning and foresight. Carol has just come charging into his office in her usual state of panic, and once again, it is Gordon's job to try to calm her down enough to understand what the problem is today.

> *Gordon:* What's the matter, Carol? You seem even more upset than usual.

> *Carol:* We've got a terrible problem. The work in the office is piling higher and higher and if we don't do something, we will never get to the bottom of it. You have to do something about Karl, he's out of control again.

> *Gordon:* Now just calm down and tell me what he is doing that you think is so out of control.

> *Carol:* He's at it again.

> *Gordon:* At what again?

> *Carol:* He thinks that he is going to catch the virus on our computer network again.

Gordon: I don't understand — didn't we install that computer antivirus program on the system last week? That should prevent any of his computer files from being affected.

Carol: Yes, we did. But that's not the problem. He's so crazy that he thinks that *he* is going to catch the virus!

Gordon: You mean to tell me that he thinks that the virus will affect his body somehow?

Carol: I'm afraid so.

Gordon: What does he think is going to happen to him?

Carol: Well I'm not completely sure, but from what I have been able to discern from his rather incoherent rambling, he thinks that the virus will begin affecting his memory and alter the way he thinks.

Gordon: This sounds weird even for Karl. I wish I could catch the virus and have my memories of him erased.

As the laugh track begins to fade, Coop comes swaggering into the office and joins the conversation.

Coop: Hello, Carol. You look particularly beautiful this morning, my dear.

Carol: Give up, would you already? I happen to be at least one female in this office who can resist your charms, Coop. Besides don't you know that you could get in trouble for violating the company's sexual harassment policies by saying things like that?

Coop: I just love it when you talk sexy to me like that!

Gordon: All right, both of you, knock it off! Coop, what do you know about Karl's latest problem?

Coop: I don't know, doesn't he think that he is going to get some sexually transmitted disease from looking up dirty web sites on the internet during company time or something?

Gordon: Today is turning out even worse than I thought it was going to be when I got up this morning! OK, we've got to do something to get this office straightened out or we are all going to be in trouble. Carol, ask Karl to come in here so we can have a meeting to begin to try to get going in the right direction.

Carol: OK, but you asked for it. You know how he is going to react to being called into your office without notice.

Carol picks up the phone and dials Karl's extension.

Carol: Karl, the boss wants you to come into his office right away. No, I don't know why he wants you in here. No, I wouldn't tell you even if I knew. No, I don't know if you are getting fired. No, I don't know if we have a severance package for people being fired. No, I don't know if your health benefits continue after you have been fired. Listen, Karl, you had better get in here right away before we both get fired!

After several minutes had passed, Karl finally comes into Gordon's office. He is obviously in a state of total anxiety.

Karl: I'm sorry it took me so long to get in here. I had to wash up a bit. I seem to have picked up some new germs in this office this morning.

Gordon: Please sit down Karl. I would like to talk to all of you about something very important.

Karl: You're not going to fire all of us, are you Gordon? Please say that you won't. I don't know where I will ever be able to get this kind of health insurance anyplace else. They will want to put me in one of those horrible HMOs that tell you what doctors you have to go to and what kind of treatment you can get. *Please*, tell me this isn't going to happen to me! *Please!*

Gordon: Calm down, Karl. That's not what I asked you to come in here to talk about. Although after that performance, maybe it wouldn't be such a bad idea! But seriously, what I am most concerned about is the way we seem to work together around here. The problem is that we don't!

Coop: What do you mean, that we don't? Do you mean we don't work or that we don't work together?

Gordon: We don't work together as a team. I don't deny that everyone is trying hard to get their jobs done. In fact, everyone works very hard. I see you working overtime and through your breaks, almost every day. I'm not suggesting that we need to work harder, just smarter.

Karl: You mean that I'm not getting fired?

Gordon: No, Karl.

Carol: Not today, anyway!

Gordon: That's the kind of thing I want us to stop doing around here. We all need to support one another and work together as a team — not just pick on one another.

Coop: I like that team idea. Do you think that we could have some cheerleaders? I have a suggestion for Captain of the squad.

Carol: I'm sure you do.

Gordon: Could we get back to the topic I want to talk about? Thanks. Now, what I think we need to do is to develop some specific goals that we want to achieve as a team and then develop a plan to achieve them. The first thing I think we need to address is how we get the work done.

Carol: Well, I guess what happens is that you give me the orders and tell me how to distribute them to the others each day.

Gordon: How is this working out?

Coop: Not very well. Because we never know what orders we are going to get, there is never any way that we can prepare for them. You know, to get ourselves organized before the day begins or to get a head start in any way.

Gordon: I'm not sure that I understand?

Coop: For instance, the other day you assigned work to Karl that I was better prepared to handle, and you gave me work that he could have more easily completed. It took both of us longer to complete the work than if we had simply switched assignments that day. I had already done a lot of work on the project that Karl was doing and was up to speed on all the details. Because it was new to Karl, he had to spend most of the day learning what I already knew. I tried to help him, but I had my own similar problems with the assignment that you gave me.

Gordon: I don't understand why you two didn't simply switch your assignments that day? It seems ridiculous that the two of you wouldn't do such a thing once you realized how much more efficient you both could have been by doing so.

Karl: Well, we didn't know that we could. We just figured that you had a reason for assigning the work that way and didn't want to question your authority.

Coop: Yeah, and besides that, the assignment you gave me required me to work closely with that new beautiful intern we just hired!

Carol: I knew your libido was going to part of your rationale somewhere in this story!

Coop: No, seriously, I felt the same way as Karl, which in itself is a little bit scary. I just thought that you had some reason that we didn't know about concerning the way you assigned the work. Didn't you?

Gordon: To be perfectly honest, no. I didn't realize that the two of you had any prior experience in those assignments or I would have switched them. I still can't believe that neither of you said anything to me, or better yet, just taken it upon yourselves to trade assignments?

Karl: Is that what you would want us to do in the future?

Gordon: Absolutely. In fact, now that I think about it, it seems to me that we need to change the way that we give out assignments around here.

Carol: That does sound like a good idea. I've been thinking about that for some time. I think it would be better if you simply let us know what work needs to get done and let us decide how the assignments should be distributed. That would prevent the type of thing that just happened with Coop and Karl and also allow us to work better together as a team to get these assignments done.

Coop: That sounds like a great idea.

Karl: I agree.

Gordon: OK, starting tomorrow we will begin doing just that. If you have any problems doing this, then you can get me involved. Otherwise, I will leave this up to you to work out as a team. It makes a lot of sense to me and will give me more time to do other things, and I have plenty of other things to worry about. In fact, I have to travel to three of our branches during the next few days to try to get things straightened out there. It would really help me if we got this office under control so I could focus on them.

Coop: This is just a hunch, but I wonder if you might not be having the same kind of problem with the branches as we are having here?

Gordon: What do you mean?

Coop: When you visit the branches, what do you normally do?

Gordon: I do a number of things, but I guess mostly I make decisions about what they need to be doing to operate more effectively.

Coop: How's this strategy working?

Gordon: I already told you what it was like at the branches — there's even more chaos there than we have here! I guess it's because I'm not there very often.

Coop: Maybe it is because you are there too often!

Everyone in the room laughed at Coop's comment. Even Gordon managed to find some humor in his remark.

Carol: I think what Coop is trying to say, although not very diplomatically, is that maybe the reason that there is so much chaos at the branches that you have made them too dependent on you. If you haven't taught or allowed them to make those kinds of important decisions for themselves, then all of that responsibility falls on your shoulders. It also seems to me that they are the ones who would be most familiar with the day-to-day problems and be in the best positions to make these kinds of decisions. You only visit there once in awhile and couldn't be as informed about their issues as they would be.

Coop: You know, now that I think about it, the same thing basically happens to us here. While you are gone to the branches, we postpone decisions until you get back, and then try to fill you in on all the details. This not only causes important decisions to be delayed, but sometimes, no matter how hard we all try to bring you up to date, there is still a lot that is hard to accurately and completely convey to you. Consequently, there are many things that are addressed correctly. Just as we just discussed about how we are going to begin assigning work, we should also change the way that decisions are made and by whom. I think we could all be more productive if we did.

Gordon: You know, I think you are right; in fact, I know that you are right. I've got to learn to allow people to make more decisions for themselves — particularly those decisions where people have more expertise than I do. Maybe that would help all of us to get more control of the problems we face every day, rather than these problems controlling us. But I guess I am still confused about what role I need to play in getting these decisions made and the work done, particularly at the branches?

Carol: I think the first thing you need to do is make sure that the people know exactly what kinds of decisions you want and expect them to make. Then make sure that they have everything they need to make these decisions. For instance, have they received all the training they need to do the things that you will now expect them to do? If they haven't, it is not really fair to expect them to do these things with any degree of competence. They will need to know what kind of information and feedback you expect from them on what they are doing and the results they achieved. They need to know how they will be measured and evaluated by you concerning how well they are performing their new responsibilities.

Coop: They also need to have all the resources available to them to do what you are asking them to do. For example, do they have access to our company's intranet computer system? It seems to me that would be necessary to be able to quote the latest pricing plan as they change daily from the New York office.

Gordon: Those are all excellent points. I would not have thought of many of those, but they are all legitimate. I am beginning to see more clearly what my role needs to be, at least in getting this new system set up. I am confident that I can handle all of these things and will rely on this group to help me along the way. But what bothers me the most is how my boss will react to this whole idea? You know that Stan is a bottom line type of guy. All that is ever really important to him are the results. He has no time to listen to excuses about why things didn't go right. He will just start right through you and tell you that its your job to deal with the problems. All he is interested in is the answers.

Karl: Stan is not coming here any time soon, is he?

Carol: Calm down, Karl. You're starting to break out in hives again. Just the mention of Stan's name anymore gives you an allergic reaction. We had to hide you in the supply closest the whole time he was here during his last visit or you would have turned completely purple.

Karl: I can't help it. He just makes me so nervous. I think I'll be sick the next time he comes. Anyway, that's not funny. Stan mistakenly walked into that closest and found me in there.

Coop: I would have loved to have seen your face when he walked into that closet! What did you say to him anyway?

Karl: I just said how nice it was to see him and that I hoped he could come visit us more often. Then I got really sick and threw up on his shoes.

Coop: You really know how to impress the top brass, old man!

Karl: Thanks a lot. Just wait until the next time you need a favor from me. I'm not giving you anymore personal information from the secretaries' personnel files.

Gordon: I wondered why I smelled something kind of sick every time I was around Stan the last time he was here. I thought it was some new aftershave or something. I was afraid to ask, in fact I'm glad I didn't. But Karl, what did you mean when you said that you have been giving Coop personal information from the secretaries' personnel files?

Karl: Oops!

Coop: Oops!

Gordon: Coop, now you listen to me. You keep away from those files! What is in those is confidential information and none of your business. If I hear you do that again, you're fired!

Coop: That's cool. I already have all the information I need! In fact, I've got a luncheon date with that new secretary in accounting and have plenty of information on her to begin a beautiful relationship. I think I've got her number!

Gordon: No wonder, there isn't any control in this office. There is nothing confidential around here!

Coop: Take it easy, Gordon, or your drinking problem is going to get out of control again.

Gordon: What do you know about my drinking problem? I've never told anyone here about that!

Coop: Oops!

Karl: Oops!

Carol: Maybe we had better change the subject. Gordon, what are you going to do about Stan's reaction to this new way of making decisions?

Gordon: Yeah, thank you for getting me focused on the issues that we are really here to discuss. It seems to me that just because I change the way that decisions are made around here that doesn't change my responsibilities or accountabilities in any way. I am still the one who is ultimately responsible for how the operation performs. I will still be just as accountable for the results under either system.

Carol: What kind of support do you think you will need from Stan?

Gordon: Well I guess I need Stan to understand what I am trying to do as well as support it. Without his support, it will be much more difficult to change the way we make decisions around here. He needs to understand what will be different and how some of the communications he receives may be different.

Coop: How will communications to Stan be different just because we will be making more of the day-to-day operational decisions, Gordon?

Gordon: Well, it seems to me that because I won't be as involved in every decision that is made around here, I won't know all the details that I did in the past.

Karl: So, what? How does that affect how you communicate with Stan? I'm getting a little uncomfortable with what is being proposed here. What does this really mean?

Gordon: What it will mean is that I will not be the subject matter expert on everything around here. I think that has been one of our big problems. There is no way that I can know as much as each of you do about the work you do or those who are in our branches. As all of you know, Stan is the type of Manager who likes to have a great deal of information about our operations. He knows what is going on from his many years of experience in this business, and is not one to be fooled by anyone. I think he would appreciate hearing directly from each of you about what is going on rather than always getting this information from me.

Karl: That's exactly what I was afraid that you were going to say. I don't think that I could handle having to talk to Stan on a regular basis. It will make me sick for sure. In fact, I'm starting to feel sick just talking about it right now!

Coop: Someone get the wastepaper can. I think old Karl is about to blow again!

Carol: Perhaps this is a good point to end this meeting, don't you think, Gordon?

Gordon: Definitely. But before we do, I would like to say a few things that I have been sitting here thinking during this meeting.

Carol: Karl, do you think you could hold off a few more minutes? Could we get you anything, a glass of water, a new job assignment?

Karl: Very funny. No, I don't want anything right now. I think I am starting to feel a little better. But why don't you move that wastepaper can a little closer to me, just in case.

Gordon: We do need to work together as a team to make these changes go smoothly. I need to have input from each of you on what you need to be able to make the kinds of decisions and accept the responsibilities that I am proposing. I suggest that we spend some time each week for the next month or so discussing how to make this transition and how to make everyone more comfortable with their new responsibilities. We even need to look at such things as our reward and recognition systems, communications, resources, equipment, training, and even our organizational culture. I need to keep Stan informed about the process that we are beginning and ensure we have his support.

Carol: That sounds like an excellent idea. Maybe the first thing we should do the next time we get together to discuss this is to develop a plan that would outline exactly the steps that we need to take to reach our objectives.

Coop: Identifying our objectives sounds like it should be the very first thing we need to do. That way, we will all know more clearly what it is that we are trying to do. That way it will be easier to know how we are to get there.

Gordon: I totally agree with everything that is being said. I will set up the meeting and we will get started right away. I'll get with each of you to find the best time for the meeting. Is everybody OK with this? What about you, Karl?

Karl: I've just been taking my pulse; it has gone up 10 beats per minute since we began this discussion. I think that I am beginning to run a temperature, too. Carol, feel my forehead, will you, to see if I'm hot.

Carol: Karl, you are as cool as a cucumber. You need to calm down. You might find you like this new system more than you think.

Karl: Why?

Coop: Because you will have more control over your job and the decisions that affect it. I know you are always worrying about what someone else is going to do to you. This way, you will have more say in what happens and less reason to worry about what others might do that will negatively affect your work. Your problem is that you worry too much about things that you don't have any control over. This new system will give you more control over more of your job.

Karl: I guess that does make some sense. But I'm still worried about having to talk to Stan more often. I don't think he likes me very much.

Coop: Oh, sure he does. He just loves it when people throw up all over his shoes!

Gordon: OK, that's enough. Let's get back to work and I want all of you to be thinking about what we need to do to get started in changing the decision making and problem solving process around here before our next meeting.

The Wide World of Sports Analogies

Watching sports on television may be rapidly becoming the closest thing to exercise that many of us get anymore! Many people's idea of participating in sports today is playing "armchair quarterback," spending the weekends watching their favorite teams in action. Television viewers spend countless hours watching sports in the comfort of their easy chairs, while yelling at the players on the screen for not putting forth more effort. Somehow, there seems to be a contradiction in this scene. Shouldn't it really be the other way around, and the people sweating their "butts" off should be yelling at the "couch potatoes" for their slothfulness? In an attempt to help us move away from our increasingly sedentary life-styles, the following *mental* sports activities have been developed. If the mood strikes you, you may want to supplement them with some calisthenics or warm-up exercises to help get you in the mood for more sports analogies than you probably have ever been faced with before in your entire life!

In this spirit, the following section might be better termed, "The Wide World of Sports Analogies"! Although many may feel that the sports analogy has been overused in management training programs, it still provides many excellent lessons. The following are a series of sports analogies relating to the concepts of Remote Control Management, empowerment, and the teamwork that must exist in any organization to reach their goal for success, no matter if it is winning the Superbowl or increasing profits for your company.

Playing as a Team at Work

Most people usually don't associate being at work with having anything to do with play. After all, work by its very name and definition is understandably associated with something that is less than fun. Play is typically something you do when you are not working. Unfortunately, it seems that work tends to get a "bad name." People often think of work as something that is hard, tedious, boring, unpleasant, dreaded, etc. (this list could go on and on).

Have you ever wondered why work can't be more fun? Actually, there are no rules that say you shouldn't enjoy your work or that if you just happen to like your job you can't still get paid for doing it! Your work is a very important part of your life. After all, when you spend at least 25% of your time at work, you might as well make the most of it!

Believe it or not, work and play each do share many things in common. Often it is a matter of how we view the different roles we play in our lives that determines how much we enjoy participating in these activities. With the introduction of the concepts of Remote Control Management, work can become not only more enjoyable but also more rewarding as well.

Remote Control Management can give everyone a greater chance to contribute to the success of the team. It can make work seem more like play by helping you learn to enjoy the challenges and rewards of striving to reach shared goals with other members of your team.

Remote Control Management gives everyone a greater opportunity to "get in the game" at work, regardless of their position in the organization. Often, there are many talented people in an organization who for one reason or another are "sitting on the bench" and have not been given the opportunity to show what they can do. Remote Control Management demonstrates that the people who work closest to where problems and opportunities for improvement exist are the *real experts* when it come to solving these problems and in the best positions to "make the big plays."

Remote Control Management is based on the concepts of empowerment, which allows those people in positions closest to where problems exist to have the ability to take positive corrective action to improve their work, jobs, and ultimately the entire team. Empowerment helps eliminate many of the "hassles" people have had to put up with at work, as well as making their team better able to beat the competition.

Empowerment helps make everyone feel more a part of the team and responsible for its overall performance. Ultimately in sports, the success or failure of a team is in the hands of the players performing their jobs. Once the game begins, there is little the team's coach, manager, owner, or fans can do compared to the roles and responsibilities of the players on the field or court. The same is also true in the game of work. Ultimately it is the performance of the individual doing his or her job that really makes the difference. It just makes sense to give these people the opportunity to have the greatest impact on how their jobs are to be performed and more input in the decisions which affect them.

Remote Control Management helps people work more effectively as a team and proves to have many benefits. People's jobs are becoming more enjoyable and their overall performance is improving, as they are now finding better solutions to problems that have existed for years. As one employee said, after the concepts of remote control management and empowerment were introduced into the workplace, "Our workteam has learned that none of us are a smart as all of us!."

One person might look at what appears to be an impossible task and ask, "How am I ever going to get this job done?" Along comes another person who asks, "What can I do to help?" Soon another person pitches in and another and another and another. Before long an entire team of people are working together on the job and soon complete the assignment. This simple example is what teamwork is all about. It is the combining of efforts by a group of people all focused on reaching the same goal that allows the greatest accomplishments to be achieved. Team efforts enable even the biggest of jobs to be completed, from winning the championship to meeting the requirements of your customers better than the competition.

A team working together can accomplish more than any of its members could as individuals working alone. It is the combined efforts of the team members that is the true strength of the team. Team members also provide backup support for one another. A player may take a greater chance trying to catch the ball, knowing that there is someone else there to back him up just in case he is not successful.

Team members can also be inspired by other player's performances. Often a team rallies or comes from behind as a result of one player's success. One person's accomplishments, often enable other players to make winning plays. Players will often pass the ball to other team members in better positions to make the play. When a team begins to really work together and build upon each other's talents and successes, they can become nearly impossible to beat.

Responsibilities of Team Members

A member of any team has a responsibility to both himself and to his teammates. A team's performance is made up of the results of all of its member's individual performances. Each team member must strive to do his/her best to reach their own goals and personal performance standards. Teamwork can help take an individual to higher levels of performance by the support other team members provide one another. Each player must perform to the best of his or her ability, not just for themselves, but also for the team.

Most important to a workteam is that each person supports the team and contributes to its success in whatever way they can. Workteams often seek to find better ways of getting the job done than the often inefficient methods of the past. Workteams help utilize the talent and expertise of each of their members. A member of a workteam must have the same kind of commitment as does a player on a sports team as they strive to become champions. Both an athlete and a member of a a team at work must strive hard to reach their goals and ultimately be better than the competition in order to be successful.

Every sporting activity has different requirements for each of its players to meet. Common to all team sports is the need to have all players working together to reach their shared goals for success. Each player contributes to the overall team effort. However, some players make greater contributions to the team than others. Why? Is it because of their ability, motivation, or the position they play? Similarly, at work, why do some people make greater contributions to the team and have more impact on the overall results than others? Are similar factors which make an athlete more successful on a sports team present at work? How can an athlete or someone at work improve his/her performance to reach both personal and the team's goals? How do personal goals lead to team goals, and what is the relative importance of each? There is a great deal of individual effort in every team victory. It is individuals that make up a team. Everyone plays an important role in any team's victory, no matter if it is in sports or at work.

Your Role on the Team

In sports, each player has different responsibilities depending on the position played. In one way or another, each position is designed to help the team beat the competition. The responsibility of some positions is to prevent the other team from scoring. For other positions, the focus is on scoring points for their own team. In some circumstances, players perform both of these responsibilities, while others have more specialized jobs and functions. Regardless, every player is important to the team. What is your role on your team at work and how does it support your team's overall performance?

The Role of the Coach

What is the role of the coach on a sports team and how does it relate to that of a supervisor in the workplace? In many ways, these roles are also very similar. In both roles, each person has been given responsibility for the overall performance of their team. The main objective of both roles is to help people perform their jobs to the best of their ability and to work together as a team. Every coach or supervisor is unique in his/her overall approach and methods for getting this job done.

One of the many changes with the introduction of empowerment and remote control management systems is the way those in leadership positions lead people. Traditionally, the boss told the workers what work to do and they did it. Today, with these new concepts becoming increasingly popular and successful, the role of the supervisor is different. With the concepts of empowerment becoming an important part of the workplace, instead of giving orders, the supervisor's new challenge today is to help employees make decisions which affect their jobs. With this increased responsibility, empowered employees are now performing jobs and tasks typically done by those in higher positions. Employees are making critically important decisions previously only made by their supervisors.

Why this change? Again as mentioned earlier, those who work closest to where problems exist are in the best positions to make decisions concerning solving these problems. These people are the *real experts* when it comes to finding practical and effective solutions to correct and prevent problems from recurring in the future. An excellent comparison is found on the baseball field. Who is in the best position to decide what pitch to throw to the batter? Is it the coach, the pitcher, the owner, the fans? The answer is, of course, the catcher. The catcher works closest to the batter and has the best perspective on how to pitch to him. In many ways, the concept of empowerment has always been part of sports. The work world is just beginning to catch up and get into the game!

How is being a member of a team at work like playing on a sports team? The following are examples of different roles and responsibilities that members of sports teams play and how they relate to those of members of teams at work. Think about how some of these roles and responsibilities in sports compare to those that members of your team play at work.

Baseball

On a baseball team, players must perform a number of different roles. Each team member must be responsible for playing a position on the field as well as taking a turn at bat. The batter must face the entire opposing team as he or she steps up to the plate and tries to hit the ball in hopes of scoring runs for the team. At the same time, all nine players on the other team will be doing everything they can to prevent the batter from being successful.

In business, this same scenario also takes place in many similar ways. A business must try to score "runs," or in other words, make profits for the team. However, there will always be competition out in the field who will be doing everything they can to prevent your team from being successful. Who will ultimately claim victory in this contest? There are many factors that affect and determine the results. The overall strength of the team is certainly an important factor. However, equally important is the attitude the players have about themselves and their team. Having a positive attitude about your work can have a great effect on the results of your efforts. How many times have you watched a baseball team that everyone expected to lose the game come away with a victory despite the odds against them? How can this happen? Most likely, that team had a more positive attitude about winning. A winning attitude can overcome many obstacles that may exist between you and your goals.

Every baseball player hopes to hit a home run each time at bat. In baseball, every player gets a turn a bat regardless of the position played. Too often in the workplace in the past, only certain employees have been given the opportunity to get a "hit." By giving everyone a turn at bat, your team has a greater chance of scoring points against the competition. Depending on a few players or even one individual to hit all your team's runs can be risky. This game plan may work well in the short term but may not work long term, even if you have the "Home Run Champion" on your team! What if he or she is having a bad day or has to leave the game? A team could find themselves with no one else that can hit the competition's "fast ball."

Managing by remote control can help give everyone a chance to have a turn at bat, not just players in certain positions. By giving everyone the opportunity to "hit the ball" your chances of scoring against the competition are greatly improved.

Home Plate

Where is "home plate" for your team at work? What opportunities do you and your teammates have to "hit the ball" at work? Does everyone get their turn to step up to the plate? Has everyone been given "batting practice" and instruction on how to hit the ball or in other words, perform all of the tasks required to get the job done when given the chance?

- What or where would "home plate" be at work as it affects your work group?
- What are some of the opportunities you have to "swing at the ball" on your job?
- Does everyone get their turn to step up to the plate?
- What are the toughest "pitches" thrown at you at work?
- What would be the equivalent of hitting a "single" on your job?
- What would be a "double"?
- A "triple"?
- What would be a "home run" at your work?
- What would be "striking out"?

Even professional baseball's superstars strike out sometimes. Striking out is part of any game. You can get so worried about striking our or failing that you can't hit the ball. You can not expect to hit a "home run" every time you step up to the plate.

- At your place of work, if you strike out will you get another chance at bat? How do you get another chance to step "up to the plate"?

Taking the Field

Players on a baseball team must be able to play positions on the field when it is the other team's turn at bat. Each player must be able to play one or more of these more specialized positions as well as be able to get hits at bat.

People at work often must also be able to share certain responsibilities with other team members as well as having their own specialized skills and tasks to perform. The more positions that players are able to perform, the more flexible and stronger the team becomes.

- What are some of the responsibilities that are shared among the members of your team at work?
- How can these shared responsibilities be better learned by each team member?

- Does everyone on your team accept their responsibilities to perform these tasks?
- If not, what can be done to help everyone accept this responsibility?

Throwing the Ball

When the ball is hit, it is up to the team on the field to try to stop the runner's forward progress. Their goal is to get the runner out, or at least limit the number of bases he or she is able to advance. To accomplish this goal, the players will, depending on the position they play, either try to make the play themselves or throw the ball to another teammate to try to get the runner out. By working together, an outfielder and infielder can achieve that which neither one could accomplish alone.

At work there are also situations when it is possible to make the "play" or solve problems yourself, but also other times when you must work together to reach your shared goals.

- What are some examples where it is important for one player on your team to throw the *ball* to another?
- What happens if someone tries to make all the "plays" at work alone and never "throws the ball" to anyone else?
- How can your work group better learn to "throw the ball" to each other when necessary?

Football

Football provides a different kind of team challenge for its players. Football involves a great deal of specialization among its players. For example, in football only a few players ever get to touch the ball. In fact, most of those on the field never even get close to the ball. Football consists of many support roles designed to allow other players to score points for their team. Often, little is ever heard of the tireless efforts of the offensive linemen who, play after play, provide pass protection or open up holes in the defense for the ball carriers to run through.

Without the efforts of these support players, touchdowns could never be scored by the team. Similarly, even these support players can not do the job all alone. There must also be skilled performers capable of maximizing the opportunities these support players create. Sometimes all they can provide is a glimpse of daylight, an instant for another player to make his or her move.

For the runner, this is often all that is needed to gain valuable yardage. Often it is the lineman and running back's ability to work together on a play that allows the team to make forward progress down the field. Each yard the team gains is as much of a credit to the linemen who opened the hole as it is the runner who carries the ball. On a football team, everyone contributes to their success or failure — not just one player or a select group of individuals.

- On your team at work, are there certain positions that provide support for other positions? What are some of these positions?
- Are there other positions and people who get to "run the ball" and receive more of the attention and recognition? What are some of these positions?
- In your work group, how do these "support" positions enable other people to do their jobs?
- What would happen if these support positions did not provide their services for other positions?
- On your team, how can those in "support" positions and those who "carry the ball" work better together to strengthen your team?
- How can those in support positions on your team get more of the attention and recognition that they deserve?

Playing Defensively

There is an old saying, "The best defensive is to take the offense." Unfortunately, in sports or in business, this is not always possible to do. There will be times when the competition has the ball and is driving forward trying to score points against your team. In these situations, all you can do is to play defensively, trying to stop their progress and, hopefully, get the ball back. In football, a team's defensive strength is often the critical factor needed to defeat the competition. By stopping or even shutting down the other team's offensive efforts, you can take away their ability to score against your team.

- How does your team at work play "defense" and in what kinds of situations is this necessary?
- At work, how can you regain "possession of the ball" and again begin playing "offensively"?
- What would be your team's best defense against the competition?

Levels of Defense

There are a number of levels of defense a football team must have to prevent the other team's offense from breaking through and scoring a touchdown. A football team's primary line of defense is typically the defensive linemen who are positioned to stop the offense at the line of scrimmage before they can make any yardage. The linebackers provide backup support in case a runner gets through the defensive line or the quarterback is able to get the pass off to the receiver. There is even a defensive position called the **safety** that provides additional backup support in the event that all of the other levels of defense break down. Sometimes all of the levels of defense work effectively, resulting in a gang tackling of the runner or receiver. Other times, none of these systems work as they were designed, giving away valuable yards and points to the competition.

At work, there also need to be different levels of defense or backup systems to prevent problems from occurring that eventually could give away valuable business to the competition. Team members must help and support each other to perform their jobs. As on a football team, there will always be occasions when people are going to need to serve as a backup or replacement for a co-worker. On the job, there are times when one person needs to be available to step in and "make the play" for another person, just as a linebacker would for a defensive lineman. No team in sports or at work can rely entirely on one player or a certain group of players to make every "tackle" on every play.

- Are there different "levels of defense" at your place of work to ensure that the requirements of your customers are met? What would be some of these levels of defense?
- How do players on your team provide backup support for one another?
- How could this support be improved among your team members?

Basketball

Teams do not always consist of large numbers of players. Basketball is an example of a smaller team consisting of only five players, each sharing many of the same responsibilities and roles. In basketball, players need to be able to quickly adapt to the many rapid changes in the game. Possession of the ball can quickly go from one team to the other, requiring players to change from offensive to defensive roles in a matter of seconds. It is as important for a player to be able to help regain possession of the ball by rebounding a shot or stealing a pass as it is to score baskets. Each player must constantly make decisions whether it is better to pass the ball to a teammate who may be in a better position to score or to try to make the shot himself.

There is also a unique event in the game of basketball called the "free throw." Basketball players get the opportunity to try to make free throws as a result of infractions of the rules by the other team. When a player steps up to the foul line to shoot a free throw, all of the pressure is on him or her to be successful. Sometimes the entire team must depend on this single individual's ability to make the basket. Everyone's efforts on both teams during the entire game can come down to this last shot. All the action stops as the player dribbles the ball, sets to shoot, and releases the ball, sending it sailing through the air, hitting the backboard and rolling around the rim. The crowd rises to their feet as everyone waits anxiously to see if the ball will drop in the basket. Does the ball go in? You decide!

- What are some situations at your work when a small group of team members need to share duties and responsibilities?
- What are some examples of your team members having to make decisions concerning "passing the ball" or "trying to make the shot themselves?
- What would be an example of a "free throw" at your place of work when your entire team's success may depend on the performance of one individual?
- How can your team better provide support for this individual?

Hockey

The game of hockey is one of the roughest sports to play, and also requires players to make "pass or shoot" decisions, much like those in basketball, An entire hockey team must also depend on the performance of a single key player — the goalie. It is the goalie's responsibility to prevent the other team from scoring by guarding their net and stopping the puck. Hockey players can also be forced to spend time in the penalty box for breaking the rules of the game.

- Does your team depend on a single individual to play "goalie" to prevent your competition from scoring? If so, who would this individual be, and how can other team members help him or her perform this important job?
- What would be your "penalty box" at work?
- How can you and your team avoid the "penalty box" at your work?

Rowing Crew

On a rowing crew, everyone must work in perfect synchronization with the other members of the crew. No one can be out of time with the other rowers. A rower out of time with the rest of the crew can actually be counterproductive to the team's overall efforts.

On any team there are similar situations in which all the members must work together with perfect timing.

- What are some examples of situations when your team needs to work together as a synchronized unit?
- What happens if your team members are out of synchronization with one another?
- How can this problem be avoided or corrected?

Relay Race

In track, there is the relay race in which each runner must pass the baton to the next runner. The passing of the baton is a critical part of the race. This is when valuable seconds can be lost or the baton dropped, causing the relay team to be eliminated from the competition. Each runner, once handed the baton, must run as fast as possible to the next runner or to the finish line. Each runner must do his or her part to keep their team competitive in the race and put the last runner in a good position to reach the finish line before the others.

- Are there times in your work group when one team member must pass the "baton" to another team member? What are some of these situations?
- What are the consequences if the "baton" is dropped during this hand-off at work?
- How can your "hand-offs" at work be made smoother and more efficiently?

Auto Racing

In auto racing, a driver and his or her car depend on their pit crew to keep them in the race. The pit crew must work not only quickly, but also precisely to get their car and driver safely back in the race. In only seconds they perform services on the car that would typically take a much longer time under normal everyday circumstances. Both the driver and the pit crew are part of the racing team and work together to make it possible for their car to be the first to cross the finish line and get the checkered flag.

- Who would be the "pit crew" at your place of work?
- How important are they to your work group's overall performance?
- How can they get more recognition for the job they do?
- How can your team better support your "pit crew" at work?

Volleyball

In volleyball, each player rotates positions after each point. By doing this, every team member has a chance to play each position, including serving the ball to the other team. Everyone gains first hand experience concerning what it takes to play each position on the team.

- Are the players on your team able to perform each other's positions? If not, how much stronger would your team be if everyone was able to perform all the positions on your team and why?

Tennis

Tennis is a sport which can be played by single opponents on either side of the net or which can also be played as doubles. In a doubles match, two players cover the same amount of court area as the single player would normally play. In a doubles match, the performance level of the two-person team is greater than one player could ever expect to achieve. Each player is responsible for their area of court and also to provide backup for the other player should he or she not be able to get to the ball. Doubles matches require both individual skill as well as teamwork to play competitively.

- Are there jobs at your work that if you played them as "doubles" rather than "singles" you could perform more effectively and efficiently? What would be some of these opportunities and how they being presently "played"?
- Are there times at your work when you could use some help from another member of your team "getting to the ball"? Are there occasions when you could help another member of your team members in a similar way? How can your team help "cover" each other better to help get the jobs done?

Golf

Golf is typically an individualized sport in which players concentrate on their own score and performance. However, there is a popular variation of the game played by teams of golfers that is often called "Captain's Choice," "Best Ball," or "Scrambles Matches." In this format, each golfer takes his or her turn hitting each of the team's shots. The team then selects the best shot and disregards the others. This procedure continues throughout the entire game. The final team score is the result of the combined best shots of all of the players. Most likely, the final score is much better than any one of the individual players could have ever hoped to achieve alone. Everyone feels they contributed to the team's efforts, as even the weakest player's shot will typically be selected at times during the game. The players can immediately see the benefits of this teamwork and that their combined efforts will exceed that of any one of them.

- What are similar examples at your work where a team's efforts will greatly exceed that of any individual?
- How can everyone's efforts be better utilized to improve the overall efforts of your team?
- Do you believe it is better to measure individual performance or a team's overall performance? Under which measurement system do you think that everyone will feel more a contributing member of the team and why?

Putting It All Together

Let's look at the characteristics or qualities that make teams successful in the sports activities previously mentioned and see how they may apply to your team at work. Check if each of the following is a strength or weakness for your team at work:

Strengths and Weakness in Your Team at Work

Strength	Weakness	
_____	_____	Hitting tough "pitches" thrown at you
_____	_____	Everyone getting a turn at "bat"
_____	_____	Throwing the "ball" to other players in better positions to make the "play"
_____	_____	Playing positions that support other players ability to perform their jobs
_____	_____	Playing defensively when necessary
_____	_____	Regaining control of the "ball"
_____	_____	Players providing backup for one another
_____	_____	"Gang tackling" with everyone in on the play
_____	_____	Taking advantage of "free throw" opportunities your team may get
_____	_____	Adapting to the rapid changes in the game
_____	_____	Playing "goalie" by defending the goal
_____	_____	Ending up in the "penalty box" for breaking the rules
_____	_____	Having the right timing and synchronization
_____	_____	Passing the "baton" to someone else at work
_____	_____	"Pit crews" to keep your team in the race
_____	_____	Doubles matches when pairs of players work together to increase efficiencies of both people
_____	_____	"Captain's choice" activities in which everyone gets a "shot at the ball" and a chance to contribute to the team's success

Game Summary

- How can your team maintain and continue to develop its strengths?
- What can you do to help your work group or team improve in those areas you marked as weakest?
- How can the concepts of remote control help you work better together as a team?
- How could managing by Remote Control help your team be better able to meet your goals, both individual and shared?

6 The Remote Control Manager

Leading the Pack

There is a story about leadership that illustrates its liabilities probably as well as any other told. The leader in this case is not a highly educated and talented CEO of a major multinational conglomerate but, rather, a dog. But not just any dog, this is a bloodhound, trained to lead man, with his inferior sense of smell and even direction, on the trail of a scent to some ultimate destination. Picture a scene with tens of people following behind this dog through a wooded area. Each of them is totally focused on the dog's every move. Where will he lead them to? Will he lose the scent? When will he finally take them to where and what they wanted to find? The dog suddenly turns in another direction, heading south now with the group of humans obediently following his change in course. He turns west, then north again. The humans again follow. What has the dog discovered? What secrets will he lead them to? What is the dog thinking, assuming (of course) that dogs have the ability to have such thoughts? The answer is, the dog is saying to himself, "I can't smell a damn thing!"

This could just as easily be a story about leadership in many businesses today. The organization obediently follows the lead of the chief, assuming that he knows the direction in which they should go. Unfortunately, in many cases, the manager may not be able "to smell a damn thing" either! Instead of following the "scent" to the successful obtainment of their goals and objectives, the executive has lost the trail. The entire organization may be wandering about aimlessly following their leader's instincts, rather than a

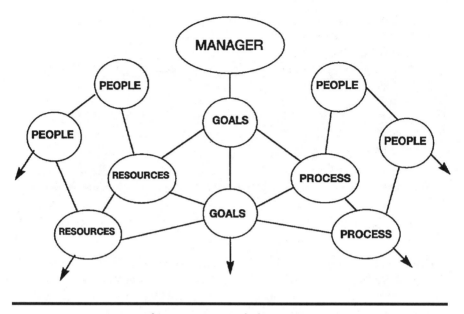

The Remote Control Manager

trail that leads to somewhere they had planned to go. But how does the manager get back on the "scent"?

Remote Control Management can help provide this direction that may have been lost. Sometimes the manager's "sniffer" is not as accurate as it used to be! They lose the confidence in their instincts. They may ask for more and more data and, even armed with this arsenal of information, can not make a decision. One of the most difficult things for many managers is moving up in the organization and no longer being in touch with the operational aspects of the business. They begin to lose their point of reference. Their world suddenly changes from solving operational problems and being expert on the details to one of dealing with abstract strategies and concepts. Their "sniffers" may not be wrong, the trail may be "cold." It's like the dog that everyone was following. There may have been absolutely nothing wrong with his ability to follow the scent, providing that there was one to follow. His lack of success may not have been his fault at all, but rather that of those who put him on the trail. Perhaps too much time had passed and there was no scent left to follow. Things change at an incredibly accelerating pace nowadays. Yesterday, the trail may have provided all the information that would have been necessary to find whom or what they were searching. But today, the trail may be somewhere else. Where they were looking was yesterplace will do nothing but put them farther and farther away from what they are searching to find.

The model shown on page 176, shows how a Remote Control Manager influences what happens in the organization. The Remote Control Manager gets the job done through others. However, contrary to what common sense might tell you, this more indirect method of managing can result in better, more informed decisions and methods of getting the job done. The Remote Control Manager influences the resources, work processes, and ultimately the goals of the organization but mostly through the actions of other people. It is like putting decision making and problem solving in the hands of those who know their way through the woods because they walk through them every day. They understand what is involved in getting things done in the organization and what resources are needed. They know the shortcuts and the parts of the trail to avoid. The skill that the Remote Control Manager must have is the ability to listen to the input that he or she receives from their direct reports. They are giving the Remote Control Manager eyewitness accounts of what is happening in their working world on a daily basis. Anything else would be more or less a "secondhand" account of the realities of the workplace. Which would be more accurate and useful? What type of information would you as a manager rather make "big picture" decisions based upon?

Another problem is that managers tend to forget is the "hassle factor" of getting things done in an organization. They forget the complexity of work. From their current perspective, they just tell people to do things and they get done. If they don't get done properly, then it becomes their job to deliver some kind of consequence. It all happens rather effortlessly, at least for the manager. However, someone has to put the effort into getting the requested task done. Even the most simple of tasks can become burdens if there are obstacles in the way of getting them completed. The role of the Remote Control Manager is to work to remove as many of these obstacles as possible. Unfortunately, many times management tends to create more obstacles than they remove. They may not always even be aware that they are causing this affect. In one company, the Vice President of Operations was touring one of the company's facilities and saw a calendar from a tool manufacturer on the wall in a maintenance shop. On the calendar was pictured a scantily clothed young woman holding one of the tool company's products. The VP said, "I want that picture taken down. We have diversity programs and sexual harassment policies that say that we will respect the rights of all of our employees. I don't think that this picture supports those policies. Also, I bring many important people to this plant including our biggest customers. Some of them might be offended by this type of picture." Of course, the vice president had every right to take such action, even a responsibility to do so.

However, his actions had more far-reaching affects than he realized or even could have imagined. The Plant Manager of the facility was understandably very upset that this incident had occurred at his facility and felt personally responsible. He wanted to ensure that no similar embarrassing event would ever occur again, at least during his tenure, the direction of which he was beginning to worry about. He ordered an audit of all calendars in the facility and that each one be judged for its decency and appropriateness. People started coming into his office with their wall calendars for him to judge. He struggled with questions such "would a picture of a attractive fully dressed woman in an automobile or a vacation site showing people sunbathing on the beach be appropriate?" Would anyone possibly be offended by these pictures? Just to play it safe, he ordered that all wall calendars, regardless of whether they had pictures or not, be taken down throughout the facility. Unknowingly, this edict took away a valuable planning tool for many of the people in the facility. Wall calendars allowed everyone quick reference to dates in order to schedule their work. Particularly, those who worked in planning and scheduling positions struggled to find other ways to have this information readily available. They began developing creative ways to disguise this type of information or at least hide it. Calendars were placed under glass on people's desks and quickly covered up with papers when they knew their boss was coming. They were hidden behind doors or tucked away in closets. Worse yet, word got around to the other facilities in the company about the incident, and they, too, started enforcing similar "no calendar" policies.

In another company, a CEO once remarked to an assistant, after touring a number of his company's manufacturing facilities, "Why is it that all of our plants always smell like fresh paint?" Perhaps he realized that the facilities painted their plants to try to make a more favorable impression during his visit and was simply acknowledging the fact that this occurred. Regardless, what is most significant about this kind of activity is the distraction that this kind of visit can create from what the real order of business should be at the facility. Managers should work to reduce this churn, not create more. Too often they fail to realize just how much power and influence they have on those who work for them. Like the "no calendar" policy, subordinates may create entire systems designed to meet what they perceive to be the expectations of the boss, only causing needless inefficiencies and hassles for everyone.

Entire meetings involving many busy people are often held in organizations every day to try to understand what their leader wants. Entire processes may be developed to try to deliver what they think the boss wants. When the boss does show up, they proudly parade their ideas or changes in front of him in hopes of approval of the fulfillment of his wishes.

Unfortunately, the reaction from the boss and ensuing dialog often goes something like this:

> "Why in the hell did you do that?"
> "But that's what we thought you wanted, sir?"
> "Who told you that?"
> "We thought you did, sir?"
> "Like hell, I did!"
> "What is it that you would like us to do?"
> "Anything but that; now change it!"

And so it goes. More time and energy wasted without really accomplishing a thing! At best, the organization ends up just where it started but only after expending a great deal of resources getting there.

These are pitfalls that a Remote Control Manager must avoid. Even worse than not adding value to the organization is to cause it to become less efficient because of your influence as a manager. Remote Control Managers have the potential of both adding value to their roles in the organization as well as to those who report to them. This worthy goal can often be best achieved by the right mix of involvement and independence provided to direct reports. Part of the art (or is it a science?) of being a Remote Control Manager is learning what this blend should be in each situation. This implies that there is no absolute right or wrong mix of these attributes. What is most important is what works best in each particular circumstance.

These decisions should be made based more on the factors which exist in any given organization than on some predetermined set of guidelines. Some workplaces may need more of a manager's attention and interaction. Others may function better left to work out problems for themselves. The degree of autonomy or direction a Remote Control Manager provides will vary in each situation to which the concepts are applied. The point is that, to a certain degree, even a Remote Control Manager must remain involved in the area or process he or she is responsible for managing, depending on their needs. To become completely detached would cause another set of problems, many of which may be worse than being overly controlling.

When should a Remote Control Manager's influence be present in those parts of an organization for which he or she is responsible? The answer is: *always*. As long as the Remote Control Manager has overall responsibility for some aspect of the business or operation, then he or she must be always be involved, at least on some level. Again, the manager's accountabilities don't change — it is the way in which they are exercised. To do otherwise would be abdicating your management responsibilities.

Which is the more difficult system to manage? Is it harder to empower others who work for you to accept greater responsibilities, many of which would have normally landed on your desk than to do the work yourself? Again the answer is the same: *always*. Although your common sense might tell you that having others perform the tasks that you presently do might sound like it would save you time and effort, this probably won't be the case, at least not at first. Yes, eventually as those who report to you become more skilled at performing these responsibilities you will not need to be as directly involved. But there is an important distinction that needs to be made between accountability and responsibility. For the purposes of Remote Control Management, responsibility is defined as those duties or tasks that are required of a person in performing his or her job. Part of the person's responsibility is performing these tasks to a desired level of competence. Accountability is ensuring that these responsibilities are fulfilled. The Remote Control Manager is still accountable for the fulfillment of the employees' responsibilities.

The Virtually Remote Manager

Accountability is ensuring that the desired results are achieved. You can still be accountable for a function and be some distance from where the actual work is being performed. In many circumstances today, managers are accountable for functions of the organization on the other side of the globe. Distance does not make someone less accountable. And herein lies the challenge. How do you still get things done as a manager when you can't always be there, particularly when your accountabilities keep growing and growing each day? The answer — become a Virtual Remote Manager.

When you think about something that is virtual, you picture something that only exists in one's mind. Virtual is more of an mental image, but one that still can seem to be as real as if it existed in a physical sense. Management in many working environments today is becoming more and more virtual rather than actual as the span of responsibilities is being extended beyond anyone's previous expectations. The Virtually Remote Control Manager exists within each person in the organization to some degree. The challenge of management today is to help this ability in each employee to emerge.

The Virtually Remote Manager's most important tool is information. Information is powerful, but only if you apply it. The Virtually Remote Manager manages information, not people. In this work environment, the manager enables people to manage themselves. This is a slightly different form of what has typically been referred to over the past decade as self-managing or self-directed teams. The difference is that, at least in theory, self-managing or self-directed teams provide their own direction. There is no management representative who officially provides this direction. The whole concept is that through empowerment the people on the team make all the decisions and perform all of the functions of a supervisor or manager. But can such a team truly ever exist? Doesn't everyone have someone that he or she must answer to? Someone in management must have accountability for the results of such a team. Surely no organization would allow any part of it to function without someone being accountable for its results. All of us have a boss in one form or another. No one is without accountability to someone. Even the Chief Executive Officer has others he or she is held accountable to, to meet the requirements of the job, be it the Board of Directors or the shareholders of the corporation. None of us gets completely off the hook.

In reality, even those work environments who call themselves self-directed or managing most likely are really a Virtually Remote Controlled workplace. There certainly is someone who is quietly and perhaps silently providing direction. By not openly acknowledging the existence of this manager, it may only serve to confuse everyone involved. It could cause people to have false expectations about how much authority and decision making ability they truly have in actuality. It may open up questions such as, "I thought that we were given the authority to make that decision," if they are ever "overruled" by some higher authority on a matter of critical importance to the organization. And inevitably, this is going to happen. This causes people to lose faith and confidence in the system. They lose trust in those who set up the system and may even feel deceived.

Wouldn't it be better to set up a more realistic system that is designed to achieve the same or similar results but without this potential Achilles heal? People have no problem being told that they will be managed by someone. Effective leadership provides people emotional security. People want and need to have effective and strong leadership. This is very evident every 4 years when a U.S. Presidential election occurs. The whole country and even the world, is drawn into every step of the process. The nightly news gives us the day's soundbite from each of the candidates' campaigns. We watch closely to see who will stumble and who will emerge victorious. Much of our emotional energies are invested in this important contest. Our futures, it appropriately seems during these critical periods in history, are being held in the balance as the winner is projected by the television networks often even before the last ballet is cast. Why is this such an important event every 4 years, even in those elections when it is pretty evident who the ultimate winner will be? What if, instead of this process, we were to become a self-managed country? Imagine what that might be like! Would it be any different in a business if such a situation ever truly existed?

The reason why you probably shuddered at such a thought was the images that such a system might have conjured in your mind. Our course, we need leadership. When people are asked to recall the most effective leader one has ever experienced in their lives, typically strong emotions are associated with that relationship. Maybe this person was a teacher, a coach, or possibly a boss or supervisor. People can tell you very specifically what made this person such a good leader and the positive effect that they had on their life. To try to take away this potentially supportive role in any workplace would be not only mistake, but an objective you would never really want to achieve. Instead, it is more realistic and desirable to include leadership in your organizational design, but in a capacity which would allow the everyone's greatest potential to be achieved.

The concept of the Virtually Remote Manager allows such an organizational structure to exist. It is a new form of self-management, but acknowledges the necessity of leadership. The Virtually Remote Manager can be both a concept and an actual person, at least most of the time. The Virtually Remote Manager is always present. It is a self-regulating and constant force. It integrates any number of other management functions into a single focus, controlled by those affected by its influence. The concept of the Virtually Remote Manager exist in each person in the organization. It is what manages the organization when the manager is not physically there. Actually, this concept is nothing new. What directs someone when the boss is gone, even for an instant? The Influence and direction of the boss still remains. In traditional terms, this influence needs to be renewed with some frequency in order to maintain control and direction in the organization. The Virtually Remote Manager concept challenges this paradigm of thinking about how long a time can pass between a manager's personal involvement and contact with those under his or her responsibility and still achieve the same or better performance.

The following is a story about a workplace just beginning to embrace the concept of becoming a Virtually Managed workplace. In this story, a very well-respected supervisor named Harry is about to retire. As the organization struggles with the question of how to replace this extremely valuable influence, they realize that instead of replacing Harry physically with another supervisor that they could continue his positive impact of the organization in a virtual manner. In this case, Harry's retirement did not mark the end of his contributions to the company, but marked a new beginning of virtual management for the department he ran for so many years. Virtual Managers don't necessarily have to retire, as was the case with Harry. They can be present in many different locations at the same time, increasing their impact in ways never before conceptualized in most current philosophies of management. As you read this story, look for ways that Harry's influence continues at least virtually in the organization.

Harry's Replacement

"Congratulations and have a happy retirement. We are going to miss you!" read the card to Harry that was signed by everyone who worked at Simpson Enterprises, a small privately owned company with one location and approximately 500 employees. Harry Bailey had been a supervisor for the company nearly as long as they had been in business and had been in charge of the facility's largest department for most of his career. As a young man, Harry had only worked for the then struggling new company for a short period of time before Mr. Simpson recognized his leadership potential and moved him into his present position. Everyone, including Mr. Simpson, credited Harry with helping build the company into its present size and success. Many of the company's policies and procedures had been developed with the help of Harry over his long and successful career spanning nearly four decades. Harry had input in virtually every hiring decision during his more than 38 years with Simpson Enterprises, and there were many who would say they *owed* their careers to him.

"Who is going to replace Harry?" was a frequent question around the company, as his retirement date approached. Everyone who worked for Harry had the greatest respect for him and worked particularly hard to meet his high standards and demand for quality workmanship. Who could fill Harry's "shoes" was a good question. No one else in the company commanded the respect or stature Harry had earned over the years. Everyone waited anxiously for Mr. Simpson to announce his decision. There were even rumors that someone was gong to be brought in from outside the company to fill the position.

When the day of Harry's retirement finally came, his replacement was still not announced. If Harry knew who it was to be he was not saying. When asked, he would simply reply, "Mr. Simpson will share that information at the proper time." No one seemed to know if that meant that someone from inside the company would be promoted into the job or that there would be someone brought in from another company. At Harry's retirement party, Mr. Simpson gave an emotional speech thanking him for the many contributions he had made during his years with the company and for his friendship. Before the party ended, Mr. Simpson announced that there would be a meeting for all employees at 8:00 a.m. the next morning. Everyone was sure that there must be someone new coming in to replace Harry who would be introduced at the meeting the following morning.

As everyone gathered in the conference room the next morning, anxious to hear the announcement that there had been so much speculation about for such a long time, they all kept looking around for a new face to appear, but Mr. Simpson came into the conference room alone and asked for their attention.

> He began, "We are all going to miss Harry. But now we need to look ahead to the future. I know that you all have been very anxious to hear who will replace Harry in this important position. I am sorry if I've kept you in suspense for so long, but this was obviously a very difficult decision to make. In preparing for this decision, I have been doing a great deal of reading as well as attending seminars about new concepts that are being introduced in many companies today. I have been particularly interested in something called Remote Control Management and the concept of the virtually remote manager. This involved simply giving many of the traditional responsibilities of supervisors to those whom they supervise. The supervisor's roles are changing and becoming focused on strategic issues rather than the day-to-day operational responsibilities. Regardless of what you call it, the whole idea is to give people the opportunity to self-manage themselves — in other words, to make the decisions that their supervisors used to make. I believe that with the caliber and experience of the people working here that we should have no problem implementing this new concept."

> "Then who is going to replace Harry to help us work this way?" one of the employees asked.

"That's the whole point. We're not going to replace Harry, at least not with another supervisor, if that's what you are asking. Instead, we are going to replace him with a whole department of people — those of you who worked for him all these years!"

There was complete silence in the room as everyone was shocked at this announcement and the idea of Harry not being replaced. No one had ever even considered this as a possibility. Mr. Simpson asked to meet with the people in Harry's department after the meeting to further explain to them the work in this new environment. "I realize that this comes a great surprise to all of you, but I believe that once you have a better understanding of these concepts you will become much more comfortable with the whole idea. Harry and I have spent a great deal of time talking about this, and he agrees that it will be an excellent way to operate your department. He, as I do, has the greatest confidence in each of you," Mr. Simpson explained.

"So you are saying that Harry agrees that this is a good idea and that we will be able to run the department as well as he did?" asked one of the employees who had worked for Harry for years.

"Yes, in fact, we both believe that you will be able to do it even better! You will be able to because of the many benefits and effectiveness of teamwork. Instead of just one person's experience and opinion making critical decisions we will have the benefit of all of your experience and knowledge. Harry was so excited about this new approach that I asked him to come back to work with you for a while as a consultant to help you get started. In the meantime, I would like you to spend the rest of this morning discussing how you can work more effectively as a team," explained Mr. Simpson.

"I just can't believe the things I'm hearing around here today," said Mary Brooks, who had worked in Harry's department for the past 12 years, after the group was left alone to discuss the changes which were abut to take place. "I don't understand how we are supposed to take over Harry's job and work without his help or guidance."

"I don't know about that," said Tom Franklin. "I've been reading about these new concepts lately. Many companies are starting to operate utilizing these kinds of management concepts that involve giving people more responsibilities and say in how they perform their jobs. They are beginning to make the types of decisions that their supervisors and managers used to."

Roger Perkins, who was listening to what Tom was saying, added, "You know, I've been thinking about all of this, and I'm really not as concerned about us being able to continue to get the work done without having a supervisor around. When you think about it, we have actually been going in that direction for some time. Harry gave us more and more responsibility over the years. Maybe Harry had some idea this was coming years ago and started getting us prepared."

"You know, I believe you are right," added Mary. "I worked for Harry in this department for a long time, and things did begin to change in the past few years. I can think of many times Harry would answer my questions by asking me what I thought we should do."

"He started doing that with me, too," added Vince Nelson. "I learned a great deal about our operation and business as a result. There were even times when what I suggested we do turned out to be a mistake and Harry let me do it anyway, even though he knew I was wrong from the beginning. He would just say that I would learn more from my mistakes and would be less likely to make them again in the future than if he corrected me every time he thought I was not doing something the right way," he added, smiling as he remembered several such occasions."

"Perhaps we are farther along toward working this way than we may think, "said Alice Miller. "If you remember, Harry stopped giving out work assignments each morning some time ago. Instead we would have a meeting and discuss the work that was to be done and decide who would do each job. I really didn't think that much about it at the time. It just worked so well that it seemed like a natural thing to do. I guess we were beginning to become a self-managed team even then."

"Imagine, we've been a self-managed team all this time and didn't even know it!" said Mary.

"You know, I agree with Roger that it's not assuming responsibility for the operation of our department that worries me. It is all the other things that Harry or any supervisor is responsible for that I don't understand," said Tom.

"What do you mean?" asked Mary.

"Well, things like what happens when someone calls in sick and has to be replaced or how to handle conflicts that come up between people," replied Tom.

"Yea, and what about giving discipline? Are we supposed to fire people? I'm not sure I want to be part of anything like that!" added Roger.

"There's something else I just thought of. You know how Harry used to give each of us a performance evaluation each year. I liked that a lot. At least I knew where I stood with him afterward and usually he gave me feedback about how I could do my job better," said Tom. "Who's going to do this now?"

"It's getting close to noon. We had better go to lunch and then get back to work before things get too backed up. Maybe Harry can answer our questions when he is here tomorrow," said Mary.

"I sure hope so!" said Tom.

"Welcome back, Harry!" everyone said, when he came into the conference room the next morning. "We knew you couldn't stay away!" joked Mary.

"Well, it certainly is hard to leave all my friends here but I am retired now and looking forward to it. Mr. Simpson and I have talked many times about the idea of this department becoming more self-managed or managed remotely. He and I both want to make sure that you get off in the right direction. With a group with as much ability and talent as you people have, I have no doubt that you will be successful," Harry said

"We were all talking yesterday," Tom began, "and we have a lot of questions. We all feel fairly comfortable with the idea of accepting more responsibility on our jobs and for the operation of the department. Looking back, we realize just how much increased responsibility you have been giving us over the years. What we are most concerned about are the other aspects of a supervisor's job," explained Tom.

"I understand your concerns and even anticipated them. Mr. Simpson and I attended several seminars to learn more about this concept of self-management, or what's now beginning to be called Remote Control Management. We learned that there are no absolute right or wrong ways to do things. What is most important is that the employees feel sense of ownership of their team and its actions. We heard the word "consensus" used often, but with a slightly different definition than I had remembered from my school days," Harry explained. "It is important for you to work towards consensus as you make decisions together on any issues you may need to deal with, including such things as performance feedback, enforcement of rules, discipline, and even terminations."

"We're not too sure we want to get involved in some of those areas!" said Mary.

"To tell you the truth, I wasn't very happy to do many of those things myself," said Harry. "But unfortunately, sometimes they have to be done. Along with increased responsibility comes certain things you must do."

"Yes, but it is one thing for a supervisor to do those things and another for us. We still need to work with each other afterwards," said Vince.

"That's where consensus comes in," explained Harry.

"I'm not sure that all of us are ever going to completely agree on anything, particularly things as sensitive as the ones you just mentioned," said Tom.

"That's exactly what I used to think consensus meant as well, Tom. What we learned is that consensus means that everyone on the team is at least willing to support an idea, even thought they may not necessarily totally agree with it. If there is not consensus among the team members on a particular issue or decision, then a different action plan should be developed which everyone can support, or change the one you have to meet this objective. Consensus is one of the basic principles of teamwork and would serve as a guide in making these difficult decisions a team must make. However, there is more to managing a department than just enforcing the rules. Maintaining effective communications throughout the department is essential for its success. I think this is why I believe so strongly in this concept and in giving everyone more responsibility for the management of the department. When everyone is involved in decisions in an organization you cannot help but have effective communications," Harry explained.

"Are you saying that when there is a problem we should meet as a team to discuss how it should be handled and come to a consensus of what we are going to do?" Mary asked.

"I think that it should be left up to your team to decide how you are going to resolve problems. However, what you suggested sounds like a very good idea!" Harry answered.

"Yes, but the difference now is that you're not going to be there to lead us in the right direction or settle disputes and differences of opinions we have," Vince pointed out.

"I'm certain you will continue to have those disagreements, maybe even more of them at first. But I feel you need to have confidence in your ability, not only as a team but also as individuals to resolve these conflicts."

"How will we be evaluated? We always received feedback from you on our performance each year. Who's going to do this now?" asked Vince.

"That brings up a very interesting concept and approach to this type of job performance feedback that has been utilized by self-managed teams at many other organizations. It is called 'Peer Feedback' and is just what its name implies. Peer Feedback involves each of you receiving information from your fellow employees concerning your performance. This way, you can learn how you are perceived by your co-workers and how to be a more effective member of the team. You not only hear more than one person's viewpoint, as was the case when I completed your evaluations, but how your peers feel about working with you as a member of the team," Harry said.

"I'm not sure I like this idea very much!" said Mary. "I'm afraid some people's feelings may be hurt."

"There may be times when this information may not be so easy to receive or even accept. But you must accept it, particularly when there are a number of sources that say the same thing. What everyone needs to keep in mind that the purpose of this type of feedback is not to hurt people's feelings or embarrass them, but rather to help them maintain or improve their performance so they can be a more effective and contributing member of the team," Harry explained. "Besides these things that we just talked about, there are many other areas and responsibilities your team can become more involved in, said Harry.

"Isn't that enough already?" said Mary.

"I understand that all this will feel a bit overwhelming at first, but I'm sure as you get more involved in making decisions, you will grow to appreciate and even need greater responsibilities. For instance, what about when we hire new employees who will become part of your team. Who should be involved in the interviewing and selection process?" Harry asked.

"I have always thought that we should be the ones to make those decisions. After all, you are the ones that have to work with new employees and need to be involved in their selection," answered Vince.

"Like so many other aspects of working in a team environment, it just makes sense that you should be," said Harry.

"How do we get started?" asked Tom.

"I think you are already off to a good start. I would suggest that you spend the rest of the meeting talking about how you will organize yourselves regarding work assignments and how to handle the other administrative aspects of the department. I know that each of you is familiar with the paperwork and other reports required to be completed each day. I *do* suggest that you continue to meet on a regular basis to ensure that you are communicating effectively with one another. This way, when problems come up, you can discuss them right away to begin to get them resolved. Most importantly, you need to realize and remember that you are not in this alone. You have the support of Mr. Simpson and the entire organization, and when you need help all you have to do is ask. I realize that the concepts of remote-managed teams may seem brand new to you, but they have actually been around for a very long time. Remote-managed teams are built on the trust and respect members have for one another. I believe in each of you and know that by working together you will continue to be successful in the future," Harry concluded.

"I didn't want to say anything in front of Harry," said Mary, after Harry had left the team to meet by themselves. "But I just don't see how this whole idea is going to work. We are all just going to end up arguing with one another all the time. This empowerment idea might sound good in all those books and seminars that Harry and Mr. Simpson went to, but it will never work in a real-life work setting like ours. Somebody has got to be in charge around here to make sure that the work gets done and everyone doesn't just goof off all the time!"

"I agree with Mary, said Art Graham, a newer member of the team. "I have only been in this department for a few months; how am I supposed to self-manage myself when I don't even know what to do?"

"Maybe we should go talk to Mr. Simpson and tell him that we don't think that this is a very good idea. That way he can get started finding another supervisor to replace Harry," suggested Vince.

"Wait a minute," interrupted Tom. "I don't necessarily agree with that idea. As I said the other day, I've heard a lot about this concept lately, and I personally would really like to work in this kind of environment. I have a good friend who works for another company that has been very successfully utilizing this kind of a team concept for several years now and he really likes it. I think we need to at least give it a chance before giving up on it."

"Tom's right. We have to at least give this idea a fair chance," offered Roger. "I agree with the things that Mr. Simpson said the other day — that we could do the job better than Harry did."

"You had better never let Harry hear you say that!" Mary warned.

"I'm not saying anything against Harry in any way. There isn't anyone I have more respect for than Harry. What I *am* saying is that all of our experiences and knowledge working together will be greater than any one person's could ever be — even Harry's!" Roger explained.

"I guess I have to agree with that," said Mary. "In fact, there were occasions when I didn't feel that some of the assignments Harry would give to us should have been our top priority at that moment. There were many times when we had customer complaints about our service because we were not working the right things at the right times. It wasn't Harry's fault that this happened. He couldn't have known all the details that all of us knew that might have prevented these problems."

"Why didn't you say something to Harry at the time? Harry is a reasonable guy. He would have listened to you," said Art.

"I just never thought it was my place to tell Harry how I thought he should run the department. After all, he was the boss and we were supposed to do what he said to do," Mary replied.

"I guess that is what empowerment is all about, and why things need to change," said Tom. "Everyone is finally beginning to realize that the most qualified people to make decisions about a problem are those who work closest to the problem."

"We need to start talking about how we are going to organize our work and how assignments are going to be made. Harry did start giving us a great deal of freedom concerning job assignments, but he still got involved in any conflicts or problems that would come up. Who's going to do this now?" Vince asked.

"Why can't we rotate these assignments on a weekly or monthly basis? That way it would be fair to everyone," Art suggested.

"I'm not so sure that is a good idea," said Roger. "For one thing, we are not all trained on every job."

"Couldn't we ask Mr. Simpson to give us time to do more cross-training so we could all learn each other's jobs?" offered Alice.

"I'm sure he would support that idea. Particularly in the slow business season which is coming up," said Mary.

"I think that all of us learning each other's jobs is a great idea and we will function much better as a team as a result of this cross-training. However, there may be alternatives to job rotation," said Tom.

"I'm really surprised to hear you say that, Tom," said Mary. "I thought you were all for the idea of becoming more independent?"

"I am!" answered Tom. "I am not saying that there is anything wrong with rotating jobs, and it may be a very good idea for us. I just think it is more important that we are all able to do each other's jobs so when we are needed in a certain area any one of us would be able to help," he explained. "We also would have a lot more flexibility in job assignments by being able perform each other's jobs," he added.

"That does make sense," said Vince. "On a football team you wouldn't want your halfback playing on the offensive line, but you would want him to be able to block incoming linebackers coming crashing in to stop the play!"

"Vince, I knew you would work football into this discussion somehow!" joked Mary.

"You're right about that. Vince is about the biggest football fan I've ever known," laughed Roger. "But I do think he is making a good point. Many of the same factors that allow a sports team to be successful would also apply to us. We need to set goals for ourselves and work together to meet them. The most important thing is that our team is successful. If the team wins, we all win!"

"I agree, but what should be our goals?" asked Art.

"I think we need some help with that question," replied Roger, with the agreement of the rest of the group.

"Let's ask Mr. Simpson and Harry to help us chart our direction and define what our team goals should be," suggested Tom.

"This is sort of like trying to decide what we want to be when we grow up!" laughed Alice, with nods of agreement from several others.

"There is something else I just thought of. Maybe we could visit my friend's company that I was telling you all about, where they have been utilizing these concepts for several years. I'll call him tonight to see if he can set it up, if that's OK with everyone?" Tom suggested.

"Sounds great. Let's do it!" Mary and several of the others said.

The next morning, Mr. Simpson and Harry met with the team prior to the beginning of their shift. After listening to the team's request for help in setting goals, Mr. Simpson said, "One of the things we learned about moving in this direction was that it was important to develop a Vision Statement to describe what we are trying to accomplish in this process. I agree that it would be an excellent idea for your team to develop your own goals you want to achieve," he said.

"What should be our goals?" asked Mary.

"I guess I would like to try to answer this question," said Harry. "The way I see it is that how you are going to work together in the future is not going to be that different than the way things were when I was your supervisor. Think about what has been important up until now and you will see what your goals should be in the future."

"When you put it that way, creating a vision and goals for our team will not really be all that difficult," said Tom. "We still need to keep safety as our number one priority on the job."

"Also, meeting the requirements of our customers, as well as productivity and keeping costs down will all continue to be important in everything we do. I guess our goals will not change as much as the way we go about reaching them," said Roger.

"Why don't we all think about what should be included in our Vision Statement and share our ideas the next time we meet," suggested Tom. "Oh yeah, I almost forgot. My friend came through and is setting up a meeting for us to visit with his team this Thursday after work. I hope everyone can make it. He said they have helped several other companies get started in establishing their teams so they understand what we will want to see when we get there."

On the following Thursday, they all met at Tom's friend's company for the visit. They assembled in the company's conference room following a tour of the facility. John Kimble was the spokesperson for his team. "I would like to welcome all of you to our facility. Tom has told me a lot about the new concepts being introduced at your company and I believe we have many things to share that will be helpful to you. We began the team concept here about 2 years ago and we feel it has been very successful. Since then, our team has improved our productivity by 17% and our customer charge backs have decreased a total of 29%. We have also established a new safety record for the number of safe days we have worked and recently received our company's top safety award," John explained as he pointed to an award plaque on the conference room wall.

"Those really are impressive results," said Tom. "I see you have a number of charts and graphs on the wall. What do they all measure?"

"I'm glad you asked that. Our team sets our own goals for such things as productivity, quality, customer satisfaction, cost reduction, and safety. These charts are kept current by our team members and help us monitor our progress in reaching these goals," John explained.

"What happens when you reach a goal?" asked Roger. "Do you have to set a harder goal for the next time?"

"Sometimes," laughed John. "The team will get together and make these kinds of decisions," he explained.

"What other kinds of decisions does your team make?" asked Roger.

"We make almost all the decision that affect our work. For instance, we have a team meeting for about an hour each week to discuss different things that have been going on. Sometimes we invite guest speakers in to talk to us, such as the Operations Manager, Safety Director, Quality Assurance Supervisor or even suppliers and customers. We also have a brief meeting before the beginning of each day to talk about how we did the previous day and assign jobs for the shift to the team members," explained John.

"That's a big question that we have," said Tom. "How do you decide job assignments?"

"Actually, that's one of the things we decide in our daily meetings. We don't have any set rules for job assignments, just that we all take turns doing each other's jobs so we all are familiar with and able to do them all. We have a sort of pact among our team that we will help each other out in performing our jobs. This means that everyone must be able to go where the work is. For example, before we began the team concept, each person had a particular assigned job. That job had a specifically defined set of responsibilities that the person had to perform. If the person got caught up during the day, he or she was not expected to help out anyone else on their job. For one thing, usually they weren't trained or qualified on the other jobs, only on their own. This is where the benefits of the team approach comes into play. Now, everyone has been trained to perform all the jobs. When people have extra time, they go and help out another person who might be behind," John explained.

"Wasn't this difficult to get people to do?" asked Vince.

"Yes, but only at first," answered John. "All it really took was for you to realize how much easier your own job could be when others pitched in and helped you when you got behind for everyone to realize the benefits of teamwork."

"You were talking about how you assign different jobs. Could you give us more details?" asked Tom.

"That's right, I didn't go into much detail on that. Actually we have gotten away from the traditional job titles we had in the past. As I said, they had a tendency to confine or restrict the responsibilities of our employees. In our daily meetings we review the work that needs to be done that day and agree on what each person is going to do. What someone's actual job title is, is not as important as it used to be. What is most important is getting the work done, not so much who does it."

"Isn't it hard to get everyone to agree on something like that? There must be at least some disagreements about who does what jobs that day?" asked Art.

"We used to have some squabbling about who was going to do certain things, but we seemed to have gotten pretty much away from that. Actually, the way we decide job assignments is by volunteers. If the team feels someone is not sharing fairly in certain jobs, they will tell the person," said John.

"Don't people get upset when they are told this?" asked Tom.

"Yes, sometimes they do. That is why everyone tries to make sure they take their fair share of turns on all the jobs," explained John. "It is really surprising how well everyone can get along concerning things like this when you really begin working together as a team!"

Tom added. "Why don't I give some of the other members of our team a chance to share their experiences."

Kevin Jensen, who had worked for the company since it began 12 years ago, was the first to speak, "Well, I've worked here before we had teams and now that we do have them I have to say that I like our present system much better, but I would not have said that at first. I didn't think I would want the extra responsibility of making decisions that can affect our entire operation. I guess I used to think that should be someone else's responsibility. However, I have come to accept this added responsibility and even like it today. I would not want to go back to our old way of doing things," he added.

"What is it that you like about it?' asked Mary.

"I guess I like the fact that I can make a difference. Now I can use my experience and knowledge about my job that I have gained over the years. I remember many times in the past that I had better ideas about how we should do things that I never had the opportunity to share. Now all that has changed, and I give my input every day!" Kevin replied.

"How do you receive feedback about your job performance?" asked Roger. "We've been hearing a lot about a system called Peer Reviews, in which team members provide this feedback to each other."

Scott Harvey, a young man who had been sitting quietly in the back of the room replied, "We do have a system similar to what you just described. We call it "Team Counseling." Twice a year we fill out an evaluation form on each member of the team. We basically developed the form ourselves so we all agreed on what should be included and what should not be on the form. Most of the questions have to do with how effectively the person works with others and how well he or she accepts a share of the responsibilities for the work of the team. We designed the questions to address the person's work characteristics, rather than his or her personality traits. Everything that is evaluated about the person must be job related. This way everyone is less sensitive about giving and receiving this feedback," Scott explained.

"So, is this system working well?" asked Mary.

"Yes, I would say that it is," Scott replied. "We were all a little nervous about it at first, but today we all a lot more comfortable. I really feel that the feedback I receive about my performance has actually helped me do my job better. Fro instance, the last time I was reviewed, several of the team members commented that I had been trying to do too many things at the same time and not getting anything totally completed. Consequently, everyone else had to finish my work when I would run out of time. When I was told about this I realized that they were absolutely right. I am glad I know that I was doing this so I could correct this problem. We try to also provide support to team members in trying to improve an area identified as a weakness."

"Do you ever give this feedback to someone face to face?" asked Tom.

"Yes, a team member can request a special meeting to talk to the group as a whole or can just talk to certain people individually about how they evaluated his or her performance," Scott answered.

"This is really beginning to sound like a better way to evaluate our performance than the old way of only receiving feedback from just your supervisor," Mary observed. "And it doesn't sound quite so threatening to me now!"

"I'm sure you are going to find a lot of things about working in this type of work environment are not nearly as threatening or scary as they may have seemed at first," said John. "I think I speak for all of us when I say the most important thing to remember is that you need to stick together as a team and support one another. You will be amazed at what you can accomplish when you work together as a team."

"I have a question that I am very curious about," said Tom, "what is the supervisor's role in this system?"

"Let me take this one," replied Jack Craven, who had been supervisor for the company for the past 18 years. "Over my career as a supervisor I have seen my role greatly change. Being an effective supervisor used to be defined as making sure everyone did what they were told to do. Today, as part of the team concept, my role is more as a support person to the team helping others make decisions concerning what they need to do. I spend most of my time helping the team perform their work. I take care of many of the essential functions of the team such as long term planning. This may include ensuring that materials are ordered in advance that the team may need and keeping abreast of trends in customer orders and reacting accordingly. I also could be called the resource person for the team. Whenever we need to request money for more capital expenditures, I help the team members make their proposals to management. One of my major duties is to provide training for team members. Sometimes I may provide this training personally and other times I arrange for outside sources to provide it. I am finding that I don't need to spend nearly as much time in the production area as I used to. This gives me the opportunity to focus on these other areas that allow me to be much more effective as a supervisor than my old role allowed me to be. I guess you could say that I am supervising more by Remote Control! But, there are occasionally times when I still have to play the traditional role of a supervisor, although this is becoming less and less frequent."

"When would you need to do this?" asked Mary.

"For instance, I might need to step in to resolve conflicts or stalemates when the team simply can not come to any kind of consensus concerning a problem and other circumstances like that," Jack replied.

"Do you have any teams that do not have a supervisor?" asked Tom.

"Yes, we have several departments which operate without supervisor," Jack answered. "In these departments, the team members take turns serving in a leadership capacity. It is not only good developmental experience for the team members, but it gives each of them a greater appreciation of what it is like to be in this position. They tend to be much more supportive of their co-workers when it is their turn to lead the team!" he added. "In other words, everyone takes a turn in the barrel and is more appreciative of how difficult this role can be!"

"That sounds like an excellent idea for our team," said Tom. "We need to talk to Harry and Mr. Simpson about it when we get back. We don't want to take too much of your time here today, and we realize how busy you are. Thank you for all the information you shared with us. I know it will help us out a great deal."

"Of all the things we have talked about today," John summarized, "I feel the most important thing to remember is that you can not be afraid to ask for help when you need it. I am sure you will, as we do, have all the support you need from the top of your organization to be successful as a team. We look forward to hearing more about your progress and will be available to help anytime. I'll be following your progress through Tom and will give our team periodic updates," said John.

The next day the team met with Harry and Mr. Simpson to share what they had learned about the team concept and becoming more self-managed.

"It certainly sounds like you had a very successful visit. You have heard many of the same things that we learned as we prepared for these changes here," Mr. Simpson said. "I can see that you are becoming as convinced as I am that this is the best way to operate your department."

"I'm even becoming a believer!" Mary said smiling. "But we saved the best for last. We want to share with the both of you our team's Vision Statement:

The Vision for Harry's Department

Harry led our department for many years and his friendship and caring for his employees will never be forgotten. Today, we are a team and are learning to work together to accept the responsibilities for the success of our department. Each of us plays an important role in our team's efforts and everyone must share in the work equally. Each of us must help and support one another for the benefit of the team. Each of us has our own unique abilities and knowledge that we must share with the team to help us reach our goals. We must be honest with one another and provide constructive feedback to one another to help improve our performance. Harry taught us well and we feel prepared to accept these responsibilities that we have been empowered with today. We feel confident that with the support of the entire organization and Harry's continued guidance that our team will be winners.

7 Surfing the Channels

There is no doubt that the television remote control device has completely changed our viewing habits. Instead of watching just one show, you probably switch through any number of channels using this incredibly useful "labor-saving device." However, is it really as entertaining to watch television like this if you are not the one controlling the clicker? How much fun is it if someone else has the clicker and is on a "surfing safari"? Not so much fun anymore, is it?

As a personal challenge to begin learning to "let go" of authority in your life, if this is not already the case, try letting someone else in your home have control of the remote control clicker as you watch television together next time. Explore your emotions and feelings during this exercise. Afterward, go back and reflect on the following questions about this experience:

- How did it feel to give up this control to someone else?
- Did you feel that you had any ability to watch the program(s) that you were interested in seeing? Why or why not?
- Did you feel that you had to have the Remote Control in your possession to see the programs you were interested in?
- Did you watch something that you would not have normally seen? If so, did you enjoy the program?
- Was there more communication between you and the person who was in control of the clicker than usual?
- How do you think you could have had more input concerning what channels clicked on the set under these circumstances?
- Do you think that this experiment will alter the viewing habits of you and the other person who had this newly discovered control of the

remote control? In other words, do you think that you will ever get it back?

■ What have you learned about managing people at work as a result of this exercise?

If you are not typically the one who controls the remote control clicker at home, ask for it for just one evening. Reflect on this experience by asking yourself these questions:

■ How did it feel to have complete control of what channels were on the television?

■ How was this different than having someone else decide or change the channels you want?

■ Did you watch any different programs as a result of having the clicker in your control than you normally would have?

■ How do you think the usual "clicker controller" felt about you having the remote control in your possession?

■ Was there more communication between you and that other person?

■ How was it determined what you would watch? Was this different from how this decision was normally made? If so, how?

■ Overall, was your viewing experience more or less enjoyable than it is when you don't have control of the clicker?

■ Would you like to continue to have control of the clicker in the future?

■ Do you think that who will have control of the clicker in the future in your home will change as a result of this brief experiment?

■ If you were to somehow gain control of the clicker in your home, would you "manage" it differently than is presently the case? If so, how?

■ How do you think the other people in your home would feel about this change?

■ What have you learned about managing people at work as a result of this exercise?

Actually, surfing the channels can be a very educational experience. We all need to expand our horizons. Channel surfing takes us to places and shows that we would have never seen otherwise. Be it a program on fishing, cooking, art, drama, comedy, or whatever, even our momentary stop on that channel introduces us to something different. We all have a tendency to stay in our comfort zones, both in our personal and working lives. We can get stuck in a "management rut" always doing things the same old way — or at home, watching the same shows day after day or week after week. Instead of whizzing past the "back" channels of your cable offerings, spend a few minutes exploring what they really have to offer. You might just learn things that you didn't know or actually find new programs that you enjoy even more than what you typically watch.

Learning what other organizations or even other parts of your own company are doing can be an enlightening experience. These efforts are often referred to as benchmarking or best practices. They are the currently politically correct terms for stealing other people's ideas! But these are ideas for which others do not claim copyright or ownership and which they are willing to share. Most people are proud of what they have accomplished working together as a team and are happy to help others achieve the same results. As they say, "imitation is the greatest form of flattery." This was the case when the employees in Harry's department visited Tom's friend's company to learn from their experiences. They learned that their concerns and challenges were not unique. As one person was once heard to say, "It seems that we have the same problems, but under different rocks!" Often seeing that someone else is actually achieving what you are striving to do can motivate you to reach your own goals. Benchmarking can make the impossible seem possible when seeing it being practiced in real life! You may also see different practices and skills being utilized that you never considered before. Instead of "reinventing the wheel" you can start from a different level and achieve greater success. So often, we keep looking under the same "rocks" for different answers to our problems. It is not until we expand the world of possibilities that might exist to finding solutions to our problems that we can really make progress in eliminating them and preventing their recurrences. It is like the old saying, "If the only tool you have is a hammer, you tend to see every problem a nail." What benchmarking and best practices do is to give you more "tools" to use in achieving your goals for organizational change.

However, leaving what you are comfortable and used to is much easier said than done. Even the chair that you sit in at home to watch your favorite TV programs can become a habit nearly impossible to break. Do you ever feel like Archie Bunker on the classic TV show, *All in the Family,* about a "lovable bigot," as you ask others to let you have your favorite chair? Archie, of course, never felt the slightest remorse when he ordered his son-in-law (unaffectionately referred to as "Meathead") to get out of his chair. To him, it was a right that was bestowed upon him like a throne. In fact, this chair became such a symbol of American culture of the times that it is now on display at the Smithsonian Institute.

To further demonstrate just how difficult it is to change what you are comfortable with and used to doing, try the following brief exercise that Archie certainly would have had problems completing and no doubt would have greatly upset him. First, fold your arms in front of you as you normally would do. Now, repeat this exercise, this time reversing the way that you fold your arms. If you normally place your right arm over your left, instead fold your left arm over your right. How does this feel? Probably, it is very uncomfortable. Try this same exercise with your hands interlocking your fingers together. Now, reverse the way you do this. Again, it is probably very uncomfortable as well. How many times do you think you would need to repeat this exercise before it would become natural? They say that it takes 21 times to make something new really a habit. But do you really think that a lifetime of folding your arms left over right or right over left can't be reversed in just 21 repetitions?

How, then, can it be expected that work habits acquired over an entire career as a manager or supervisor can be reversed in a brief period of time? The obvious answer is that this would not be a reasonable expectation. Becoming a Remote Control Manager is something that must be approached with both patience and a plan. This plan needs to part of the overall business strategy of the organization. This should be part of the Sanctioning and Design Team functions of the organization. To simply command that managers and supervisors will change a lifetime of management habits as part of some new program just announced would be like expecting them to never fold their arms the same way again starting tomorrow. It would be like trying to move Archie out of his comfortable chair.

This is another reason why "bottom-up grass roots" approaches to organizational change do not normally work very well. It is only through a top-down approach to organizational change that issues such as the role of the manager or supervisor can adequately addressed. First, you must ensure that they understand what it is you are expecting of them. Again, what they will hear may sound something like this, "We are going to have the people who work for you make most of the decisions that you have been responsible for on your job all these years and we want you to help us to do this. By the way, we don't have a clue as to what you will be doing in the future in this new scheme of ours, but don't worry, you are going to play a very important role. We will tell you about it as soon as we figure it out for ourselves!" Telling managers or supervisors that you will explain to them exactly what their new role in the organization will be as soon as you figure out what it will be just doesn't help them become motivated to work towards the success of this plan. Making it worse is asking them to *trust* you while you figure it out. Until you can explain just what this vision is that you have for their future, they won't feel very confident or secure.

This vision should be projected about 3 years ahead; after that it would probably be purely guess work. In this "high beam" view ahead, the role of the managers and supervisors needs to be defined in as precise terms as your current understanding of the changes being introduced will allow. An excellent source of data for this future vision can be obtained from the "Today and Tomorrow" exercise. Their future role is obviously to be found on the "tomorrow" list. Once this has been identified, you can begin working *backwards* to develop a plan for providing the support, training, resources, etc. necessary to allow them to evolve into this new role. As always, the more that those who will be directly affected by this process are involved in its design and implementation, the more supportive they will be.

Beginning with the top of the organization, everyone's new roles and responsibilities need to be identified and explained to everyone affected by these changes. It should be the responsibility of the top management of the organization to either identify these new roles or sponsor this function to be completed. The Steering and Design Teams can be invaluable in achieving this objective. It is not fair to those whose job's will be directly affected (which is probably just about everyone in the organization) to begin this process until a through plan has been developed and approved. To do otherwise will only cause confusion, false starts, and disappointment. In the absence of such plans, organizations often become quickly disillusioned by these concepts because they have not done anything to support their success.

Again, there is no "magic dust" that can instantly transform an organization from where it is today to its desired goals. These goals must be established, approved, designed, implemented, and supported in order for success to be achieved. All this doesn't happen without at least some sacrifice and pain. As much as we would like to guarantee that no one will be adversely affected by the organizational changes that are being introduced in the workplace, this may not always be possible. For example, at a small electronics company, the concepts of self-management and remote control were introduced. The President of the company, when announcing these changes, told a group of managers that no one's job would be lost as a result of these new concepts.

Unfortunately, he soon learned that he could not keep this promise. With his guidance, the company developed a strategic plan for implementing these changes and developed the necessary steps to begin the process for changing the roles of the managers and supervisors in the organization. Decisions were beginning to be moved to lower and lower levels closer to where the work was being performed and to the real experts. Almost everyone had adjusted to these changes. That is, everyone but one manager named William. William just couldn't seem to understand what was expected of him in this new organizational design. While other managers were learning to become more focused on longer term strategic issues rather than day-to-day operational tasks, William continued to want to lead in the same way he had for the past 20 years. This soon became a significant problem, as often William's actions were inconsistent with the way everyone else was now trying to operate. Often his actions were counterproductive and even destructive to the team atmosphere that they were all trying so hard to achieve. It became apparent to the company's president that he needed to take action or everything he was trying to achieve would be threatened by William's failure to adapt to the new corporate culture that had been created. After wrestling with every alternative he could think of, there finally was no other recourse to take but to end William's employment. The president called William into his office to give him the news that he would be terminated. This was made even worse because of the statement the president had made as these new concepts were being introduced into the organization.

More appropriately, the president should have told the supervisors and managers that the new concepts being introduced were not designed or intended to eliminate anyone's job. However, everyone must be committed to learning to adapt and work in the this new empowered environment. There might be those who would have problems adapting and they would do everything that they could to support people in this transition. However, just like so many other things in life, there can be no guarantee that no one will be adversely affected by these changes.

In another company, a similar story occurred, where a supervisor with many years of service also struggled with the role that he was expected to play in the new organizational design based on remote control management principles. After several years, it became apparent that he was not going to ever successfully make the transition to becoming a remote control supervisor and his employment, like William's, was also terminated. When the Human Resource Director told him the news and began reviewing his termination benefits, the supervisor interrupted him and asked this question.

"I don't understand what is going on here anymore. I've been with this company for many years, almost 17 in fact, most of that as a supervisor. When I first became a supervisor, everyone used to tell me what a good job I did. In fact, I have a file full of commendations for the work that I did. I even got a letter from the plant manager of this facility at the time, telling me that I was one of the very best supervisors that he had ever worked with. Then a few years ago, my performance evaluations began going down in their ratings. This kept going on until it got to the point last year that I was in the lowest performance category, which meant if I didn't improve I would be fired, which just happened. What I am most confused about is that I never changed. Why was the company so pleased with me for so long and now firing me for the same things I always did as a supervisor?"

"The problem is obvious," said the Human Resources Director. "It is the fact that you never changed that led to your termination today."

Problems in adapting to change are not just confined to those in management and supervisory positions. After an organization similar to the one in the story, Harry's replacement had introduced the concepts of empowerment to the hourly workforce, one woman came into her supervisor's office and turned in her resignation. The supervisor was upset by this news, as he felt that she was an excellent employee and contributing member of the team. She had seemingly adjusted to the new requirements of the job and had worked hard to acquire the skills she needed to operate in an empowered, team-oriented workplace.

"I don't understand why you are quitting," her supervisor said. "We don't want this to happen. You are one of the best employees we have in our department and would miss you very much if you were to leave."

"I appreciate your saying that, but I'm not sure I really am suited very well to work in this type of work setting," she said.

"What do you mean? As I said, we are very pleased with your work and contributions to the team."

"That's just it. I'm not sure I can continue to work as part of this kind of empowered team anymore. It used to be that I just came in and did my job and left. I never really gave this place a second thought once I walked out these doors until the time I had to come back to work. Now, since empowerment was introduced around here, I have to make all sorts of decisions that I never even dreamed that I would be making. I go home at the end of my shift and find myself worrying about decisions that I made at work. Sometimes I even call the operator who relieved me to see how the decisions I made during my shift turned out. I don't want to live like this anymore. I want to find someplace else to work, where I can just put in my time and let someone else worry about all the important decisions that have to be made!"

The lesson to be learned from these stories is that sometimes people are negatively affected by changes made in the organization as it moves more towards concepts such as empowerment and remote control. One of the worst ways to introduce any new concept, be it empowerment, teamwork, reengineering, quality, or any other new idea is to disguise as something else that would otherwise be perceived as negative. Sometimes it might be believed that a reduction in workforce or some other reorganizational initiative would be more accepted if presented as associated with some other overall objective for the organization. But this approach only serves to confuse everyone concerning what is really going on.

If you need to make reductions in the workforce, then make them, and call it what it really is — a reduction. Don't bastardize concepts such as empowerment or remote control by using them as a "smoke screen" for something else less desirable. Make your reductions first, then begin introducing empowerment or whatever you want to move towards. Don't try to introduce both at the same time. You will only taint everything that follows with the same negative influence as the reduction. This may be the case of guilt by association but it still can be just as influential as in other life situations. In one major corporation, the term "Reengineering" was used interchangeably with a major restructuring effort at one of their major divisions. The word soon took on all the negativity usually only associated with the layoffs and terminations that were occurring at the time. Reengineering became a euphemism for "someone is going to be gone soon from the organization!"

Adjusting the Volume

Sometimes you need to adjust the volume for different channels you click on via your remote control. Some programs may be better viewed with the volume turned way up, and others are more enjoyable with it serving more as background sound. Different channels sometimes seem to broadcast their audio at different levels, also requiring these adjustments to be made to the volume on your television set as you surf through the channels. In the old days before remote control, it is probably safe to say that the sound level on television sets wasn't adjusted nearly as often when someone had to actually get off the couch and turn the volume knob. The Remote Control Manager must also make a *volume adjustment,* so to speak, concerning those his or her areas of responsibility. Like the term that truckers use concerning turning on their CB radios to communicate where the "smokies" are along the highway, you need to put your "ears" on. A Remote Control Manager's ears are possibly the most important tool he or she has to perform the job. However, merely hearing what others have to say isn't nearly enough. What is required is to really listen to what they are trying to tell you. This, like so many other aspects of Remote Control Management, is not an easy task or skill to learn.

The average person spends approximately 70% of his or her time communicating with others in one way or another. Of this time, 16% of it is spent reading. In our society today, we are taught to read even before we begin our school days. Children's television programming such as shows mentioned earlier, begins introducing these concepts in fun and creative ways, including huge yellow birds, grumpy characters that live in garbage cans, or pigs who are vain about their looks. We spend 9% of our communications time writing in some manner. Depending on your job, this amount would greatly vary, but it still makes up a certain percentage of all of our communications time. Much of our education is focused on helping us learn to express ourselves in written form. Talking occupies about 30% of our communications efforts. Although not everyone may have been a member of the school's debate team or have taken a public speaking class, we all do get some training in this area. In every home, a child's first words are met with the pride and adulation usually reserved for presidential inaugural addresses or graduation speeches. Speech teachers come into our grade school classes to correct our lazy "S's" or other problems that might be more easily corrected at an early age. However, we spend the majority of our communications time *listening,* approximately 45% of this time. But most people receive little or no training in their lives learning to become better listeners. Listening is the most important communications skill needed, both at work and in our personal lives. It is erroneously assumed that if someone knows how to hear that they also know how to listen. Unfortunately, this is not necessarily true.

In many societies, the most severe punishment that can be imposed upon someone is to be isolated or "shunned" by the rest of the community. Our prison systems use solitary confinement as a variation of this punishment as one of the severest of all penalties to be placed on a prisoner. All of us have a tremendous need to be paid attention to, and we become frustrated when we feel that our thoughts and ideas are being ignored. People at work also have this same basic need, naturally wanting to share their knowledge and experience and be recognized for these contributions. Often, these attempts to be "heard" are discouraged rather than encouraged, more by inattention than by any other factor. "If nobody is going to listen to me around here, I'm not going to waste my time giving them my suggestions anymore!" is a common emotional frustration experienced by many employees.

Becoming a successful Remote Control Manager requires you not only to hear what others are trying to share with you but to really listen to what they have to say. This requires not only giving others your undivided attention but listening with an open mind. If you have already made up your mind on how something should be done, then it is likely that no amount of persuasion will move you from your position once you have dug yourself in. This may be in the face of perfectly sound logic being presented to you that clearly contradicts your current thinking and rationale.

Becoming a Remote Control Manager requires you to accept the notion that other people may know something that you do not. This doesn't take away from your expertise in your field, your managerial ability, or your self-esteem. It only makes sense that others who are closest to where the work is being performed are going to acquire some degree of expert knowledge in that area. To deny this is closing the doors to an abundance of information and knowledge accessible to you just for the asking.

But this can be difficult for either party. There are just so many obstacles in the way of these messages being heard. One of the major problems with listening is that we can only speak at a rate of about 150 words per minute, but we can hear at a rate of about 4 times that level. Apparently our brains can move much faster than our tongues! The result of this phenomenon is that this gives us a lot of extra time! What we do with this extra time is the difference between effective listeners and those that hear only what they want to hear. A skilled listener spends this time really trying to understand what the other person has to say. This listener considers the emotions, circumstances, experiences, and point of view of the other person. A poor listener allows his thoughts to drift away to other things that might be on his mind. This, too, is an easy thing to do. The average high school student has an attention span of about 10 seconds. As adults, we do only slightly better with an average of 17 seconds. Thus, it requires a great deal of discipline to really give someone your undivided attention.

We also listen with our eyes more than we normally ever realize. Studies have shown that we receive 55% of a message from someone's nonverbal language, or, in other words, their body language. This includes facial expressions, how one motions with his/her hands, the position one is sitting or standing in, etc. Approximately 38% of a message is received via one's voice inflections or tone. This is how our messages are heard. And incredibly, just 7% of a message is received from the actual words or vocabulary a person uses. Thus, a Manager can say one thing to those who report to him and have an entirely different meaning perceived by his audience. This can happen because his words are not consistent with his body language or tone of voice. Based upon these percentages, it is clear which of these hidden messages will make the greatest impact and impression. How many times have you heard someone say something, and when they left you said yourself, "I heard what was said but I don't think that is really what was meant?" For communications to be truly credible, all three of these communication elements — *nonverbals, voice inflections,* and *actual words* must be consistent.

To demonstrate this point, try this exercise with someone you work with whom you would be willing to have help you become a better communicator (for some people, this could be a long list!). Repeat the following statement, four different times, each time giving it a different meaning, at least to you:

"I want you to make these kinds of decisions."

The four ways to communicate this message are:

1. Statement indicating that this is solely your idea.
2. That you want to ensure that it is no one other than the other person making this decision.
3. This particular type of decision is the only kind of decision that you want the other person to make.
4. Indicating that it is your strong desire that the other person makes these decisions, but not to take any other action.

Have the other person write down what message they heard after each repetition of this statement. Compare and, possibly, contrast what the message was that was heard and what was intended by you. If there was less than 100% agreement on the intended message and the message perceived, this represents the communications gap that so frequently exists throughout the organization. The problem is that extremely important information gets misinterpreted on a daily basis as messages are transmitted throughout the organization. As you would surely agree, there are significant differences in each of the four interpretations of the statement above. Different perceptions of these differences can cause tremendous problems and losses to the company. Trust between a manager and his or her direct reports can easily and quickly be eroded by a single misunderstanding that was no one's fault, but rather simply different perceptions. Sometimes people *do* tend to hear their own selected versions of the truth. Truth, we come to learn, can be multidimensional. It depends on what side of it you are on. Regardless, it is still the truth to the person who is experiencing it. Perception is reality to the individual. Ultimately, it matters far less what you meant to say than what others think you meant. It is like the picture of the rabbit or the duck. If a person sees a duck in the picture, then it is a picture of a duck — that is, unless you can help the person see that there may also be a rabbit in the picture. This is one of the most important criteria of establishing effective communications and understanding of others. You must understand what "picture" they are perceiving from you and how that compares to the one you thought you sent.

Meanings are really found in people, not in the words themselves. It is how the person perceives the meaning of the word that is most important. But there can be so many variations and meanings of the same word that this can become a very formidable challenge. The *Oxford English Dictionary* records an average of 28 separate meanings for each of the 500 words most used in the English language.

For example, consider the word — **fast.** The following are just some of the possible meanings of this word:

> A person is **fast** when he/she can run rapidly.
> But he/she is also **fast** when he/she is tied down and can not run at all.
> And colors are **fast** when they do not run.
> One is **fast** when he/she moves in suspect company.
> But this is not quite the same thing as playing **fast** and loose.
> A racetrack is **fast** when it is in good running condition.
> A friend is **fast** when he/she is loyal.
> A watch is **fast** when it is ahead of time.
> To be **fast** asleep is to be deep in sleep.
> To be **fast** by is to be near.
> To **fast** is to refrain from eating.
> A **fast** may be a period of not eating or a ship's mooring line.

Photographic film is **fast** when it is sensitive to light.
But bacteria are **fast** when they are insensitive to antiseptics.

There is an statement that for years was often cited as an excellent example of poor communications. Although, the creator of this statement is not known or no one want to admit to ever saying this, a good guess might be that was from a high ranking politician! It goes like this:

> *I know that you believe you understand what you think I said, but I am not sure you realize that what you heard is not what I meant!*

What do you think this person was trying to say? Perhaps the person was trying to express his/her frustration at not being able to communicate with others very clearly. Based on what we see from this statement, that person had good reason to be frustrated! But the real problem was that there probably was an intelligent thought disguised in this twisted question and struggling to escape. The question you might be asking yourself is, "Do any of the messages you receive from those that you report to in your organization often sound like this?" Or worse yet, "Do any of the messages I send sound like this!!!"

Even when we *do* communicate clearly, people have a tendency to hear what they want to hear or perhaps more accurately, what they expect to hear. The following exercise demonstrates this point.

Repeat the answers to the following questions out loud three times.

1. You tie things down with a _____, _____, _____.
    (answer should be "rope")
2. A soft drink that begins with the letter C is called a _____, _____, _____.
    (answer should be a "coke")
3. The white of the egg is called the _____, _____, _____.
    If you answered "yolk" to the third question, you were incorrect. The white of the egg is not the yolk, it is actually called the albumen or egg white but most people incorrectly answer this question as "yolk." Why? Because "yolk" more or less rhymes with "rope" and "coke." It follows the pattern or sequence that has been established. It fits. Often, in our normal communications we make erroneous assumptions that, just because something fits into a pattern or our expectations, it is correct. This obviously is not always necessarily the case.

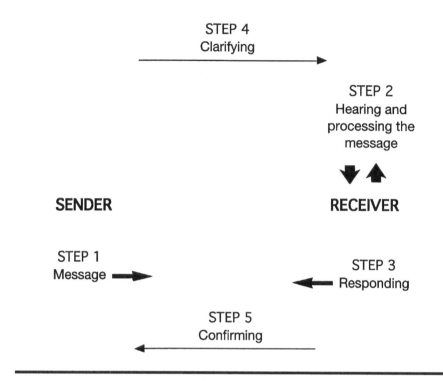

Remote Control Communications Model

A model for effective communications can be helpful to a Remote Control Manager in preventing at least some of these pitfalls and allowing for clearer, more understandable interactions with others. There are any number of communications models that have been developed over the years. However, a simpler model showing the basic component of effective communications can often be the most useful. The following is such a model that can help the Remote Control Manager achieve more effective communications (Figure 7.1).

In this mode, the 5 steps necessary for effective communications to take place are shown. In step 1, the Sender of a message verbally sends the communication to the Receiver. In other words, some kind of conversation has been initiated by the Remote Control Manager. This could be a request for information, a question, a directive, sharing of information, small talk, or just about anything. Step 2 involves the Receiver not only hearing the information contained in the message but processing this information as well. This can often be the most difficult step in the entire communications process. As just discussed, there are many barriers to this message being received the same as it was transmitted by the Sender. In addition, there may be physical barriers which further inhibit the accurate reception of the message. The world seems to be getting noisier each day. It getting harder and harder to find a quiet place to have a meaningful conversation with another person. Particularly for the Remote Control Manager, it is likely that this communication is being done remotely via some type of electronic transmitting device such as the telephone, pager, cell phone, intercom, or even a teleconference. All of these can create potential obstacles to the successful transmission of the intended message from Sender to Receiver. Also, as we become more and more global in our management responsibilities, language may play an important factor in this communications model.

Unfortunately, typically the communications process ends at Step 2. A message is sent, and it is assumed that it was fully understood by the Receiver to the complete satisfaction of the Sender. Obviously, this is not always or usually the case. Ending the process at this point causes almost all of the problems and breakdowns we have in communicating with one another. This invariably results in subsequent conversations that go something like this-

Sender: "I thought I told you I wanted X to be done?"
Receiver: "But I thought you told me to do Y!"
Sender: "No, I clearly told you I wanted X."
Receiver: "That's not what I heard you say."

Again, there could be countless reasons why this Receiver may have heard Y when the message was intended to be X. What is most important is that Y is what the Receiver perceived to be the message. Perceptions are reality to the Receiver. How could this misunderstanding have been avoided? The answer is found in Steps 3, 4, and 5 in the model. Unless the person receiving the message responds at the time of the communication demonstrating his or her understanding, there is really no way of ensuring that the message was understood as it was intended. The Sender has no way of knowing if the Receiver heard X or heard Y. Consequently, Step 3 in this process is critically important. This gives the Sender the opportunity to clarify what the Receiver said he or she heard (Step 4). Finally, confirmation of the successful delivery and receipt of the intended message is achieved in Step 5 of the process.

Utilizing all the steps in this model, the above communication between the Sender and Receiver might go something more like this:

Sender: I would like you to be responsible for this new account we just landed. (Step 1)

Receiver: I hear what you are saying and think I understand what you are asking. (Step 2)

Receiver: I believe you are assigning me to the new account. (Step 3)

Sender: I am doing more than assigning you; I want you to be responsible for everything associated with this new account. (Step 4)

Receiver: OK, now I do understand. I am to be completely responsible for this account. (Step 5)

You are probably thinking to yourself that there is no way that you are going to go through all five of these steps every time you need to communicate with someone, right? Obviously, this may get to be more irritating to others than useful. What is most important are the basic concepts of the model. For example, it is possible that in this last dialogue between what appears to a manager and a subordinate, if the process had ended at Step 2, there would have been a significant misunderstanding on what the assignment really entailed. It was only through the clarification and confirmation stages of this interchange that there was agreement and understanding concerning what was really being asked. To the extent that a Remote Control Manager can encourage and develop this level of communications with those that he or she works with, the less misunderstanding there will be about expectations on everyone's part.

One doesn't necessarily need to be educated in the intricacies of this model in order to be an effective communicator. There was a Supervisor who worked in a textile mill in North Carolina who practiced the concepts of the model for over 30 years and who probably never had any formal supervisory training — except his own common sense. Every time he would give one of the employees he supervised any kind of instructions, he would pause and then ask them to tell him what he just said. It didn't take very long before they realized that they needed to pay very careful attention to everything that he told them as they would immediately be tested on their understanding. Eventually, this supervisor had a production crew of the best listeners in the company!

The Laws of Forgetting

Unfortunately, even your best communications efforts can be all for naught if you factor in the great likelihood that people will forget what you tell them under most typical circumstances. For example, studies have shown that people forget 25% of what they hear immediately. This is very disturbing news, when you consider all the effort that you might have put forth trying to provide this information to others! However, there may be a bright side to this situation. Perhaps things were set up this way for a reason? Think about the amount of information that is being communicated today. Could anyone ever possibly absorb or process all of this data? Certainly not. Our brains actually serve as a sophisticated sorting and filtering mechanism which regulates what information we retain and discard. The only problem with this system is that sometimes the information we want to be retained is discarded, and what we would like to have been discarded is retained! Still not quite a perfect system.

The news gets worse. We forget 75% of what we hear within 2 months. Perhaps this is the usage test. Like the old saying, "If you don't use it you will lose it." As new information is constantly pouring in, storage room must be freed up to retain it. It is sort of like your clothes closet at home. If you don't wear a particular item of clothing for some period of time, you eventually will discard it to make room for your most recent purchases.

Wait — there's even more bad news. Of the 25% that we *do* manage to remember, only 60% will be accurate, plus we tend to add things that were never said in the first place. This is where the expressions such as "having a selective memory" or "telling his own version of the truth" come from. When you think about making up things that were never said in the first place, the existence of the "rumor mill" comes to mind. Why is it that everyone loves a rumor so much in every organization? What is it that makes rumors so appealing? Perhaps it is once again the tremendous need people have to be "in" on things. They appreciate hearing things that are "nice"-to-know as opposed to only that which they need to know. Sharing "nice" to know information with those who report to you builds trust and rapport with them. It also slows down the Rumor Mill, making it less of a necessity by replacing speculation with factual information.

How accurate the Rumor Mill is in any given organization is anyone's guess. Studies have shown it to be approximately 75% accurate. While at first this may seem like a rather high percentage of accuracy, is it really? How would you like all of the information you receive at work to be only 75% accurate? Although you may be saying to yourself that would be an improvement over what you presently receive, in truth this would surely not be acceptable. What if your paycheck was only 75% accurate? Directions to the hotel from the airport? How your name was spelled on your office door? If you ever want to test just how accurate rumors that get spread throughout your organization are, try the following exercise. Write down some event that is about to occur in the organization that you know about but that others may not. At your next meeting, pass this slip of paper to the person sitting next to you. Allow them to read the information on the paper but do not allow them to keep it. Tell that person to verbally share this information with the person sitting next to him or her but to not allow anyone else to hear. Tell each person to continue this exercise until everyone has privately heard the message. When the message has traveled completely around the room ask the last person to hear it to share what they heard with the rest of the group. Compare what this person says with the original message you originally wrote on the piece of paper. How similar do you think that the message will be as heard by the last person to receive it in the room to how it originally was written?

The most curious thing about rumors is how much faith many people put in them. Perhaps it is like another old saying, that "there is a little truth in every rumor," that gives them so much credibility. It is not unusual to find people who would be far more likely to believe a rumor heard in the office regardless of how preposterous it may sound than anything that the company may officially communicate.

The Laws of Remembering

Fortunately, there are laws of remembering as well as forgetting. The first is the Law of Recently. We remember best what we heard last. In many ways, all of us are communications experts in our own right. If we were not, we would never have been able to achieve any of the successes we have experienced in our lives. We are already aware of this concept and most likely practice it on a frequent basis. For instance, what is it you say to someone after giving them important instructions on something before you part company? Probably, you say something like, "And don't forget what I told you about making sure that we meet the customer's deadline," or "Remember to be sure to call when you get there." We want this critically important information to be the last thing they hear from us to make it more likely to be remembered.

The second law of remembering is Frequently. We remember what we hear most frequently. The information that we use on a daily basis at work is usually quickly remembered. We easily remember our addresses, telephone numbers, directions to our offices, names of our co-workers, etc. But do you still remember the telephone number of someplace that you might have lived 10 years ago, other than where you grew up? It is probably less likely that you would remember that number, particularly if you haven't had any use for it for the past 10 years. Another good example is your Social Security number. Most people can easily recite the nine random digits of their Social Security number. Why do they remember such a thing? Because you frequently are called upon to provide this number as part of your everyday life. If you didn't have it memorized you would have to keep looking it up and slowing down the processing of things important to you such as applications, passports, insurance claim forms, etc. But what about another far less frequently used number in your life, but one that might have equal if not greater importance — your driver's license number. Could you recite this number without looking? Most people probably can not. But it is an important number. Trying cashing a check without it or not having it available when you get stopped for speeding by a State Trooper. Most people do not know this number by heart because it is used relatively infrequently. And when it comes to needing this number to show to State Troopers, the less often the better!

Impact is another fundamental of remembering that relates to how things are presented to us. This is perhaps why certain songs we hear seem to stay with us for many years. Dramatic lines from television shows and movies can often be recalled years, even decades, later. For instance, what was the most famous line from the Clint Eastwood movies about a detective named Dirty Harry? Almost anyone could identify this line as, "Go ahead punk, make my day!" But for many of us, we may not have seen this movie for over two decades. Why would we remember such a thing? It is just something about Clint Eastwood's dramatic impact while talking to you with a gun pointing in your face that tends to stay with you for a while. We also remember that which has the greatest impact on our lives. We remember significant experiences, particularly those that shape and direct our futures.

Finally, we remember that which we have the greatest **application** or use for. This may be similar to the concept of frequency, but with a slightly different twist. We may not use something with great frequency, but when we do, it is something that really sets itself apart. Again, the comparison between your Social Security number and Driver's License number would be appropriate examples. You have a greater application for your Social Security number than your Driver's License number, and thus more readily know it. Your birthday may be another similar example. There may actually only be a limited number of occasions each year when you are actually required to provide this date, but when it is needed it is critical to accomplishing whatever task you have undertaken. It is a useful if not essential piece of information needed to go through life.

The following is a story about a young CEO who learns about the need to not just hear but really listen to what others in the organization had to say.

Another Viewpoint

At the age of 41, Stephen Madison had become the youngest Chief Executive Officer in the company's history. He had established an impressive performance record for the company with sales nearly double those 5 years ago when he first took over as CEO. He had the reputation of being a smart businessman who was not afraid to try new things. He was a dynamic young leader who was well respected and liked by nearly everyone who worked for him. He was also known to be very aggressive in his management style and accustomed to getting his own way.

Under Stephen's leadership, the company had undergone many changes. Like so many other companies, there had been a major restructuring of the organization in the past several years. The result was a more streamlined and efficient organization better able to succeed in the increasingly competitive marketplace. However, these changes created greater demands on everyone on every level of the organization. Stephen was constantly searching for new ways to improve the organization and develop the employees to be more satisfied with their jobs and better able to meet these increasing demands. He had recently learned more about the successes that other companies were achieving through empowering their employees to have greater decision-making and problems-solving responsibilities and accountabilities concerning their jobs. He was so excited about the potential benefits of these concepts to the organization that he decided to introduce the subject at his next meeting with his staff the following week.

> "Good morning ladies and gentlemen, "Stephen began the meeting. "I'm going to get right to the point. We are going to begin empowering our employees in our organization and this is how we are going to do it," he told the group.

> Stephen's staff was very interested in the subject their boss had just introduced. Most of them were familiar with the concept of empowerment and these success that many other companies were experiencing with this management philosophy. However, accustomed to working for Stephen, they were used to simply listening to how things were going to be done in their company rather than participating in the decision making process.

"Miller, call a meeting of all the company's Human Resource Managers for next week so we can tell them about this new program. I've already contacted a consultant recommended to me to talk to your group on how to get started. He's available next week. You can call him after this meeting and make the necessary arrangements," Stephen instructed Tom Miller, the corporation's Vice President of Human Resources.

"I don't think that next week is a good time for the meeting," Tom Miller said. "I know of several other things going on that will cause scheduling conflicts, and besides, that is not very much notice about the meeting. The Human Resource Managers are all extremely busy these days and I think we should at least give them enough advance notice about meetings so they can rearrange their schedules with the least amount of disruption to their operations."

"Next week is the only time the consultant is available and that is just because someone else canceled. If we don't get him next week, it will be at least 6 months until he is available again, and I'm not going to wait that long," Stephen said, interrupting Tom. "I know there is a great deal going on in your area right now, but I think that this needs to be your top priority. Every day the competition is getting tougher and tougher. If we are going to remain competitive, we must find better ways to manage our operations and better utilize the talents of our associates on all levels of our organization," Stephen explained.

"I agree completely with the whole idea of moving in this direction. In fact, I have been doing research of my own on this subject, and several of our locations already have empowerment programs in place. I'm just concerned that if we are going to formally introduce these concepts throughout our entire organization, we don't get off on the wrong foot. I'm not sure changing everyone's schedule at the last minute for this meeting is the best way to get started in moving in the direction of empowering our associates. As a matter of fact, it may be perceived as being contradictory to the very principles we are trying to promote," Tom tried to explain.

"Like I said, this is the only time that the consultant is available. There is no choice. Your people will just have to understand. The meeting has to be next week," Stephen ordered, as he was completely out of patience on this subject.

This discussion and interchange between Stephen and his staff was not unusual. Typically, the decisions and action plans for the company were made by Stephen. His direction for the company was usually correct and produced favorable results. The problem was that no one, not even Stephen, can be 100% correct all the time. There are many situations when a variety of viewpoints and experiences are beneficial and needed. This situation was further aggravated by the fact that Stephen did not recognize that this was a problem. From his perspective as CEO, he believed that it was his responsibility to lead the organization and make decisions. Although this was certainly true, Stephen did not yet realize or appreciate the need to empower others in the organization who may be in a better position to make certain decisions which affect their areas of responsibility and ultimately the entire corporation.

"Now let's move on to other business," Stephen said. "Henderson, I want you to change your marketing plan to include a greater concentration in the southwestern part of the country, based on a report I just read," Stephen ordered as the remainder of the meeting continued in a similar manner.

After the meeting, John Henderson, Vice President of Marketing, and Tom Miller talked on their way to the elevator. "I think that empowerment will be a good thing for our company, "John said. "We are all aware of the benefits of empowering our people and allowing them greater ability to be involved in their jobs and in making decisions that affect our entire operations. I think that we are just beginning scratch the surface of the potential talents of our people. "I just hope that these concepts will be utilized on all levels of the organization."

"You mean like on the vice-presidential level?" Tom knowingly replied.

"Exactly!" said John.

The following week the meeting with the consultant was held at the corporation's headquarters. The Human Resource Managers from all of the company's locations were contacted and told they were to attend.

"What's this meeting all about?" Jack Sterling asked Clyde Anderson, another Human Resource Manager, as they took their seats in the conference room shortly before the presentation was to begin. "I didn't really get much of a chance to look at the agenda or material that was sent out. We sure didn't get much notice about this meeting. I really had to do some scrambling to rearrange my schedule to be here today. What was so urgent they had to rush us here without any advance notice?"

"As I understand it, we are going to talk about the idea of establishing Empowerment throughout our organization. They brought in some expert to talk to us about these concepts and how to begin moving in this direction. I don't know either why this was set up in such a rush. I had to cancel several very important things to be here myself today. My guess would be that the boss ordered that the meeting would be today and wouldn't take 'no' for an answer!" replied Clyde Anderson, who had flown in from the West Coast to attend the meeting.

"That sounds typical of the way we do things in our company nowadays! At least at our level in the organization," replied Jack Sterling.

"I agree. Maybe the ideas and philosophies we are going to hear about today will help us become more involved in the decision-making process concerning what the policies are going to be from the top executive level of the company," replied Clyde.

"I'm not so sure when they talk about empowerment that they are thinking about our level of management. My impression is that they just assume that the higher you go in the organization the more empowered you become. You and I know that this is not necessarily true!" said Jack.

"I agree with you on that point as well. A good starting point would be to empower us to be able to set and keep our own work schedules and time commitments!" Clyde answered, as their conversation was ended by the beginning of the presentation.

"Good morning. I'm Charles Bradner, President of Bradner Associates. We are a consulting group specializing in helping companies like yours in beginning the process of change necessary to achieve an organizational culture supportive of empowerment," Charles Bradner said to the group of Human Resource Managers. "It is a pleasure to be with all of you today and I appreciate you all being able to attend on such short notice." There was a considerable reaction from the group as a result of his last comment, interrupting him for a moment as he waited for the noise from the audience to quiet down before he could continue his presentation. "I believe the things I have to share with you today will not only be interesting to you, but also extremely helpful as you move toward a more empowered workforce and organization in the future. First, I would like to share with you some of the basic principles of empowerment."

The consultant wrote the following on the padboard:

E veryone

M ore

P articipate

O nging

W e

E xcited

R esource

M easurable

E ffective

N atural

T eam

"Now let's look at each of these principles in relation to the others," Mr. Bradner continued. "**Everyone** must be **more** involved and **participate** in the management of your company and in making decisions which affect their jobs and the organization. This must be an **ongoing** process in which your associates view the organization as '**we**' as opposed to management vs. the employees. Empowerment will allow your associates to become **excited** about their work, finding it more challenging and rewarding as a result of their increased involvement. Your people should be a **resource** to your organization providing valuable input resulting in **measurable** results concerning how to become more **effective** and efficient. You will find that empowerment is a **natural** part of the **team** process in which each member plays an important role."

During the remainder of the day, the consultant had the Human Resource Managers break up into small groups to discuss the changes which needed to take place in order to achieve empowerment in their organization. With the help of the other Bradner Associates representatives attending the meeting, each Human Resource Manager developed his or her own specific plan to begin this change process.

Charles Bradner concluded the meeting with the following comments, "Today, each of you have developed a comprehensive plan designed to help your organization utilize your most important resource — your people. Everyone, regardless of their position in your company deserves to be treated with the same amount of respect and appreciation. Each of us needs to be given the opportunity to fully utilize our abilities and talents to reach our highest potential for the benefit of both the individual an organization. The empowerment process we have begun today will help you reach this very important goal. Many companies like yours are finding that their leaders must manage their businesses more from a distance than ever before. This new concept of Remote Control Management must be based on these same principles of empowerment. The role of leadership will always be critical to any organization's success. It is the way leaders lead that is changing. Leaders today are finding they can't always be physically present to make sure things run smoothly. They need to manage more remotely, utilizing concepts such as empowerment to meet the increasing demands and scope of their jobs."

After the meeting, Jack Sterling and Clyde Anderson talked about the presentation. "I feel that I have a much better idea of what empowerment and remote control management can do for our organization and am looking forward to establishing these concepts in our facility," Jack Sterling said.

"I agree," said Clyde Anderson. "But, I still would have appreciated more than a week's notice about the meeting. This is just one example of the type of things that need to change in our company. We need to have more respect for the capabilities of everyone on all levels of our organization," he said.

During the next several months there were many changes made throughout the company. Their associates were given greater opportunities to make decisions and share their ideas and experiences. There were already measurable improvements in the company's performance as a result of these changes. Needless to say, Stephen Madison was very pleased with this progress.

"Call Miller and make arrangements for me to visit one of our facilities so I can meet with some of our associates to learn more about these changes that are taking place through empowerment and what that consultant called 'Remote Control Management.' I've got time next Tuesday. Tell him to make the necessary arrangements," Stephen told his secretary.

"Mr. Miller is not going to like this short notice again!" the secretary thought to herself, but she knew better than to say anything.

Stephen Madison and Tom Miller were met at the airport by Jack Sterling as they stepped off the corporate jet the following Tuesday. At Jack Sterling's location, empowerment, and Remote Control Management was achieving very impressive results. Since the concepts were introduced a few months earlier, they had already turned their operation from one that had been losing money for the past several years into a profitable one. Jack Sterling had arranged for a group of associates from their most successful department to meet with them. Stephen had a keen interest in anything that could have such a turn around effect on the performance on one of the company's poorer performing operations and looked forward to their presentation.

> "It is a pleasure to be here today," Stephen began the meeting. "I have heard many good things about what your team has accomplished during the past few months and I would like to add my personal appreciation and congratulations to each of you. Today, I would like to learn more about how you went about achieving these successes and what changes were made that allowed them to happen."

Jack Sterling began with an overview about the way they had introduced the concepts of empowerment at their location. He explained that they began with meetings for all associates and their supervisors to talk about everyone's present roles in the organization and how they should change in the future to improve both the quality of the associates' jobs as well as the effectiveness of their organization. Everyone agreed that the idea of giving associates more responsibility concerning their jobs was the natural and right thing to do. They began to identify the most important tasks which needed to be performed and who should be responsible for each function. Each associate began rotating job assignments according to a schedule developed by the team. This way everyone gained a better appreciation for each other's roles and responsibilities, as well as developing greater job-related skills. The end result was an organizational structure different from what they had traditionally been accustomed to, but one in which each associate felt a greater sense of ownership and part of the entire team. Communications throughout the organization had been greatly improved by informational meetings held by the Operations Manager with all the associates on a monthly basis. Daily team meetings were being conducted in every area to discuss the work that was to be performed and receive input from associates about how it should be accomplished. Many of the duties that had formerly been the responsibility of supervision were now being performed by those who reported to these positions. Supervisors were now doing more planning rather than troubleshooting as they typically had done in the past. They were beginning to become Remote Control Managers, finding that they could now focus their attentions on more strategic issues rather than day-to-day activities. As a result, many potential problems which could affect the customer were now being identified before they occurred and corrected. There was a great sense of pride throughout the organization in what they had accomplished working together as a team.

The group was a bit reluctant at first to speak up, with such important visitors present, until Kyle Davis, a young man who had been with the company for less that 3 years was the first to speak.

> "I think what has made a big difference is that we are now given the chance to make decisions that we never had in the past. Instead of the boss telling us what we are supposed to do and when we are supposed to do it, we now make these kinds of decisions on our own. Even after being with the company only a few years, I still have many ideas about how I can perform my job better and make our operation run better."

> "I feel like we are being listened to more now than before these changes were made," offered Shirley Smith, who had been with the company for over 25 years. "After all these years, I am finally being asked what I think, rather than just being told what to do. We've all had a lot of good ideas about how we can make things run better around here but we never were really given the chance to be heard before."

> Stephen asked, "Could you give me examples of some of the changes that are making such a big difference since we began introducing these new concepts in your workplace?"

> "Well, just last month I made a suggestion that involved the way we receive orders from customers," Shirley Smith offered. "For years we have been sending orders back and forth between departments in our organization unnecessarily. I guess we were doing this to try to make sure the order was allocated to the right department, but the end result was the customer getting upset because of these delays. I came up with a new system that ensures that the orders are being processed correctly and in a timely manner, sometimes cutting the order cycle time in half."

> "That's great!" said Stephen. "What did your supervisor say about your suggestion?" he asked.

"Both my supervisor and the Facility Manager thanked me for sharing my suggestion. They said they wished that I had not waited so long to come up with my idea to change the order-processing system, as we could have prevented a great deal of problems caused by delays in meeting our customer's orders over the years. We have even lost some customers because of these delays that we would not have happened with this new system. I told them that I did think of it 5 years ago and have been trying to get someone to listen to my idea all this time!"

Everyone laughed at her story, including Stephen. "Listening to what people have to share concerning their work experience and knowledge is perhaps a way to better utilize our company's most valuable resources — our associates' ideas. I'm beginning to realize that this has been an significantly under-utilized resource for a long time!" Stephen concluded.

"Before you leave, Mr. Madison, there is something I would like to share with you," said John Hawkins, an associate of the company for 10 years. "I would just like to say that I think what you are doing with our company is the best thing we have ever done. I now feel a greater sense of ownership for my work and my area of responsibility than every before. I now know what my responsibilities are and am able to have more control over how I am to meet these responsibilities. I know that it is up to me to see that my work gets done and done right. If it doesn't, then I have no one to blame but myself."

"I think that it is just a matter of having respect for people and their abilities," added Shirley Smith. "I believe you get back what you give in life. If you treat people with respect, that is what you will get back! Respect isn't something that just people on your level of the company need. It is something that everyone needs," she said. We all need to think more about how we would like to be treated and extend these same courtesies to others that we work with. There really isn't anything new in what you are calling managing by Remote Control. It really is nothing more than the Golden Rule that we all learned as kids in grade school."

On the flight home that evening, Stephen was uncharacteristically quiet. He was thinking about what he had heard from the people they had visited earlier that day. "I guess if there is anything to be learned from the visit today it is that how we treat our associates can be the most important factor in our success as a company. Everyone needs to be treated with respect on all levels of our organization, just like Shirley Smith taught me today," Stephen finally said as he turned off the overhead reading light and shut his eyes.

> "I wonder if he really understands that people at the higher levels of the organization need to be treated with respect as well?" Tom Miller thought to himself as he reviewed his notes from the day's visit.

> "Tom, I would like to have a staff meeting as soon as possible to discuss this visit and get a progress report on what is happening at our other facilities concerning our associates having more control of their jobs as we saw today and our managers manage more remotely. I wonder if the same things that Shirley Smith talked about today are also an issue other places in our organization. Please check with everyone and see when it would be most convenient for us to get together again and let me know the date for the meeting. I'll move my schedule around to accommodate whatever is best for everyone else."

> "I think we are finally beginning to make some progress!" Tom thought to himself.

Remote Control Communications

Television programming today is becoming much more than merely entertainment. We receive many different types of communications via our television sets. Much of this information is communicated to us via commercials, infomercials, and news reports. Again, taking lessons from television's tremendous ability to keep millions of viewers in touch with what's going on in the world each day, let's look at each of these communications tools as a Remote Control Manager might in his or her organization.

Commercials

Commercials are the lifeblood of the television industry. Even channels that don't depend on private sponsors still have their own version of commercials. For example, the pay movie channels spend most of the time they are not actually showing movies promoting themselves and their service. Even the public broadcasting channels still try to get into our wallets through pleas for pledges and donations. Everyone has something they are trying to sell or promote; it is only the delivery method and approach that changes.

What does the Remote Control Manager want to promote or sell? What's on their agenda, so to speak? For the Remote Control Manager, the process itself is what would be most important. The Sanctioners in the organization may not be completely "sold" on the idea of managing from a distance as the concept promotes. They may consistently need to be convinced that this is the best way to manage the organization and that the company's assets aren't being put unnecessarily at risk. To some extent, either to a greater or lesser degree, those who are being managed remotely may also need to be frequently "advertised" about the benefits to be achieved through this management approach. This is not to imply that there should be anything less than a "truth in advertising" standard involved in these internal commercials, but sometimes, people need to be reminded of the benefits of what they are buying. Often, the features of the product go unnoticed by the buyer unless the salesperson points them out. The car buyer may not be aware of the special safety features that are part of the structural design of its frame. The beer consumer may not realize that his favorite brew contains less calories than the largest competitor or that the recipe was handed down from the founding fathers of our country.

Similarly, employees who are part of a Remote Control Management system may not realize all that they have accomplished working together. They would appreciate hearing more about their accomplishments that may not be readily apparent to them. They would also enjoy being presented in a favorable light to the upper levels of the management of the organization. Who wouldn't? Just think about what a commercial for a team managed by Remote Control might be like? It might just go like this:

Remote Control Commercial — *Take One*!

Announcer: Managing by Remote Control features benefits never realized in the more traditional methods of management.

Pictured is a team of employees in a meeting room discussing a work problem. They are charting data on a padboard, noting the trends that they have observed. Their voices are now able to be heard as the announcer stops talking and music fades. You can hear them discussing the numbers that are being analyzed on the chart, each person taking a turn to speak and supporting each other's observations. There is a sense of camaraderie and cooperation among the team members. Spirits are high, and everyone seems to enjoying the role they are playing. The camera begins to zoom in on one particular team member until it is focused solely on this person.

> *Team member:* I'm glad to be part of this team today. Since we began managing our department this way, all of us have taken on greater responsibilities on our jobs. Our manager no longer needs to constantly be checking up on us or telling us what work we need to do. In fact, we only occasionally ever see the manager anymore. We realize that he has many other responsibilities and doesn't need to be involved in every detail of the work we perform. He has provided the training and support we need to work independently and responsibly.

The camera pans back to the entire group, as they continue to discuss the problem they are working on.

> *Announcer:* Remote Control Management is enabling everyone to add value to their jobs. The manager is now able to work on more strategic issues that will help move the organization towards its goals. You won't see him in this scene. He is working on how he can make this organization better able in the future to beat the competition. He has empowered those who work for him to focus on meeting the requirements of their customers today and solving any problems that might arise. He is available if they need him and provides the support and resources the team needs to be successful

The camera again focuses close-up on another team member, as she turns to the audience viewing at home.

> *Team member:* Remote Control Management makes all of us feel like we are a more important part of the team. I feel like I am making a much greater contribution at work and even look forward to coming here each day. Remote Control Management is helping everyone be more successful including the company.

> *Announcer:* Remote Control Management — giving everyone more control of their jobs.

Informercials

What would it be like if there was one of those informercials that you see late at night, that try to sell you on all the wonderful features of the product they are advertising but in an informational format. These paid advertisements sometimes deceptively confuse factual news reporting with selling. If only everything they claimed their products can do was true! Our lives truly would be better as they claim they could be! The following is a paid advertisement on a product that can help you become a Remote Control Manager. Please have your credit card number ready when you call the number on the bottom of the screen to order.

"The Following is a Paid Advertisement ..."

2:30 a.m., Saturday morning. The late show and last of the decent movies are over. Only test patterns or a soccer game from Bolivia is on the remaining channels your cable offers.

> *TV Announcer:* Are you tired of the same old management style in your Organization? Are you working harder but enjoying your job less? Do you feel that no one appreciates the job you are doing?

Pictured is a manager sitting at his desk with papers strewn all over it. He has his sports coat off, tie undone, and hair disheveled. His telephone is ringing, pager is going off, computer's printer spitting out E-mail messages by the dozen, fax machine spilling recently received documents onto the floor, the secretary is bringing even more documents into his office, and the boss has just sent someone down to tell him that she wants to see him right away.

> *TV Announcer:* Does this seen look familiar to you? Are you at the end of your management rope? Then try Remote Control Management if you want the very best. Remote Control can help develop your staff to reach their highest potential both as individuals and as a team. Learn how to how to delegate in a way that makes others glad they have more work to do. Turn even the most negative employees into highly motivated business partners. Give your work group that drive that enables professional sports teams to become champions. Turn average employees into superstars. Become the

envy of your peers as they watch you shoot up the corporate ladder on your way to a really high paying job at the top.

The next scene shows the same manager from the previous scene, but this time his office is as neat as a pin. His desk has nothing on it, his telephone is quiet, and no one is rushing into his office with urgent requests. He has his sports jacket on and every hair is in place. He is leisurely chatting on the telephone, laughing at something the person on the other line has just said.

> *TV Announcer:* This is what the Remote Control Manager, easy-to-use, 12-step process can do for you. Turn chaos into productivity, complaints into compliments, waste into finished product, down-time into efficiency. Get control of your job and your life.

Become a Remote Control Manager in just a few minutes a day. Today we are pleased to be able to provide this limited offer to learn how to master these incredible new management skills. But hurry, this offer will only be available for a short period of time. Be the first in your company to use this amazing concept and become the envy of the corporation. Call this toll-free number to receive more information and learn how to order the Remote Control Manager system. All major credit cards accepted. If only it was really just that easy!

News Reports

Most of us have learned to depend on our local as well as network news programs to provide us with the information we need to live in our world today. We may tune into the morning news shows, watch the evening news with our favorite anchor person or stay up to catch any late breaking stories on the 11 o'clock news. These programs give us a summary of what's happening not only in our area but around the nation and world. We are provided the latest sports scores and what to expect the weather to be in the immediate future.

Where does a Remote Control Manager get his or her news? Information is the most important tool that a Remote Control Manager can have. Where the Remote Control Manager gets this information and how accurate and reliable it is, become some of the most critical aspects of being able to effectively lead others in this indirect manner.

Thus it is critical that a Remote Control Manager is "tuned in" to what is going on in his work world around him. With the virtually limitless ways to stay in touch today, there really is no reason for a Remote Control Manager not to be able to keep informed about what is going on in his area(s) of responsibility. Again, just because a manager may not be there physically he or she is not absolved of managerial responsibilities. It just changes the way these responsibilities are carried out. But this style of "downstream managing" is almost totally dependent on the quality of the information that the Remote Control Manager receives.

Our electronic and computer age today is constantly providing new and more effective tools to communicate with one another and thus constantly providing new opportunities to manage remotely. The Remote Control Manager has communications tools that just a few years ago were not available were available or only to a select few. For example, today most managers have the capabilities to utilize fax machines to instantly transmit documents anywhere and anytime. Fax machines are becoming as common as the telephone, being found in homes, small businesses, your local sandwich shop, everywhere!

The personal computer is revolutionizing the way we communicate both at work and at home. The popularity and populating of the Personal Computer in nearly every workplace has created the capability to send accurate, current, and detailed information in just seconds to recipients anywhere in the world via E-mail networks and the World Wide Web. The PC is also connecting the world on-line through the Internet, transforming offices and homes into virtual libraries and storehouses of information at the mere push of a button. Eventually, the Internet will have as great an impact on our lives as such innovations as the telephone and television had in shaping our present culture and lifestyle. Organizations are developing their own intranet systems which link together all of their facilities through a common database, accessible to anyone on the system. Electronic mail is beginning to become more and more popular as a replacement for internal "paper" flow, eliminating the expense of physically moving documents from location to location and the delays involved in this process. On-line "chat rooms" are popular today with people who want to link up with others with similar interests around the world to discuss or learn more about a particular subject. People can have on-line access to celebrities. Video conferencing is beginning to become more and more a practical reality for businesses as well as individuals, as Internet technology is providing more and more possibilities.

In addition to the world of possibilities that the Personal Computer and its laptop mobile version has created, there are still many other new ways for the manager today to stay in touch with those in remote parts of the organization. Cellular telephones are making it possible for you to be in touch with anybody just about anywhere, anytime. Traveling no longer needs to take you out of touch of what is going on back home. Pagers can deliver messages to you anywhere you may venture on this globe via communications satellites providing you with a wide variety of information and options.

Any or all of these communications tools can be utilized by the Remote Control Manager to provide the "News Reports" needed to stay in touch with what is going in his or her areas of responsibilities. The amount of detail that the manager chooses to stay informed about will vary from one individual to another. Some managers want to stay abreast of the details, while others may instead prefer only summary reports. This is more a matter of style than anything else. The most important factor is that the Remote Control Manager remain in communications and in touch on some level about what is going on in those locations where he or she has empowered others to work more independently.

The Remote Control Manager may not be present but he or she still needs to be accountable for understanding that aspect of the operation for which he or she is accountable. To the extent that the Remote Control Manager utilizes these new communications tools, the more effectively he can find that balance between being involved and being absent at the same time. Again, Remote Control Management is not abdication of responsibility, but a different way of being accountable. Communications and information are critical to achieving this objective.

The greatest advantage that these new ways of communications provide is the ability for the Remote Control Manager to be many places at the same time. Electronic messages allow everyone to instantaneously send and receive information. The Remote Control Manager can be virtually "beamed" into many locations, at the same time utilizing the new technology available today. The Remote Control Manager's "grasp" today can extend much farther than his "reach" of just a few years ago. Building trust from a distance can be enhanced by the use of these new electronic communications tools.

However, these new communications tools can also become a problem to the Remote Control Manager as well. Staying too closely connected electronically to those areas for which you are responsible can become counterproductive to the objectives of Remote Control Management that you are trying to achieve. You need to be able to maintain an appropriate distance from your direct reporters to enable them to be able to make their own decisions. The proliferation of the personal pager worn by so many people today is possibly doing more to inhibit the concepts of Remote Control

Management than to help it. Here's a challenge — turn off your pages or leave them at the door. This is similar to what outlaws were required to do with their gunbelts on the old TV westerns before they came to town.

Should, Could, Would

It is sad, but unfortunately true, that common sense isn't always common practice in business today. Inconsistencies, illogical decisions, violations of policies or even laws are experienced on a daily basis by employees on all levels of an organization. This creates a gap between what **should** be, what **could** be, and what **would** be in the organization. This gap is similar in nature to that mentioned in the beginning of this book concerning organizational capability and individual competencies. In these gaps lie the opportunities to improve and grow.

Also unfortunate is the fact that often we get caught in the middle of these gaps. We get so frustrated with what should be, could be, and would be that it is hard to stay motivated to continue to improve and grow in our jobs and careers. The Remote Control Manager is vulnerable to these same problems.

Managing in this way can bring with it many uncertainties. There are many things that might become obstacles to trying to work in this way. These might be characterized as the "should be's." Examples of shoulds might include such things as the following:

> "There **should** be more training provided to employees so they can perform all the tasks we are asking them to be proficient in today."

> "I **should** have more support from my boss in order to manage others remotely"

> "There **should** be more resources committed to this process."

> "Someone **should** make it clear what is expected of me in this position."

> "I **should** get paid more money for the job that I am doing."

Should statements like those above do little or nothing to help any of these situations or circumstances. They are basically merely problem statements and not much more than complaints. And there is typically no shortage of complaints in most workplaces!

What is needed is to turn **shoulds** into **coulds.** This can do more than simply put words together that happen to rhyme. The following are the previous **should** statements that have been rephrased into **coulds.** Notice the difference from their original format and the actions that they can create.

"If we don't have time to do training during the workday, we **could** work overtime to get it completed."

"If I provided more information to my boss about what I am trying to accomplish, I **could** have a better chance of getting his support to go forward with this initiative."

"I **could** make sure that the right people are aware of the resources that we need for this project."

"I **could** go to my boss and ask specifically for direction and guidance."

"If I **could** add value to this job, I would have a stronger argument for getting more money."

Finally, you need to identify what **would** happen if the **should's** and **could's** were achieved. The following are the would's that would result from each of these statements:

"More training **would** increase productivity and efficiency."

"Getting my boss's support **would** enable me to be able to do this job in half the time."

"If we had the resources we needed, we **would** be able to get this project up and running ahead of schedule."

"If I understood the direction this job is to go, I **would** be able to make better decisions concerning what I need to do."

"If I found ways to add value to this job, I **would** be more satisfied, get better results, and would please my supervisor."

Filling the Gaps

The challenge for the Remote Control Manager is to fill these gaps between **should, could,** and **would. Should's** make people feel that they are victims.

Everything seems to be out of their control. They are instead completely controlled either by other people or circumstances. They have learned to be helpless. The more a Remote Control Manager can help others stop being victims and start taking control of their own working lives, the more successful everyone will be in this process. Using the "Should–Could–Would" model below, identify each of these factors as they might be viewed by those that you supervise. Begin with the should's, then could's, and finally the would's. Use this model to help the people you supervise to begin thinking in terms of **could** and **would,** rather than simply as **should.** Identify the gaps that exist between each of these factors — in other words, what needs to be done in order to go from **should** to **could,** and **could** to **would.**

The Should–Could–Would Model

Should—(gap)→Could—(gap)→Would		
(What's wrong?)	*(What you could do)*	*(What would happen if you did?)*
_____	_____	_____
_____	_____	_____
_____	_____	_____
_____	_____	_____
_____	_____	_____
_____	_____	_____
_____	_____	_____

Remote Control Programming

The videocassette recorder or VCR has also revolutionized not only our television viewing habits, but even our lifestyle. Now, in the comfort of our living rooms we can view recently released movies on video cassettes, instead of standing in long lines to buy tickets or sitting in crowded movie theaters in back of people with big hair blocking our view of the screen! The VCR has also given us the capability to shift time around in our lives. No longer do we need to miss our favorite programs or live televised events because of other commitments in our lives. All we have to do is program our VCRs and choose when we want to watch the programs of our choice rather than to have this decision dictated to us by the TV Guide's programming schedule for the week. VCRs give us tremendous options and flexibility to choose the time and date of a number of different programs to record while we are away from our sets. The only problem for many of us is trying to figure out how to actually program the damn thing!

Recent studies have shown that the vast majority of VCRs in our country today are right now flashing 12:00 where the current time should be displayed. Several innovative companies have tried to simplify this process with voice command systems, but even they can be intimidating. The manufacturers repeatedly claim that you do not need an electrical engineering degree to program your VCR or that "even a child could do it." Yeah, right! The fact is that our homes are full of electronic devices with capabilities that we may not nearly be utilizing to their fullest potential. Unfortunately, we may be doing the same thing with many of the employees who work for us. Like VCRs in most homes today, both the manager and those who report to them have many more capabilities than those probably being utilized at the present time.

Often, it is just a matter of investing the time and energy to learn to use all of the features, and it is not as complicated as it first appears. Like anything else, programming your VCR gets easier with practice and experience. Similarly, you may need to reprogram your Management VCR. But this VCR stands for **Variable Core Responsibilities.** The biggest obstacle you may face is how comfortable you presently are with the way you manage today. This is called your **Management Comfort Zone.** It is what you identified as your management style on page 89. No matter how hard we try, we can never completely alter this comfort area for ourselves. We may learn new skills, attend countless seminars, change our habits, and improve our relationships with others, but there will always be that giant invisible rubber band that is trying to pull us back to where we are most comfortable. Being aware of this phenomenon is important, because it can present itself when we may be least expecting it. Often, stress or other emotional situations will drive us back to this comfort zone. For instance, multilingual people tend to swear in their native tongues.

Moving from our management comfort zone takes a bit of getting used to on everybody's part, but others, including those who report to you, will in time become more comfortable with these changes as well.

Reprogramming Your Management Variable Core Responsibilities (VCR)

Instructions:

Step 1 First, identify the management responsibilities that you wish to empower others to learn to accept. This may require some additional skills and tools to be utilized.

Step 2 Let everyone who is directly or indirectly affected by these changes know what you are planning to do. Make sure that this communication is in all directions. It is very important that this step is not skipped. Extremely important in this part of the process is to have the support of your boss. Omitting this step could cause major problems with this reprogramming later on in the process.

Step 3 Continue these discussions with your boss about what your new role can and should be in the future. Both of you need to have a clear understanding of how your job will be affected and changed as a result.

Step 4 Get input from those whose jobs will be affected by these changes concerning the best ways to move these responsibilities to them. Identify what training is necessary, what resources are needed, what communications are required, and other support to be provided.

Step 5 Identify a transition period for these responsibilities to be transferred. There may need to be some duplication of efforts before these responsibilities become totally reassigned.

Step 6 Ensure that those who have assumed these new responsibilities are both comfortable and competent in performing them. Do not move on to the next step until this has been completed.

Step 7 Give those involved in this transfer process the chance to perform these responsibilities on their own. Provide frequent feedback, particularly in the beginning of this process, and coaching as needed.

Step 8 Keep in mind that you will need to repeat this process for yourself as your core responsibilities are changed by your boss.

Reruns

What would television be without reruns! There might just be a lot more empty air time! When you think about it, television embraced the concept of recycling long before the environmental issues ever came into vogue. Reruns are actually nothing more than recycled programs. Doesn't this make you wonder why reruns are so often the best shows on TV to watch? Maybe this is because the networks can't resell the bad programs that nobody wanted to watch in the first place. What we see in reruns is often the best shows from a previous season or even era of television. Without reruns our children would never have the chance to see Lucy working on a chocolate packaging and trying to eat all the pieces that were passing her by too fast to wrap or get stuck in a giant meat freezer and come out as frozen as a popsicle!

As a manager at work, you may also experience reruns of sorts. In this spirit of conservation of resources, let's call these **Recycled Lessons in Management.** Actually, when you stop and think about it, we are usually challenged with basically the same problems over and over again, but with different variations — the same problems but under different rocks. The difficulty is that often we fail to recognize them as being familiar and try to find unique solutions, when we already know what the answer should be. Thus, we constantly are learning the same lessons over in both our personal and work lives. Reruns might be fun to watch when there isn't anything better on TV, but most of us are far too busy to constantly be repeating the same mistakes and never learning from these experiences. An example of a Recycled Lesson in Management might be time wasters that many of us experience. These may include poor planning, lack of organization, unclear priorities, lack of delegation, etc. After we get done working frantically as an important deadline approaches, only barely meeting the time requirements, you would think that we would learn our lesson! But, sure enough, we find ourselves in the exact same predicament on the next major project.

A Remote Control Manager needs to break this cycle and maximize the learning opportunities that are presented to him or her. It is in these lessons that some of the greatest personal and professional opportunities for growth may exist. A good way to **capture** these valuable lessons in to record or log them somewhere for future reference. To begin this process, try using the following format to keep these lessons for future reference.

Remote Control Manager's Recycled Lessons in Management Log

Recycled lesson	Date	Action taken	Results	Do differently next time?

Your Career As a TV Show

Imagine for a moment that your career is a television show! When you think about it, there are many similarities and comparisons that might be made. For example, both your career and a TV show involve a cast of characters who play various roles. Some of these roles are very important, while others are more supportive and in the background. In both, there is a certain amount of "behind the scenes" activities that have to occur before any production can begin.

In both your career and a TV program, someone needs to provide financial support for it to continue to exist. There needs to be someone in charge, directing what happens to the main players and the scenes in which they will appear. This leader must ensure that overall, the objectives and goals of those who are providing this support are constantly being met. In either case, it will be the customer who ultimately decides if either is successful or not.

Answer the following questions concerning how you would envision your career as a television show:

- If your career was a TV show, which one (either currently of the air or not) would it be?
- How could your career be adapted to fit the story line of the show?
- How would the star of the show play your career? Would this role be funny, suspenseful, mystery, etc.?
- What would be the plot?
- What part would your boss play in this TV show about your career?
- What would be the season's final show be about in order to hold viewer's interest until next season begins?
- What might be a "spin-off" show that your career might create?

Ten Steps Toward Remote Control Management

As in any process, there are certain steps that you need to take to be able to reach your ultimate objective or destination. The following are 10 steps to help you begin this process or expedition (as opposed to a journey!) of becoming Remote Control Manager.

Step 1: Establish what your working relationship will be like with those who report to you as part of your Remote Control Management initiatives

It is important to make it clear to everyone what you envision your working relationship will be. This may involve how much detail you may expect from them relating what is going on in their areas of new responsibilities. It may also address what kinds of decisions you are empowering them to make. However, again you need to make it clear that you are not abdicating your overall accountability for the function of the operation or business you are empowering them to manage. You are still an important part of the management process. Your accountabilities have not changed, only the way you will meet those objectives — through others. This should establish the basis of your working relationship together from this point on in the remote control process.

Step 2: Set and communicate clear expectations

Let people know what you are going to hold them accountable for and what they will not be accountable for. It is important to tell them the goals that you expect them to achieve, the timeline that they have to accomplish these goals, and how they will be measured against this goal. People also need to have an idea of what the results of reaching the goal will be. So often, unclear expectations concerning goal accomplishment only lead to frustration and disappointment. People also need to know what the consequences are for not reaching a goal. If they are going to be severe, this certainly needs to be communicated. This way, there should be no surprises at the end concerning outcomes either positive or negative.

Step 3: Manage the way you say you are going to manage

If you say that you are going to manage by remote control, then you need to do it. Sometimes organizations present themselves as being an empowered work culture, when in reality they are more traditionally managed than anything else. This can happen for any number of reasons, such as a lack of agreement within the organization's hierarchy concerning which philosophy they should follow. In some circumstances, there may be an advocate of empowerment concepts in a high management position who is setting expectations for the culture of the organization. However, if this vision is not implemented throughout the organization, this label may be attached to various aspects of the system merely to placate the executive. Conversely, there may be a lack of support from the upper levels of the organization that prevents the full implementation of the concepts, such as empowerment. This can create a situation in which people feel that they have to disguise or even hide what they are doing to give employees more responsibility and decision making ability. Thus, it is important that you "walk the talk." If you say that you are going to manage by remote control, then don't show up all the time and try to make all the decisions for everyone! This will only confuse everyone and cause them to lose faith and trust in you as their leader. It would be better not to create any expectations than to have them only turn out to be false.

Step 4:   Expect and create excellent communications of a frequent basis; become a good listener

You should let people know how often you expect them to communicate with you and in what ways. Set up some kind of routine communications schedule to ensure that you are in regular contact with those whom you are going to manage remotely. The more predictable these communications, the better. This way everyone can incorporate these communications opportunities into normal work routines and know when they can ask for or share important information with you. Let people know what kind of information you expect to receive and in what detail. However, if you begin asking for too much detail, you might run the risk of negating the very concepts you are trying to achieve. Your direct reports will have to develop methods to gather and share this level of detail with you, thus necessitating a great amount of effort for possibly limited return. It also will give everyone the feeling that you are checking up on them.

Perhaps the most important communications to establish is for you to be a good listener. Don't prejudge or jump to conclusions before you have heard all of their thinking and rationale. Remember why you wanted to establish a Remote Control Management culture to begin with. Keep in mind, they are there — not you! You need to appreciate their point of view and opinions. This doesn't mean that you can't still overrule those whom you have empowered to make decisions. You are still accountable. But if you are going to do this, it should be done only with a full understanding of those people's thinking and rationale.

Step 5: Visit remote locations and talk to people in person

Just because you are a Remote Control Manager, it doesn't mean that you should never show up! People want to have access to their leader. They want him or her to understand what is going on in their part of the organization. They are proud of their accomplishments and want to show them off to the boss. The trick is not to show up so frequently that it appears that you are just "checking up" on people, or so seldom that it seems that you don't care. Somewhere you need to find the appropriate balance between these two extremes.

Step 6: Be receptive to changes suggested by people working at remote locations

Again, these people are there all the time and you are not. Don't reject their ideas too quickly and without understanding them. Often, managers get caught in a sort of **time warp** concerning change. In other words, they remember another time, possibly when their job responsibilities took them closer to the problems being reviewed, when the factors and circumstances were different. Their current perspectives may have made sense at that time but no longer are valid. However, they can't seem to mentally get caught up. They continue to see that part of the organization and decisions affecting it as it was, not as it is today. This is a common occurrence when managers are promoted through various positions that now report to them.

As a manager you need to rely on expert judgment. As a Remote Control Manager you should realize that in many cases this judgment is not your own, but that of those whom you have empowered.

Step 7: Become linked electronically to remote locations

As discussed earlier, technology is making it more and more possible to manage multiple locations remotely. You need to take full advantage of this technology and use it in creative ways. The possibilities are virtually limitless concerning the amount and frequency of the information that can readily be made available to you. This information can be "real time," meaning constantly current as you access it. One word of caution, be careful that you manage this information and it does not manage you. You can find yourself still micromanaging remote parts of the organization with all these data. You can easily find yourself trying to do something based on this information and again negating what you are really trying to accomplish by giving those closest to this information the ability to act upon it.

Step 8: Share your authority

Authority needs to be shared and delegated to those you empower. With empowerment needs to come at least some authority. This is perhaps the greatest act of faith that you can give to someone. An individual must be allowed to have the authority to make the types of decisions and take the necessary actions that enable him or her to perform his or her job in a remote control managed work environment.

Step 9: Be an advocate, not a critic, of your remote locations

Sometimes managers get frustrated with the performance or lack thereof, of certain locations for which they are responsible. They may begin to place blame or unduly find fault with the people who are assigned to the location. Perhaps they do not want to accept responsibility for the location's lack of success. Rather, they point fingers at them, even "bad mouthing" them for their shortcomings and failures. In short, they become their greatest critic.

It is much more productive to be an advocate of the people at the remote locations that you manage. Talk positively of their notable efforts and provide support in helping them achieve better results. As much as you might like to in these types of situations, you still can not abdicate your management responsibilities and accountabilities as they relate to these remote locations.

Step 10: Provide remote locations with the resources they need to operate

As a manager, you probably are constantly receiving requests for additional resources from everyone who reports to you. It is part of your responsibility to protect and conserve the organization's financial resources as much as possible. When you are not there, it is often easy to lose touch with what is truly needed to operate and what is not. It can be difficult to discern this information as all funding requests naturally come to you as being essential to one degree or another. This, again, may be more a matter of perspective than anything else.

Regardless, it is very important that you ensure that remote locations *do* have the resources they need to effectively operate. You need to compare what the requesting location has in relation to other similar locations to ensure that they are being treated fairly. "Fair" in this context means that they have the same potential capability to produce equally or better than others who already have the resources. If not, it is not fair to expect them to produce at the same level unless there is some other way in which this gap can be filled. It would be foolish economy to save money by denying resources causing a particular part of the organization to be put in a competitive disadvantage situation. In the long run, you may lose much more than you save.

Challenges Facing the Remote Control Manager

With the trend towards increased workloads, limited resources, and greater profitability goals in many organizations today, there is no shortage of challenges for managers. Naturally, becoming a Remote Control Manager is also not without its challenges.

None of the steps previously described are easy to accomplish. For example, with these increased workloads, Remote Control Managers might be expected to be responsible for any number of locations worldwide. With these expanded responsibilities, it is easy to lose touch with these facilities. They become more and more isolated from what is going on in the rest of the organization, as the Remote Control Manager is often the **linking pin** for this connection. Similarly difficult is keeping these remote locations in touch with the organization's overall business objectives and goals. They need to be constantly updated on these changes and to understand how they contribute to the achievement of these objectives.

Absence may make the heart grow fonder in personal relationships, but not in business. A Remote Control Manager faces the liability of becoming a mere figurehead, rather than a leader to the parts of the organization for which he or she is responsible if they become too distant or detached. If the manager has completely lost touch with what is going at a remote location, he or she is not in a position to provide leadership or direction. This is the other end of the continuum from becoming overcontrolling. Both extremes can be detrimental to the overall success of both the remote location and the organization.

By definition, a Remote Control Manager acknowledges and is willing to accept the opinions and ideas of those he or she is responsible for managing. This can put the manager in a precarious position. The Remote Control Manager thus accepts the fact that there can be many more ways than one to do things. By accepting this fact and practicing it, there can become inconsistencies throughout the organization. This can create perceived or even real discrepancies which the Remote Control Manager must accept accountably. Consistency has long been the cornerstone for most policy and practices in an organization. Without this consistency, new problems and concerns may arise that the manager may not have had to face in a more traditional organization.

Because the Remote Control Manager is going to be less involved in the day-to-day activities than he may have otherwise been, he could find himself in a position when he must make important decisions based on limited information. This can make someone feel very uncomfortable. Again, this requires the Remote Control Manager to place his or her complete trust in others and in the information that they provide.

The Remote Control Manager needs to give people the tools, knowledge, trust, support, and confidence they need to manage themselves and grow both professionally and personally. At the same time, the Remote Control Manager still needs to accept the ultimate responsibility for their performance and success. This can seem like trying to push the buttons of your TV Remote Control device in the dark. You may not feel that you are really in control anymore. Accepting this uneasiness and uncertainty can be a real adjustment, particularly for those who are used to being in control.

The Remote Control Manager must make decisions concerning whether it is a matter of teaching people the skills they need to be managed remotely or a matter of creating an environment supportive of Remote Control. In other words, is it a matter of people knowing what to do or of being given the opportunity to do what they already know how to do?

Often, managers must deal with organizational inconsistencies. That is, two seemingly contradictory factors that seem to be working against one another. Many of these are created by the organization itself. Often, we are truly our own worst enemy! For example, organizations often set goals for one thing, but continue to have systems in place that reinforce just the opposite. For example, an organization may go to great efforts to promote the concepts of teamwork, but still reinforce individual performance. Consequently, employees get the wrong message or a "mixed message" at best. This erodes their confidence and trust in the management of the organization and particularly in their leaders.

The ultimate question to be asked of the Remote Control Manager is: "Do you believe that if the people who report to you were given the necessary training and opportunities for advancement they could perform at a higher level in your organization?" If the answer to this question is "yes," then your organization is probably a good candidate for a Remote Control Managed work environment.

Of course, we constantly must live with the realities of limited opportunities as they relate to expectations. Will developing people beyond the performance level they currently occupy in your organization create expectations that can't be fulfilled? This is a judgment call that each Remote Control Manager must answer for himself. We need to deal with these situations as they arise, each on their own merits.

Another major challenge for a Remote Control Manager is to keep everyone focused and working on the right things. Efficiency is doing things right. Effectiveness is doing the right things. If you are going in the wrong direction, you don't want to do it well! In the following story, a manager helps provide guidance to someone who has started going in the wrong direction. Like the story in Chapter 4 about David helping Helen to learn to become more of a Remote Control Manager, often it is the system itself that prevents the concepts of teamwork from being consistently practiced throughout the organization:

The Competition

"If we get just a few more sales this month we will beat the East Coast office in Philadelphia again!" said Joe Kramer, Manager of the Midwestern regional office. "That will make the third straight quarter this year we have come in ahead of them! I can't wait to call Dan Sanders, the Philadelphia Office Manager and rub it in!"

"How are you doing it? I remember just a few years ago when that office always had the highest sales of anyone in the company," asked Janet Henderson, a Marketing Manager for the company visiting the Midwestern office.

"I would like to think that it has something to do with my great management and leadership skills!" joked Joe. "But seriously, I have to credit the hard work of everyone in this office. I have never worked with a better team of people in my entire career. They have really aggressively pursued new accounts throughout our region, and the results are beginning to show in increased sales. In fact, we are developing a new customer that really has great potential for becoming our largest account. We feel that they want to see if we can meet their requirements better than their present supplier before making a commitment to giving us their total business. They like to build a relationship with one supplier and source all their business to that company, and we intend to be the office to land this big account!" Joe proudly bragged. "Our team is really going to be on top then. The Philadelphia office will never catch up with us, and Sanders will be eating our dust! It just proves what teamwork can accomplish!"

"Aren't you missing the whole point about teamwork?" questioned Janet.

"What do you mean? This office works together great as a team. All of us help each other out whenever we can. There are many times when one salesperson will make telephone calls or even visit another person's account to help them out. We share every bit of information we can with each other to help develop new sales leads. It is incredible how much one small bit of information learned by one salesperson can open up doors for another. In fact, we have started having weekly communications meetings for just this purpose. If someone is out of town, we will hook them up on a conference call so they can still participate in the meeting. We have learned that we can accomplish much more as individuals by working together as a team. The team develops and implements their own sales plans and works out any problems or conflicts that might exist among themselves. What is good for the team is good for the team members. Sometimes this might be a little bit hard to see at first, but we have proven over and over again that teamwork pays off in the end. I don't know how you can say that we don't work together as a team." Joe replied.

"I didn't say that you don't work together in the office as a team. It is obvious that you are doing a great job in that area. What I am saying is that you are losing sight of who the competition really is," Janet replied.

"What do you mean? We all know who our company's competition is. We get memos from the Home Office nearly every day about them. We have meetings about the competition all the time. They follow what we do and we follow what they do. In fact, as you know, we just came out with a new product specifically designed to compete with theirs," Joe said.

"What I am saying is that to listen to you, one would think that the Philadelphia office was your competition," Janet explained.

Joe thought about her comment for several moments. He was beginning to get very uncomfortable with this conversation. Janet was obviously trying to make a point to him about competition, but up to now he had failed to recognize that there could be anything wrong with his office striving to have the highest sales in the company. "Well, I guess in a way the Philadelphia office is our competition as well. We both want to be the best in the company and at the end of the year only one of us will be on top. What's wrong with that anyway? It's just healthy competition. We don't go around stabbing each other in the back. We still realize that we work for the same company. Besides, if there was something wrong with us competing against each other, why does the company offer incentives and have contest for the most sales each year for the sales offices?" Joe replied, becoming more defensive.

"I understand what you are saying," said Janet. "We do many things in the company to promote this kind of competition. But I don't agree that it is always positive for the company as a whole. For example, have you shared any information about your new account with the Philadelphia office?" she asked.

"Are you crazy!" exclaimed Joe. "Most of this customer's offices are located up and down the East Coast. If Sanders ever got their business, we would never be a able to catch up with them!"

"But wouldn't the Philadelphia office be better able to service this account than your office here in the Midwest?" Janet asked.

"Well, I suppose they could. But that wouldn't help our office very much, would it?"

"Which way would our company have the best chance of getting and keeping them as a customer in the long run?" Janet probed.

"I guess I would have to admit that the Philadelphia office would have a better chance of keeping them as a customer. I also have to admit we have missed several opportunities to give them better service already, because we are so far away from their locations. I see your point but what are we supposed to do, just give away all of our best accounts to Sander's office?"

"Well, aren't there accounts that the Philadelphia office has that have locations in this part of the country that you could serve better than they can?" Janet asked.

"Yes, I guess there are, but Dan Sanders would scream bloody murder if we ever interfered with his accounts, even if they happened to have offices in this part of the country. They are still his accounts. You keep talking about teamwork, but what kind of teamwork would it be if we were out there trying to steal each other's accounts? I'll admit, we do compete with each other to be the best, but we play the game fairly!"

"You're still missing the point," Janet continued. "What I'm talking about is that the Philadelphia office and your office need to work together as a team, rather than as opponents. As you said, we *do* all work for the same company. If the company as a whole is not successful, none of us will be successful. It seems to me that you and Dan Sanders are playing a win/lose game. Each of you is trying to come out ahead at the expense of the other," she explained.

"What's the alternative?" Joe asked.

"Well, I think you should seek a win/win situation," Janet explained.

"I don't understand how we can both win. There are always going to be winners and losers. That's just the way the game is played!" Joe replied.

"Maybe that's the way the game used to be played, but things are changing in our business and in the markets we serve. The competition is getting tougher and tougher every day, and if we don't work together to make our entire team better, we all could end up being the losers. It is tough enough out there to get business today without becoming our own competition. Just think how much better both of your offices could meet the requirements of your customers if you worked together s a team to better serve them? That would be a win/win scenario. Everyone wins and no one loses!"

"Actually, the more I think about it, there is a great deal we could do to help each other. There are many sales leads that we stumble on almost daily that can't help us but could be of benefit to the Philadelphia office. I am sure the same is true for their office as well," Joe said.

"What keeps you from sharing this information with one another now?" Janet asked.

"I guess that we both want to be the winner," Joe replied.

"You both could be winners by working together. Just think of how much more successful each of you could be if you helped one another rather than competing against each other."

"You know, you just might have something there," replied Joe. "Those bonuses are based on sales volume, and if we both could increase our sales by working together everyone would win. We could even set goals for our offices' combined sales and help each other reach them. Working together I'm sure we could both exceed our present sales levels. I guess that is what is meant by a win/win situation you mentioned. I'm sure there would be other benefits to working as a team that may not show up immediately in increased sales but are just about as important." Joe remarked. "For instance, our customer relations would improve with the better service we could provide them. The customer doesn't care which office of ours gets credit for the sale. All they care about is the quality of the service they receive. As far as they are concerned, we are all the same company. I guess sometimes we get so caught up trying to be the best sales office in the company that we forget about the most important person in our business — the customer," Joe concluded.

"Sounds like you have a brand new challenge!" said Janet.

"You're right about that!" answered Joe.

"Well, good luck, Joe. I'm sure both your office and the Philadelphia office will end up winners!" Janet said as she put on her coat and got up to leave.

"Thanks for helping me see that we need to work together rather than competing against each other. Now if only I can convince Sanders," Joe said, as he waved good-bye to her.

As Janet walked out the door she could hear Joe picking up the telephone and say, "Sanders, this is Joe Kramer. I hope you are sitting down because have I got a deal for you that you are not going to believe!"

Remote Control Management Gains

Remote Control Management can create a greater sense of ownership on the part of employees on all levels of the organization, even at remote locations. This is perhaps its greatest benefit. Because people on all levels of the organization are involved in the process, they will have a greater acceptance of change and its effect upon them. Because people are involved, there may be less finger pointing and playing the "blame game." All of this can lead to better morale and a more positive attitude on the part of everyone in the organization.

It is in this type of work environment that individuals have the greatest chance of reaching their fullest potential. This leads to a more effective and efficient organization, better able to meet the requirements and demands of its customers.

Remote Control Managing can solve many problems that more traditional direct supervision may not be able to, including dealing with the increasing scope and responsibilities of many managerial positions today. The Remote Control Manager can create a work environment based on teamwork throughout the organization. Teamwork can make average people great. And the bottom line is this — when the team wins, everybody wins. This is what makes great companies.

Remote Control Emmy Awards

Each year the television industry gets together at the Emmy Awards to recognize those who have made significant contributions in their work during the past season. Imagine that there was such a thing as Remote Control Emmy Awards in your organization. These awards would be presented to those individuals that you work with who made outstanding contributions to the concepts of Remote Control. Just imagine the lights, limousines, tuxedos, and designer gowns. Of course, there would also be the media and critics on hand to report on how terrible everyone looked in their expensive clothes and jewelry!

Who would receive these awards for their performance or would be most likely to be recognized in this way at a future date? It is your job to decide who will receive the following Remote Control Emmy Awards in your organization

"And the envelope please ..."

Best Supporting Remote Control Role   _____

Most Creative Use of Remote Control   _____

Best Remote Control Director   _____

Best Adaptation to Remote Control   _____

Best Remote Control Leading Role   _____

Most Dramatic Remote Control Role   _____

Best Remote Control Technical Support   _____

Best Variety in a Remote Control Role   _____

Best Sponsor of Remote Control   _____

Best Suspense in a Remote Control Role   _____

Best Remote Control Comedy   _____

Best New Remote Control Program   _____

Best Produced Remote Control Program   _____

In conclusion, if you should receive one of these coveted awards, what would be your acceptance speech? Remember to keep it brief before the music starts playing or we have go to a commercial. And remember, you need to thank all the "little" people who helped make this award possible for you to receive!